Resilient reporting

MANCHESTER
1824

Manchester University Press

Resilient reporting

Media coverage of Irish elections since 1969

MICHAEL BREEN, MICHAEL COURTNEY,
IAIN MCMENAMIN, EOIN O'MALLEY, AND
KEVIN RAFTER

Manchester University Press

Published by Manchester University Press
Oxford Road, Manchester M13 9PL
www.manchesteruniversitypress.co.uk

British Library Cataloguing-in-Publication Data is available

ISBN 978 1 5261 1997 1 hardback
ISBN 978 1 5261 1999 5 paperback

First published by Manchester University Press in hardback 2019

This edition published 2022

Typeset by Toppan Best-set Premedia Limited

Contents

Figures

Tables

Authors

Michael Breen is an Associate Professor at the School of Law and Government, Dublin City University. He is the author of *The Politics of IMF Lending* (Palgrave Macmillan, 2013) and many journal articles on key issues in political economy. He was the recipient of an award from the Irish Research Council in 2015 to study the relationship between the media and financial markets, using new techniques from computer science.

Michael Courtney is a Statistician at the Central Statistics Office in Dublin. He held an Irish Research Council Government of Ireland Postdoctoral Fellowship at the School of Law and Government, Dublin City University, from 2014 to 2018. His research includes quantitative analyses of political communications in the context of parliamentary speeches, news media, and extremist propaganda.

Iain McMenamin is Full Professor of Comparative Politics and Head of the School of Law and Government, Dublin City University. His book *If Money Talks, What Does It Say? Corruption and Business Financing of Political Parties* (Oxford University Press, 2013) won the Brian Farrell Prize of the Political Studies Association of Ireland for the best book in political science published in 2013.

Eoin O'Malley is an Associate Professor at the School of Law and Government, Dublin City University, where he is also Director of the MSc in Public Policy. He is the author of over forty peer-reviewed articles in political science and the author or co-editor of four books, including (with Sean McGraw) *One Party Dominance: Fianna Fáil and Irish Politics 1926–2016* (Routledge, 2017).

Kevin Rafter is Full Professor of Political Communication and Head of the School of Communications, Dublin City University. He is Chair of the Compliance Committee of the Broadcasting Authority of Ireland and was the independent rapporteur to the talks that led to the formation of Ireland's minority coalition in 2016. He is co-editor of *Political Advertising in the 2014 European Parliament Elections* (Palgrave Macmillan, 2017).

Acknowledgements

The authors would like to acknowledge funding support from the Faculty of Humanities and Social Sciences at Dublin City University, which facilitated data collection for this project and also assisted in the publication of this book.

Support from the Broadcasting Authority of Ireland and the Department of Communications, Climate Action and Environment helped with data collection on broadcast programming in the 2016 general election.

The authors are grateful to Heinz Brandenburg, Stephen Cushion, Liam Kneafsey, Ana Langer, Gary Murphy, and Theresa Reidy, who read some or all of the previous versions of the manuscript. Their generous and insightful feedback – and that received from those who participated in a workshop in June 2017 – is also appreciated. We would like to thank the University of Notre Dame in Dublin for hosting this workshop.

Early versions of this research have been presented at meetings of the American Political Science Association and the Political Studies Association of Ireland, as well as at seminars in the DCU School of Communications and DCU School of Law and Government, and we are grateful to the participants for their helpful comments and suggestions. Michael Breen also acknowledges the support of an Irish Research Council Government of Ireland Research Project Grant.

Resilient reporting: An introduction

Good journalists are plain speakers and clear writers. Journalists, and political reporters in particular, are expected to provide a public good of information, debate, and scrutiny (Schudson, 2008: 11–12). Unlike most providers of public goods, however, journalists generally cannot refer to a legal or electoral mandate. Instead, they must combine public service with a commercial imperative. Journalists have reacted to these contradictory pressures by developing a professional ethos or normative code. They lay claim to a public-service role through professional aspirations rather than through legal authority. Many – especially in politics – believe that journalism has lost sight of its public-good ethos. At an election rally, Donald Trump described the media as 'bad people – the worst people in the world'. At his prompting, the crowd turned to face the reporters present, yelling loudly and 'thrusting their fists' (Snow, 2017: 2). As President of the USA, Trump has continued his tirades against the media with ongoing claims about 'fake news' and unfair coverage.

Trump is an extreme case of a general attitude. In one of his final speeches as British Prime Minister in 2007, Tony Blair addressed the role of the media in a modern democracy. He labelled the media 'a feral beast', working to create immediate impact, 'which leads to sensation, crowds out a sensible debate about policy or issues' (see Blair, 2010: 648). In Poland, members of the Law and Justice party complained that an interviewer wanted to 'upset, discredit, force onto the defensive, and, in effect, humiliate' their leader (Polska Agencja Prasowa, 2011). The former French President Nicolas Sarkozy complained, 'It's Belgian roulette, a bullet in each of the barrels: if you lose, you lose, if you win, you also lose' (Leparmentier and Schneider, 2012). Irish politicians make similar complaints. During Ireland's pre-2008 economic boom, the then Irish Taoiseach (prime minister), Bertie Ahern, went as far as asking why those 'sitting on the sidelines, cribbing and moaning … didn't commit suicide' (RTÉ, 2007). More generally, former Tánaiste (deputy prime minister) Michael McDowell claimed that the media treated politicians as a 'sub-class, barely deserving of an audience' (Regan, 2010).

This theme of elected leaders focusing on media hostility towards politicians and the political system – and, more importantly, its impact on democracy – has also attracted the interest of scholars. In a critique of reporting on US politics, Thomas Patterson concluded that 'news coverage has become a barrier between candidates and the voters rather than a bridge connecting them' (1994: 25). Also in the US context, James Fallows highlighted the increasingly aggressive way in which politics is reported, with public life presented 'as a depressing spectacle, rather than a vital activity in which citizens can and should be engaged' (1997: 8). John Lloyd took up this thesis about the media's destructive impact on democracy in his assessment of primarily British political journalism as 'ravenous for conflict, scandal, splits, rows and failure' (2004: 89). Others have offered similarly critical treatment of the perceived failure of journalism and political journalism (Barnett and Gaber, 2001; Franklin, 2004). Much of this criticism is motivated by a sense of ongoing decline. A recurring theme is that the professional ethos of the media has been overpowered by its commercial logic (Blumler and Gurevitch, 1995). In this narrative, serious journalists reporting on political debates have been superseded by 'hyperactive hacks' desperately seeking to outbid each other in selling a negative story of cynical political manoeuvres.

Assessing these claims is not straightforward. We must consider different types of journalism which range from sober political reportage to soft lifestyle voyeurism. In this regard, we must decide how to categorise political coverage. We must also distinguish short-term fluctuations from long-term processes. Scholars have produced useful answers to conceptual and measurement issues but have continued to struggle with the sheer volume of writing and talking produced by the media. Newspapers are by some way the most prolific publications in human history. Even just covering election campaigns in a small number of newspapers in one country generates more newsprint than any human can manage to analyse in a meaningful way. We designed a robot to help us. In this book, we analyse twenty-five million words from Irish newspapers, television, and radio. Indeed, most of our analyses are of all relevant text rather than a tiny sample (as is typical of almost all other work in this area). We devote most of this book to exploring the richness of the resulting data. However, data is meaningless without theory. This chapter sets out our theoretical framework and previews how it will structure the rest of the book.

Studying election coverage over time

In this study, we evaluate three broad hypotheses about Ireland's election coverage since 1969. First, we look at the extent to which the norms of *critical impartiality* have survived. Second, we assess whether the media has shifted towards *hypercritical infotainment*. Third, we investigate the extent to which content has been influenced by *exogenous factors*, that is, political, social, and economic factors outside the media itself.

The media systems literature stresses the continuity of norms and institutions dating from the birth of the mass media, arguing that Western media systems reflect three categories: liberal, corporatist, and polarised pluralist. The media systems literature is nuanced and qualitative. It does not tend to present itself in terms of explicit mechanisms or hypotheses. Nonetheless, we view it as an essentially path-dependent argument. According to path-dependence, sequences matter. The press in polarised pluralist countries emerged in the context of widespread illiteracy, economic underdevelopment, and a conflict between traditional, liberal, and radical political ideologies. There was a limited market for newspapers. Initially, newspapers emerged that emphasised ideological interpretation over mass information. When polarised pluralist countries established freedom of the press and achieved universalised literacy, newspapers did not radically change their style to provide factual reporting to society as a whole. Instead, they continued to reflect the conditions at the time of their foundation, even though those circumstances had changed (Hallin and Mancini, 2004: 90–7).

The media systems approach can be interpreted in terms of increasing returns, according to which the 'probability of further steps along the same path increases with each move down that path' (Pierson, 2000: 252). If, in its early period, a media system is characterised by newspapers that try to be objective, there are likely to be increasing returns to this strategy. Readers and advertisers become used to the objective style and will not want to buy biased papers (Hallin and Mancini, 2004: 204). In turn, journalists will value objectivity and will resist attempts by owners to introduce partiality. We think the media systems approach is a path-dependent theory – it is dynamic, not static. It does not imply that if a country was once a corporatist system, it must always remain a corporatist system. But it does imply that if a country was once a corporatist system, change in the system will take the form of a branch from the original corporatist path. The framework of path dependency allows room for agency and creativity, but agency that is constrained by past choices and present structures (Neumann, 2010: 8–10).

Three broad sets of interlocking norms and institutions make up a media system: the political system and regulation; the media market; and professional norms and routines (Hallin and Mancini, 2004: 67–8). We think this, in turn, implies that change in one or more of these three norms and institutions makes systemic change, along a branch of the previously taken path, more likely. Ireland was a liberal media system at the beginning of the 1960s, when print was the dominant medium prior to the arrival of a domestic television service. Liberal media systems are a combination of historical antecedents, structural conditions, and contemporary practices and cultures. Ireland clearly exhibited liberal features: the media sector was commercial, only weakly partisan, with internal pluralism, and strongly committed to separating reporting and commentary (Hallin and Mancini, 2004: 67). The *Irish Independent* was seen as sympathetic to the Fine

Gael party but was far from a party paper. The *Irish Press* had been founded as a pro-Fianna-Fáil newspaper and was still regarded as such. Nonetheless, the papers did not display the strong ideological commitment and explicit links typical of press–party parallelism. Distinctive from other liberal systems, Ireland's media at this time was also deferential to politicians and, in particular, the Roman Catholic Church. Bishops influenced editorial copy while government ministers sought to prevent publication of stories deemed morally unsuitable, not to mind content they found politically unacceptable (Savage, 2010; Rafter, 2015).

This type of deference was undermined by nascent social change in Ireland in the 1960s and, specifically in the media sector, the impact of television. There was a shift towards weaker partisanship and a more critical approach to authority. Professional pride, more than ever, was associated with fairness and factuality in political reporting. Journalists reacted creatively to the conditions of the time, but they were, of course, constrained by existing structures. It is consistent with the path-dependent nature of the media system argument that a major change in Ireland's media system would be towards further liberalism. We call this branch of the liberal media system 'critical impartiality'. What was once a flexible non-partisanship became a more rigorous impartiality. There are various ways of defining impartiality (Brandenburg, 2005; Cushion, 2014; Hopmann *et al.*, 2017: 94–5). In the multi-party Irish context, we understand it as coverage of parties proportional to their share of seats in the Lower House of Parliament and no difference across parties in the tone of coverage. Whereas once the media had deferred to priests and politicians, it now sought to engage them in debate and hold them to account. Critical impartiality has much in common with the ethos of election coverage in the United Kingdom (Hallin and Mancini, 2004: 216), especially in the regulated broadcast sector, and with newspapers in the United States. If critical impartiality still defines the content of Irish election coverage today, it should be characterised by a consensus on impartiality between political parties and an overall negative tone in reportage.

Technology has not been an important theme in the media systems literature, presumably because it seeks to explain diversity, but technological innovations have spread around the West relatively contemporaneously. However, in a path-dependent framework, a common shock – such as technological change – would have different effects depending on the previous path. The media systems literature is replete with examples of how the effect of the introduction of broadcasting depended on the pre-existing media system (Hallin and Mancini, 2004: 97). Corporatist countries, in particular, took a distinctive approach to the governance of television. The private sector was initially excluded. Regulation was not directly managed by the state but rather by bodies on which political parties or other important social groups were represented (Hallin and Mancini, 2004: 165). The effect of television was, therefore, not purely technological. Rather, it was a combination of technology and regulation. We believe that Ireland's move (within the broad, liberal type) from a media sector defined by deference and partisanship to critical impartiality can mostly be explained by the introduction of a domestic national television service in public ownership but outside of the control of government and with a statutory obligation to be impartial (Horgan, 2001: 83; O'Brien, 2017: 112). A shift in media system subtype resulted from the interaction of the new technology with the political system's decision on regulation. In this regard, our historical experience with television suggests that we should consider social media as something that also works through the existing media system.

Many have argued that liberal media systems, especially those in the West, have moved towards what we call hypercritical infotainment. In this type of media system, politicians and the political system are portrayed negatively (Patterson, 2002); elections are framed as a political competition between ruthless and cynical players rather than a principled policy debate (Patterson, 1994; Cappella and Jamieson, 1997; Lawrence, 2000; Downie Jr and Kaiser, 2002); the media seeks out conflict in the political system (Patterson, 2002); leaders are overemphasised (Mughan, 2000; Webb and Poguntke, 2013); and coverage of leading politicians increasingly focuses on their private lives (Brants and Neijens, 1998; Langer, 2007). Different authors stress different features and there is no causal or logical priority, but these characteristics tend to appear together.

This type of media system – hypercritical infotainment – is a branch of the liberal path. It is ultimately a business strategy for commercially sensitive media driven by the need for circulation, ratings, and advertising revenues. It is viable in a context where the media is not supposed to have a political commitment. It also appears to be an outcome of changes in two of the three broad factors underpinning a media system. Hypercritical infotainment could be a response to growing pressure to increase or protect profits. Liberalisation of participation in the broadcast sector could have allowed new actors, including transnational actors, to promote a new style of political coverage. Liberalisation of content could allow new and old actors to develop new markets with more colourful political coverage (Hallin and Mancini, 2004: 217). Changes in the organisation and identity of the journalistic profession do not appear to be a major theme of writing on hypercritical infotainment. Table 1.1 summarises the three sets of factors and their relationship to critical impartiality and hypercritical infotainment.

The two subtypes are not antithetical, which is hardly surprising given that both are subtypes of the liberal media system, while hypercritical infotainment is hypothesised to succeed critical impartiality. It may be useful to offer a critique of each from the other's perspective.

First, we do so from the perspective of critical impartiality. Hypercritical infotainment is consistent with impartiality. A negative tone, the political competition frame, emphasising conflict, leaders, and the private lives of personalities are all compatible with a careful avoidance of giving an advantage to any side in political debate and controversy. However, hypercritical infotainment is not

Table 1.1 Liberal media system – critical impartiality and hypercritical infotainment

Factor	Critical impartiality	Hypercritical infotainment
Professional norms and structures	Stability	n/a
Regulation	Stability	Liberalisation
Market pressure	Stability	Greater competition
Technology	n/a	n/a

consistent with the spirit of critical impartiality. Under critical impartiality, political journalism is above all a service to democracy. By contrast, hypercritical infotainment is a business strategy. Whether it supports or undermines democracy is incidental.

Second, we adopt the perspective of hypercritical infotainment. Critical impartiality can be naive or disingenuous. It is not possible to be truly impartial. Impartial liberals are only impartial amongst options that they regard as broadly acceptable. Self-professedly impartial media systems are only impartial amongst a restricted number of already powerful actors and work to keep others out. Hypercritical infotainment can be interpreted as a populist critique of the complacent liberalism of critical impartiality.

We should stress that media systems are not completely closed. Outside factors can also impact on election coverage. In this regard, we have a third hypothesis, namely exogenous factors. This third hypothesis is diverse and we include ideas sometimes presented separately. For example, de Vreese *et al.* (2016: 27) divide our exogenous factors into the event and political system levels. However, everything we class as exogenous shares two key features which make for a distinctive view of political coverage. First, this approach looks for explanations outside the media, and we consider a range of political, economic, and social explanations. Of course, political news is, in a basic sense, always the co-production of journalists and politicians (Gans, 1979). Indeed, political journalists work hard to develop relationships with political sources, as do political actors with political journalists (Davis, 2009; Ross, 2010). At a more general level, we look at large changes in the functioning of politics, which are clearly not the creation of the media. Second, these ideas focus on change from election to election but do not predict a tendency in one direction over time. This is in contrast to the path-dependent nature of media system arguments. Exogeneity refers to the ultimate cause of variations in content lying outside the media. However, the mechanisms through which this works can be various. We think it can include conscious and unconscious processes. For example, increased policy focus due to an economic crisis appears to be a conscious editorial decision. If asked why economics coverage expanded in a crisis, journalists would reply that this was a response to the economic environment. On the other hand, external factors could potentially also affect election coverage through unconscious mechanisms. A feel-good factor, due to good economic performance, could drive a more positive tone in political coverage, even though journalists did not make an explicit connection between economic mood and political coverage or may not even be aware that content was more positive. The mechanism through which social change impacts on election content might also be relatively conscious or unconscious. Sometimes, journalists unreflectingly reproduce common cultural assumptions and aspirations. At other times, they may consciously write pieces aimed at bolstering or undermining cultural norms. Clearly, the conscious mechanism is more associated with social change than social stasis.

Our first set of exogenous factors is political. In consensual political systems, many actors – partisan, institutional, and civil society – have an important role in policymaking. By contrast, in majoritarian democracies decisions tend to be centralised in an executive controlled by one party. In consensual countries, elections rarely lead to a clear turnover in power. Indeed, it is often policy-oriented coalition negotiations, rather than elections, that bring about shifts in power. On the other hand, in majoritarian systems elections can transfer power to a totally different set of actors. Therefore, election coverage in majoritarian elections is likely to be much more 'game oriented' – winners-and-losers-type reporting – than coverage in consensual countries, which would be more policy-oriented (Dimitrova and Kostadinova, 2013; O'Malley et al., 2014). We also look at how social media may have changed election coverage by changing the nature of election campaigning itself.

Some scholars argue that a narrowing of the terms of political competition can push election coverage towards game-oriented coverage (Binderkrantz and Green-Pedersen, 2009; Strömbäck and Van Aelst, 2010). The narrower ideological and policy differences between parties are, the more the game frame dominates. This is usually interpreted as resulting in a focus on the competence of leaders and politicians (Stokes, 1963; Green, 2007) rather than policy choice. However, in a more polarised system, policy matters more and should therefore receive a greater proportion of coverage. In polarised systems, policy may also provide more colourful copy. Reporting extreme views may be easier and more entertaining in contrast to trying to tease out subtle differences amongst centrists. Commercial media may be particularly prone to this polarisation effect. A competitive election is also more exciting and easier to characterise in game terms; close elections or those with uncertain outcomes should have more game-oriented coverage (Strömbäck and Aalberg, 2008).

Our second set of exogenous factors relates to the economy, which can affect election coverage in several interesting ways. Work in psychology has demonstrated that humans tend to overrate negative outcomes relative to positive outcomes (Kahneman and Tversky, 1979). This has very broad implications, including that journalists will emphasise negative news because it is more likely to sell (Soroka, 2012). Given the importance of the economy to all elections, it could be that bad economic news influences the tone of election coverage more than good economic news. Similarly, if the economy is doing badly or is in crisis, the economy should receive a greater proportion of election coverage than during good economic times. Journalists may anchor their reaction to expectations. Changes in economic performance and sentiment may have a bigger effect than actual levels of either. Short time horizons could matter, too. Recent developments in the economy are more likely to matter to purveyors of news than long-term trends (Soroka *et al.*, 2015: 4).

Our third exogenous factor is social: we examine the effect of changing attitudes to authority and gender. Officeholders do not receive the same deference as in previous decades – people tend to see the frailty of the individual rather than the dignity of the office. This is related to the shift towards hypercritical infotainment, in which the foibles of personalities are more profitable than the policy pronouncements of constitutional officers. We also look at perhaps the most visible change in society, the changed attitude to women in public life. This tendency must be tempered by the reliance of journalists on political officeholders for access and stories.

Figure 1.1 illustrates our overall theoretical framework. We have data from 1969 to 2016 for two national newspapers, and for the 2016 campaign we have data from a variety of print and broadcast outlets. We begin with the existing literature's assumption that Irish election content started to shift towards critical impartiality from the 1960s onwards. We commence our study in 1969 – essentially, with the first national parliamentary campaign in Ireland in which television coverage had a significant impact. We expect our data to show critical impartiality in 1969. Over subsequent electoral contests, we then test whether critical impartiality endures or is replaced by hypercritical infotainment. Changes of media system subtype are large and path-dependent since they are systemic. But the absence of out-of-type change in no way suggests complete stasis. So, we also investigate the impact of political, social, and economic change, independent of the ultimate nature of the media system. We expect to see news coverage react in predictable ways to exogenous events, for instance a greater diversity in the tone of content reflecting polarisations amongst political parties.

Book structure

Chapter 2 summarises the political and media systems in Ireland, as well as outlining some of the main socio-economic changes that have impacted the country during the fifty years covered in this study. In this context, we highlight the opportunities and limitations of the Irish case for wider generalisation. This

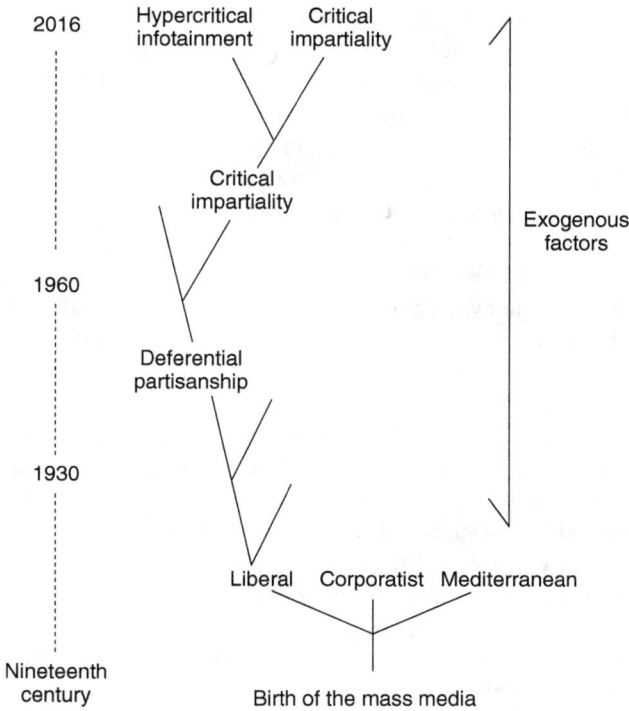

Figure 1.1 Theoretical framework

chapter also gives a jargon-free introduction to the machine learning systems that allowed us to study twenty-five million words of election coverage.

Chapter 3 looks at the general coverage of the political system in Irish elections in terms of framing, tone, and the distribution of coverage. It shows that there has been no steady increase in negativity and no increase in the political competition frame and, therefore, little evidence of hypercritical infotainment. Notwithstanding a number of fundamental shifts in the nature of Irish politics, the political system has not had any systematic influence on framing and tone. Most importantly, we present strong evidence of a tight consensus on norms of critical impartiality across fifty years and across radio, television, and print.

Chapter 4 examines how Ireland's economy has affected election coverage and discovers some interesting patterns in reporting since the 1969 contest. A bad economic performance is reflected in a more negative tone of election news, but a good economic performance has no effect. Expectations seem to matter: the tone of election coverage is associated with consumer sentiment.

Chapter 5 asks whether social change in gender attitudes and the introduction of a link between the gender of candidates and party funding in 2016 affected Irish election coverage. In earlier periods, women candidates were likely to be covered more positively, but less politically, than their male competitors. However, by the new millennium, little difference remained. Surprisingly, the media appears to have had problems adjusting to the surge in female candidates in 2016, and we can establish a general and substantial under-reporting of women candidates in that election.

Chapter 6 investigates Irish election coverage of leaders and personalities. Again, contrary to the hypercritical infotainment hypothesis, there has been no increase in focus on leaders. Nonetheless, we do see some instances of where party decisions to calibrate the leader-centrism of their campaigns are reflected in election coverage.

Chapter 7 focuses on the effect of the commercial basis of outlets on their election coverage. We do not find the association between greater market vulnerability and more negativity and more emphasis on the political competition frame, as posited by hypercritical infotainment. Instead, we stress the amount of political coverage provided by a given outlet. Those committed to politics offer a substantial amount of content in both the political competition and policy frames. Those with more marginal political content tend to stick to the policy basics and do not afford space to the details of polls and campaign strategies.

Chapter 8 looks at the election of 2011 and shows how the economic crisis at that time changed the framing of the election. Irish newspapers reacted by adopting a sharp shift towards coverage of economic policy, but this happened too late to mitigate a crisis to which media cheerleading for the property industry had contributed.

In the Conclusion, we bring together the main strands in this volume, arguing that Irish political journalism has maintained a code of critical impartiality in the face of the unpopularity of their profession, profound economic, political, and social change, as well as an ongoing revolution in the technology and business model underlying the industry. Overall, we find that, despite all these changes, over the half-century we have studied, Irish election coverage has been remarkably resilient.

2

Ireland: political, economic, and media systems

This study commences with the 1969 general election, which saw a generational change in Irish politics. Three years earlier, in late 1966, Seán Lemass resigned as Taoiseach and leader of Fianna Fáil. Lemass had been one of the revolutionary generation, who became prominent in the War of Independence (1918–22) and a founding member of Fianna Fáil in 1926. His successor, Jack Lynch, was a popular sporting figure and an experienced but cautious minister. The main opposition party, Fine Gael, also saw a leadership transition from James Dillon, a son of the last leader of the Irish Parliamentary Party, to Liam Cosgrave, the son of W. T. Cosgrave, the first Prime Minister of independent Ireland, who was head of government from 1922 to 1932. Outside the political world, the general election in 1969 was also a seminal one for the Irish media sector in that the domestic national television service, having first broadcast on 31 December 1961, was now established as an independent and critical voice. Newspaper coverage had responded to the new broadcast entrant with similar changes in reporting on political life.

We expect exogenous factors, including the political system, media system, the economy, and societal values, to influence how the media covers electoral contests. Ireland has gone through more rapid social change than most of its European neighbours. For example, during the first two elections in this study (1969, 1973), women civil servants had to leave their jobs when they married. Yet, in 2015, Ireland became the first country to legalise same-sex marriage by popular vote. In politics, the country has gone from a stable two-and-a-half-party system to having the third most volatile election in contemporary European history in 2011, and a Parliament where independent deputies held 15 per cent of seats in 2016.[1] Ireland's economy broke international records for 'rich-country' economic growth from the mid-1990s onwards, but also for costly bank bailouts after the 2008 economic crash. Despite all this change, however, the basic structure of the political system has remained constant. As well as factors exogenous to the media, there have been changes in the media sector itself. Ireland remained a basically liberal media system in all that time, one where journalistic norms emphasise impartiality and a rigid separation of reporting and commentary

– described in Chapter 1 as 'critical impartiality'. However, the Irish media market is highly competitive, comprising a variety of ownership types among its domestic players alongside significant presence from British outlets, which would suggest a movement towards hypercritical infotainment. This position will be tested throughout this volume.

Our study has a somewhat unique advantage for the wider study of political communication in that our time series from 1969 to 2016 is unusually long for studies of media coverage of elections. And although we recognise that this study is a single case, we believe that the media's coverage of Irish elections is still intrinsically important and interesting. Social science is a cumulative process, and cases are useful not because the subject is prominent but because of what it adds to our scientific knowledge. It is normal in many branches of science to generalise from a single case (de Saint-Georges, 2017: 2). As a result, we are able to make multiple within-case comparisons, thereby dampening the potential effect of Irish specificities on our outcomes. It is difficult to make general arguments about differences between one Irish election and an election elsewhere, as differences can always be attributed to national uniqueness. However, differences between one Irish election and another cannot logically be attributed to the Irishness of one of them. As we will show here, there is a great deal of variation on a number of the causal variables we identified in Chapter 1. That variation allows us to derive specific expectations for the data, enabling us to see if our hypotheses are supported by the Irish data.

The discussion in this chapter will introduce readers without a background knowledge of Ireland to the country's politics, economy, society, and media, which will be vital to understanding subsequent chapters. Moreover, the discussion will show where Ireland measures over time on the key independent variables identified in Chapter 1. The next section focuses on Ireland's political system, followed by an examination of the country's recent economic performance and social changes, and then an overview of the Irish media system.

Political system

For some, Ireland's political system was an almost prototypical Westminster system. Two large parties competed for power, and when in government, each was confident of the ability to pass legislation. Though the Parliament (Oireachtas) has two chambers – the Lower House (Dáil Éireann) and Upper House (Seanad Éireann) – the Dáil is dominant, but the executive was long thought most dominant. Ireland is a unitary state, with the central government controlling almost all of public policy. Though there is a directly elected president, the president's role is largely ceremonial and has limited practical power over public policy. Therefore, the general elections covered in this study (those to the Dáil) are unquestionably where all the real political action takes place. Other elections, local, Seanad, European, and presidential, are largely second-order elections: elections where the main issue or concern of voters is not the formal subject of the election.

While the characterisation as a Westminster system polity was reasonable in 1969 when our study begins, by 1989 it was no longer tenable (Murphy, 2016: 39–40). A number of things changed within society and the political system, though Ireland's political institutions were largely stable notwithstanding joining the European Economic Community (EEC, later the EU) in 1973. In terms of political competition and the institutional structure of decision-making, Ireland moved from being a majoritarian system towards one that could be described as a consensus system.

The most obvious change in this regard was to the party system. Though the party system might be thought to have broken down in the 2011 'earthquake' election (see Figure 2.1), this was probably the clearest manifestation of underlying changes that had taken place from the 1980s (O'Malley and Carty, 2017). The Irish party system, after it had settled down following the foundation of the State in 1922 and civil war in 1923, was usually thought of as a two-and-a-half-party system: a large Fianna Fáil party, a slightly smaller Fine Gael party, and a small

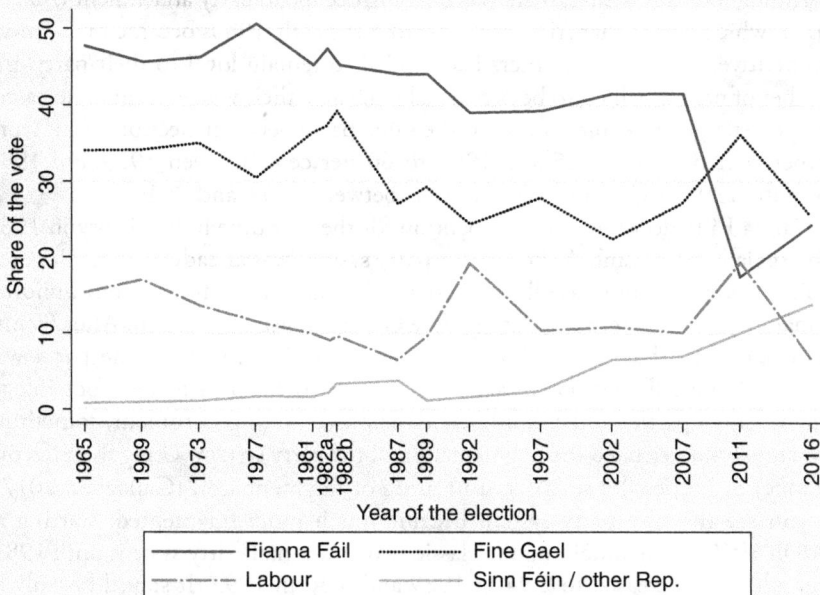

Figure 2.1 Share of first-preference votes in general elections, 1965–2016
Note: The 1965 general election is included for context.

Labour Party. Both Fianna Fáil and Fine Gael were regarded as centre-right, though Fianna Fáil usually fashioned itself as a party of the ordinary people. The party system was remarkably stable, with these three parties' support always coming in order. For example, in 1969 Fianna Fáil won 75 seats, Fine Gael won 50, Labour won 18. In all, these three parties won 143 of the 144 seats in Dáil Éireann in 1969. This three-party dominance, however, did not last.

Fianna Fáil's support has declined from a high point in 1977. This was, in part, because the party experienced significant internal divisions mainly revolving around policy on Northern Ireland, where conflict had re-emerged in 1969. These divisions – augmented by questions over the integrity of Charles Haughey, Lynch's successor as party leader – formalised with the foundation of the Progressive Democrats (PDs), a small classical liberal party formed primarily by dissident Fianna Fáil members in 1985. Ironically, the PDs would actually do more electoral damage to Fine Gael. The 1980s also saw the emergence of a small Workers' Party, which competed on the left with Labour. A Green Party was also established, while independent/non-party candidates increasingly won Dáil seats. Having ended its policy of parliamentary abstentionism in the Irish Republic in 1986, Sinn Féin, the political wing of the Provisional Irish Republican Army (IRA), gained electoral popularity following the first IRA ceasefire in 1994 and the Belfast Agreement peace deal in 1998.

Throughout this period, there was ongoing decline in party attachment (Marsh, 2017), which meant that Irish elections from the early 1980s became much more competitive. Where many voters had tended to remain loyal to their party, the number of people willing to be persuaded to change their vote evidently increased. The percentage of people voting for the same party between elections went from 84 per cent between 1965 and 1969 to 60 per cent between 1989 and 1992 (Sinnott, 1995: 147) and to 55 per cent between 2011 and 2016.

Fianna Fáil's decision to enter coalition for the first time in its history in 1989 was crucially important. Although the party system was already fragmenting, the choice of government was still a single-party Fianna Fáil administration (minority or majority) or an alternative led by Fine Gael and, usually, Labour. After Fianna Fáil decided to abandon its 'core value' of eschewing coalition, the party was able to choose different potential government partners. This made it possible to vote for small parties and still influence the make-up of government, something that arguably accelerated the fragmentation of the party system. Using the Effective Number of Parties (by seats)[2] as a measure of fragmentation (Gallagher, 2017), we can see that the party system became much more fragmented: starting at 2.46 in 1969 and maintaining the classic two-and-a-half-party system until 1987, after which it increased to 2.94 in 1989 and 3.46 in 1992. It stayed broadly at this level until 2016, when it jumped further to 4.93.

Despite this fragmentation, Fianna Fáil's 'coalitionability' made it easier for the party to remain in power. With the exception of a two-year period in the mid-1990s, Fianna Fáil led governments of various forms from 1987 to 2011. Indeed, from the start of our study in 1969, Fianna Fáil regularly achieved a majority of seats in Parliament. Occasionally, the opposition parties could agree to form an alternative administration, as Fine Gael and Labour did from 1973–77, 1981–82, and 1982–87. These coalition arrangements usually led to internecine disputes for Labour about the impact of government on the party's long-term electoral growth.

After the 1989 general election, however, the business of government formation became much more fluid. As coalitions now became the norm, Ireland moved towards a consensus system. While government remained where all the political action resided, power was spread more widely as there were more parties in government. Ministers were less likely to be policy dictators, and the Taoiseach was more constrained than previously. Other factors were also important in the shift towards a consensus system. In the late 1980s, Ireland developed a corporatist wage bargaining system, known as 'social partnership', which influenced tax and spending policy. Some ministers complained that social partnership shifted power away from the executive and legislature, as unions and employers – as well as other social partners – contributed to the formation of many aspects of public policy.

Other institutional changes over the period of this study should have led to an increased balance in power between the Government and the Dáil, at least in theory. The Oireachtas developed a committee system that made it easier to hold the Government to account. From the 1990s, a number of statutory inquiries were set up that investigated actions of politicians and would seem to indicate an increased importance of accountability procedures. Moreover, the Dáil flexed its muscles much more in the aftermath of the economic crisis in 2008, with TDs (Teachtaí Dála, i.e. Lower House members) more willing to vote against their party – something that was highly unusual before the 1980s.

The step changes in the party system of 2011 and 2016 are fascinating. Fianna Fáil formed a coalition with the Green Party in 2007, when it once more remained the largest party in the Dáil (see Table 2.1, for more information about each election). But, as shown in Figure 2.1, Fianna Fáil's support fell off a cliff in 2011, when it became the third largest party. The contest in 2011 was the third most volatile election[3] in contemporary European history (Farrell and Suiter, 2016). Despite this highly volatile election against the backdrop of dramatic economic decline, unusually no new party emerged. Sinn Féin, which had been competing in elections since 1987, marginally increased support, but Fine Gael and Labour 'won' the election, and these two parties formed a coalition government.

Five years later, in 2016, Ireland experienced yet another highly volatile election – this time, the eighth most volatile in European history. If 2011 was a shock to historic voting patterns, 2016 showed that they were continuing to dealign.

Table 2.1 Government composition, 1969–2016

Year	Government composition	Taoiseach	Government type
1969	Fianna Fáil	Jack Lynch	Single-party majority
1973	Fine Gael/Labour	Liam Cosgrave	Majority coalition
1977	Fianna Fáil	Jack Lynch; from 1979, Charles Haughey	Single-party majority
1981	Fine Gael/Labour	Garret FitzGerald	Minority coalition
1982	Fianna Fáil	Charles Haughey	Single-party majority
1982	Fine Gael/Labour	Garret FitzGerald	Majority coalition
1987	Fianna Fáil	Charles Haughey	Single-party majority
1989	Fianna Fáil/PDs	Charles Haughey; from 1992, Albert Reynolds	Majority coalition
1992	Fianna Fáil/Labour	Albert Reynolds	Majority coalition
1995 (no election)	Fine Gael/Labour/ Democratic Left	John Bruton	Majority coalition
1997	Fianna Fáil/PDs	Bertie Ahern	Minority coalition
2002	Fianna Fáil/PDs	Bertie Ahern	Majority coalition
2007	Fianna Fáil/Green Party	Bertie Ahern; from 2008, Brian Cowen	Majority coalition
2011	Fine Gael/Labour	Enda Kenny	Majority coalition
2016	Fine Gael/ independents	Enda Kenny	Minority with independent ministers; confidence and supply with Fianna Fáil

The two-and-a-half-party system that had become a system fragmented around two large parties in the 1980s was now fundamentally fragmented. Fine Gael and Fianna Fáil were the largest parties but together did not quite make 50 per cent of the first preference vote. Smaller parties and independents did well, as did Sinn Féin. In terms of fragmentation, but not in terms of ideology, the party system had started to look more like a Northern European party system, such as in the Netherlands or Denmark.

Some fragmentation was due to increased supply of, and evidently increased demand for, more diverse policy offerings among the electorate. But the narrower the ideological and policy differences between the parties became, the less likely the media would cover policy issues. Many argue that there has been a shift towards valence competition in Western democracies over recent decades (Clarke *et al.*, 2004), i.e. parties and voters agree on the ends of politics, and parties compete only in terms of the likelihood of achieving these ends (Stokes, 1963). This is usually interpreted as resulting in a focus on the characteristics of leaders and politicians, rather than policy choice.

In the 1980s, one prominent Irish political adviser claimed that there was not so much a policy space in Ireland as a policy dot. Ireland is known for its non-ideological politics. While social and ideological patterns are discernible, they are subtle and apparently ephemeral compared with those in other established democracies. The Irish Labour Party is one of the more centrist left-wing parties in Europe. At the constituency level, the electoral system produces relatively candidate-centred competition which focuses on the representation of local interests at the expense of national policy.

The emergence of new parties from the 1980s onwards also saw the emergence of broader policy offerings. The Workers' Party on the left offered a more radical alternative to Labour, and the PDs on the right were more policy-focused than Fine Gael and Fianna Fáil. The growth in the number of parties also saw the broadening of the policy space. Figure 2.2 shows parties on a scale of whether they favour market versus state solutions, based on the analysis of election

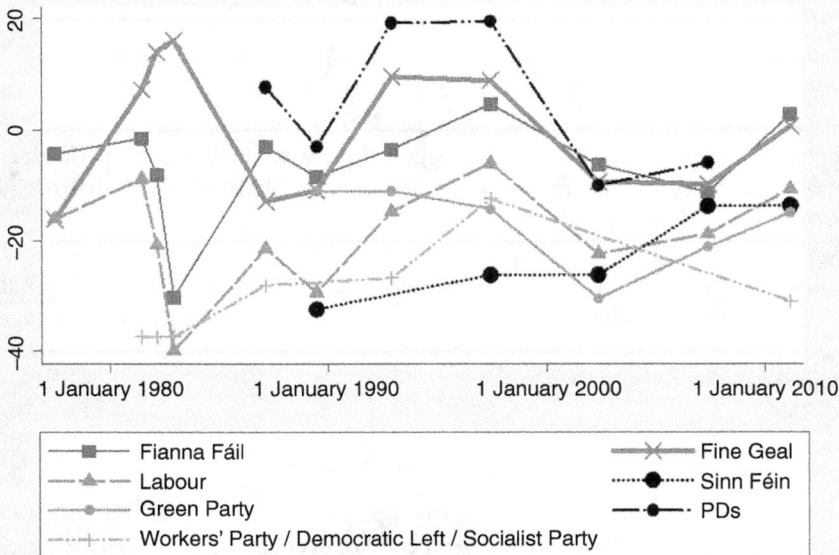

Figure 2.2 Party policy positions, 1973–2011
(Source: Manifesto Research Group)
Note: Lower scores favour more government intervention and redistribution.

manifestos. The three mainstream parties are very close in the 1970s, but Labour shifts to the left in the 1980s, and new parties expand the policy space. We see more new parties taking up more extreme positions, and existing parties seem to grow apart in 2011. If the data were available, we are confident it would show a further expansion of the policy space in 2016.

With increased policy diversity, we see increased competitiveness. A competitive election is more exciting and easier to characterise in game terms, so we would expect that close elections or those with uncertain outcomes will have predictable types of coverage. To date, the literature offers speculation rather than analysis on this question (Strömbäck and Aalberg, 2008), perhaps because measuring closeness across countries is not easy. In countries with plurality electoral systems and two-party systems, we can measure closeness as the difference between the two main parties. However, in proportional representation systems, competitiveness is not so easily quantified. The parties may appear to balance on a knife edge, but possible coalition outcomes might not.

Competitiveness of elections is thought of as being a function of several factors, including (i) entry of new candidates and new parties, (ii) greater rivalry among existing candidates and parties in elections, (iii) more intense rivalry among parties in the legislature between elections, and (iv) greater competition among the levels of government and between bureaus (Ferris, Winer and Grofman, 2014). Operationalisations of competitiveness enable the comparison of systems, rather than elections (Kayser and Lindstädt, 2015). *As such, we cannot track competitiveness over time. Ireland ranks twentieth out of twenty-three countries in terms of competitiveness, but it has a much larger standard deviation – only four out of twenty-three countries have a larger one.* The new parties in Ireland and increased electoral volatility would suggest there was increased competitiveness over time, becoming far more competitive in the 1980s, stabilising then, and becoming much more so in the elections of 2011 and 2016.

In summary, during the almost fifty years covered by this study, Ireland's politics had shifted towards consensus democracy, become more ideologically polarised, more volatile, and more competitive. To some extent, these changes from 1969 to 2016 have been gradual and, to some extent, they are turning points we can study.

Economic performance

The performance of Ireland's economy was extremely variable in the period covered by this study. After a prolonged period of decline, the 1960s were relatively buoyant, probably resulting from the decision of the Irish State to open up the economy to free trade and foreign direct investment. In the 1970s, Ireland, like other countries, suffered from the two international oil crises. Investment dried up and higher energy prices caused inflation, which put pressure on the cost of living. Ireland's response was to introduce budget deficits for the first time. After the 1977 election, Fianna Fáil funded taxation cuts and increased public spending by state borrowing. This action, however, did not stimulate economic growth, and Ireland found itself in a vicious cycle of low growth, high spending, and high unemployment. Various attempts to address this cycle failed, usually due to a lack of political will or an absence of voter demand.

There was a step change in 1987, when a minority Fianna Fáil Government replaced the Fine Gael–Labour coalition, which had been in office since the end of 1982. Though Fianna Fáil had campaigned against what it claimed were harsh cuts to public services, the incoming Government introduced significant cuts to public spending. It also backed a new system of social partnership which controlled pay demands and brought a degree of industrial peace. The partnership agreements included a steady reduction in payroll taxes. These policies – alongside an injection of monies via the EU's Structural Funds system – ultimately succeeded.

The Irish economy grew at extraordinary rates from the mid-1990s until 2007, when the country acquired the epithet 'Celtic Tiger'. Unemployment fell to nearly 4 per cent, employment doubled to over two million people in work, and Ireland – traditionally a country of emigration – saw its population rise through a combination of high immigration and comparatively high fertility rates. While growth in the early part of the so-called 'Celtic Tiger period' was caused by a significant inward-investment boom and a strengthening of the domestic economy, after 2002 the high rates of property-price growth fed consumer-led growth that was ultimately unsustainable. Irish banks fed the property bubble through lax lending funded by cheap credit available on international markets. The lackadaisical regulation of those banks became apparent towards the end of 2007 during the 'credit crunch'. On being told that a bank was within days of collapsing in September 2008, the Irish Government guaranteed the debt of all Irish banks on the basis that the banks were suffering from a short-term liquidity problem. In fact, they were insolvent, and the €70bn bank rescue was the result of what was, proportionally, the biggest banking failure in world financial history. Meanwhile, Irish tax revenues were falling dramatically. Irish governments had increased state spending in the decade from 1997, and now the Government was under pressure to reduce this quickly. General government debt increased from 25 per cent of GDP in 2007 to 107 per cent of GDP in 2011. The unemployment rate increased substantially, estimated at 14.4 per cent in 2011. Although Ireland had experienced recessions before, particularly in the 1980s, none had involved as sharp a drop in economic activity. The economy rebounded in 2016, but, as discussed in Chapter 4, progress was not sufficient to halt another dramatic election outcome. In summary, we see significant variation in economic performance over time and expect that the economy will be of varying importance in different election campaigns. Moreover, there are distinct crises which offer particular opportunities to study media coverage of elections.

Social change

The type of economic booms and busts described in the previous section is bound to have social consequences. Irish society changed radically over the period in this study. EU membership has had a hugely important impact on Irish society, and the Celtic Tiger – despite its shaky foundations – also yielded great social progress (Fahey *et al.*, 2007). Increased educational attainment may also have been a cause of a liberalisation of social attitudes.

Irish people from the 1960s onwards benefited from more formal education. Free secondary education was introduced in the 1960s, at a time when about 20 per cent of children completed secondary school, but this rose to 50 per cent by the late 1970s and reaches above 90 per cent today. Similarly, the number of students in higher-level education increased from about twenty thousand in the 1960s to over two hundred thousand in 2013. Completion rates have also increased. Over 50 per cent of 30- to 34-year-olds have completed a higher-level course, compared to an EU average of 35 per cent.

The rate of social change has been dramatic. Divorce was legalised in 1995 (a referendum on the issue was defeated in 1986). Homosexual acts were decriminalised in 1993, while the Irish voters supported the legalisation of same-sex marriage in 2015. Despite changing public attitudes, abortion was still effectively outlawed until a referendum in 2018 overwhelmingly endorsed proposals to permit a liberal abortion regime. In terms of liberalisation, Ireland no longer appears exceptional, though weekly church attendance, while falling, is still well above other European countries (Breen and Healy, 2016: 41).

In demographic terms, again the trend has been towards European norms. The Irish are having fewer babies – the fertility rate went from 3.85 in 1970 to 2.01 in 2011 (census data). Ireland's birth rate is still higher than in other European countries, but not exceptionally so (Eurostat, 2015: 29). The make-up of the population has also changed radically. For much of the period of this study, the Irish population was remarkably homogenous, white and Catholic. About 6 per cent of the population in 1991 was born outside Ireland, and much of this was to ethnic Irish parents in Britain or Northern Ireland. This figure increased to over 17 per cent in 2016, with many people now originally from Central and Eastern Europe and Africa.

In summary, Ireland's rapid change from a homogenous, conservative, traditional society to a more liberal, diverse, and globalised society would be expected to have an impact on media reporting. The move from a more authoritarian, patriarchal society to an open, liberal, and secular one means we should see less deferential coverage – and less sexism in that reportage – over time.

Media system

Ireland reflects the liberal model of media systems (Hallin and Mancini, 2004), which has a norm of impartial reporting and a rigorous distinction between 'hard news' and commentary. Media outlets are not owned by – and are usually not associated with – political parties and seem to endeavour to contain a plurality of opinions. Indeed, evidence suggests that Irish journalists do not generally express their political opinions through their reporting. Survey responses suggest that Irish journalists are much more (socially) liberal and (economically) left-wing than their paper's editorial stances and indeed Irish society in general (Rafter and Dunne, 2016).

We opted to start our study of media coverage of Irish elections in 1969, which was very much a transition election with new 'professionalism' in election campaigning, the emergence of more assertive and aggressive media coverage, and greater television coverage of politics. (The first post-television election was in 1965, but we see this as a settling-in campaign, so that by 1969 both media and political systems were better adjusted to the new service). Up to the 1960s, reporters were essentially the deferential conduits to the public of parliamentary proceedings; political scoops were few, personality politics was non-existent, while opinion polls were not available. The political journalist reported verbatim – generally on Oireachtas contributions and public speeches – and there was no room, or requirement, for analysis or opinion. This type of journalistic practice was not, however, unique to politics in the pre-1960s era. In his memoir, James Downey recalled deciding on front-page stories in the national press: 'Not many sensational political or crime stories came our way, and we often led on nothing sexier than the weather, if we got anything more out of the ordinary than freezing fog. Even more frequently, we fell back on foreign stories' (Downey, 2009: 89).

The new domestic channel gave politics an increased sense of importance, and, with their frequent television appearances, politicians and the small group of political journalists in Leinster House started to emerge for the first time as distinct personalities. During the 1960s, politicians were held to account by the media in a way not experienced previously. Reporting was less deferential and the perspective of journalists was increasingly called upon as analysis and comment was given greater prominence alongside news reporting of political developments. The nature of newspaper coverage of politics was changing. The appearance of John Healy's 'Backbencher' column in the *Irish Times* in 1963 offered a different perspective on political life from the traditional verbatim reportage of parliamentary speeches. His copy was built on an insider's view, included gossip and rumour, and, according to one assessment, 'transformed political coverage' (Downey, 2009: 81).

The Broadcasting Act of 1960 removed the Government's ability to intervene directly in broadcasting, committing the national broadcaster to 'impartial' coverage of politics and other controversial issues (Horgan, 2001: 83). The Government had expected 'impartiality' to be a continuation of the national radio's tradition of verbatim reporting of government and opposition speeches (O'Brien, 2017: 112). However, the new broadcasters were an ambitious group of new graduates who sought to introduce a more critical and dialogic approach. So, for example, impartiality meant arguing with the minister or accompanying a government statement with a statement from an aggrieved interest group.

Following the passage of the Act, numerous difficult moments had been experienced between those overseeing news coverage on the new service and the then incumbent Fianna Fáil Government. Politicians found themselves held to account by the broadcast media in a way not experienced previously in newspaper or radio coverage. For example, in October 1966 Charles Haughey, the Minister for Agriculture, sought to interfere with the content of a news report and amid subsequent controversy told the Dáil, 'when I give that advice with all the authority of my office as Minister ... that advice should be respected by the national television network' (*Dáil Debates*, 1966). A decision to send staff to cover the Vietnam War in 1967, including reporting from communist North Vietnam, was cancelled following government intervention (Savage, 2010).

TV was not just part of the media environment for the newspapers, it was also a new arena for them: the political correspondents of the national newspapers were given their own television show. This context discouraged traditional deference to the Government or outright support for one of the nationalist parties. Any journalist who did so would hand an opportunity to a competing journalist and his newspaper. Journalists were clearly impacted by these changing norms of professionalism, and these norms were formally passed down. Increasingly, journalists were graduates, including graduates in new courses in journalism and communication.

With each subsequent election covered by RTÉ, the relative importance of television over print changed. Television is now the most popular platform for accessing news in Ireland, at 73 per cent, followed by online media (70 per cent). RTÉ has the greatest reach, at 64 per cent, followed by Independent News and Media, at 44 per cent, the *Irish Times*, at 37 per cent, and breakingnews.ie, at 24 per cent. Just over half (52 per cent) of Irish people say they use social media platforms as a source of news each week. Nevertheless, traditional print media remains an extremely important source of political information for the Irish public.

The media sector today comprises broadcast, print, and online entities, including national broadcast services from the publicly owned RTÉ and TG4 and the privately owned TV3. International companies such as the BBC, Sky, and Liberty Global are active in the Irish media market, as are a variety of British newspaper groups which publish Irish editions of their UK titles. All newspaper groups are privately owned commercial operators. As seen in Table 2.2, the *Irish Times* and the *Irish Independent* are the two best-selling daily titles, but the leading British newspaper groups also have a significant presence, largely due to historical ties and close geographical proximity. Like elsewhere, digital disruption has impacted on sales and advertising revenues in the print section of the media market. The domestic economic crisis since 2008 only added to these existing commercial pressures. A number of national titles have closed, while reductions in editorial budgets and pay cuts have been the norm. Some publishers have succeeded in maintaining profitability, albeit at lower levels than previously, by means of aggressive cost-cutting. Several Irish media companies still carry large debts arising from ill-fated boom-era investments.

These newspapers are all profit-oriented, although they vary in their degree of commercialisation, largely due to their ownership type. For example, the *Irish Times* is owned by a complex charitable trust, somewhat similar to the *Guardian* in the UK. Given its trust structure, the *Irish Times* is not answerable to shareholders, as in the case of a publicly quoted company, or to personal owners, like a privately owned entity. While this trust arrangement ensures the newspaper is not exclusively focused on profit maximisation, the ownership structure does not remove a dependence on profit to ensure business viability. With a predominantly middle-class and well-educated readership, the *Irish Times* still struggled against the dual challenges of digital change and economic decline.

The situation is somewhat similar at the largest newspaper group in Ireland, Independent News and Media (INM), which is a publicly quoted company publishing the more mid-market *Irish Independent*. INM also jointly owns the *Irish Daily Star* with the UK-based Express Newspapers. Prior to the 2008 economic crisis, INM had a range of international media interests, but these have since been sold to pay down unsustainable debt levels. INM's long-time dominant shareholder, Anthony O'Reilly, was the nearest example to an Irish media baron. O'Reilly's control was challenged by another businessman investor, Denis O'Brien, who in securing 29.9 per cent ownership has pushed for a much more profit-driven approach at the media group. The other main domestic newspaper publisher at the time of the 2016 election was Landmark Media, which acquired the interests of Thomas Crosbie Holdings (TCH) in 2013. These two groups – both privately owned businesses – published the daily national title *Irish Examiner*, until July 2018 when the newspaper was taken over by *The Irish Times*. Unlike INM, Landmark did not face shareholder pressure to maximise profits to maintain dividends and share price. But a necessity to deliver profits was still a core concern, especially given ongoing operational losses and significant debts arising from the 2013 deal with TCH.

Other national newspapers in the daily market are UK-owned and produce specific editions of their British newspapers for the Irish market. This category includes the Associated Press title *Irish Daily Mail* as well as the *Irish Sun*, which

Table 2.2 Newspaper circulation

Title	1960s	1970s	1980s	1990	1999	Jan.–Jun. 2009	Jan.–Jun. 2014	Jan.–Jun. 2015	Jan.–Jun. 2016
Irish Independent	180,801[1]	167,000[2]	191,000[3]	152,000	166,000	152,204	112,383	109,524	102,537
Irish Times	35,024[4]	57,443[5]	86,000[6]	94,000	113,000	114,488	80,332	76,194	72,011
Examiner	–	–	–	57,000	61,000	50,346	35,026	33,198	30,964
Daily Mail*	–	–	–	4,000	6,000	52,144	50,032	50,037	46,578
Daily Mirror	–	–	–	60,000	62,000	64,194	50,263	43,250	38,294

Sources: Data for 2009–16 from News Brands Ireland (newsbrandsireland.ie); data for 1990 and 1999 from Barrett (2000); data for the 1960s, 1970s, and 1980s: [1]1963, [2]1973, [3]1980, [4]1960, [5]1970, [6]1982.
*An Irish edition of the Daily Mail was introduced in 2006.

is published by what is now known as News UK and Ireland (from the Rupert Murdoch stable of media interests). The Trinity Mirror Group publishes the *Irish Daily Mirror*. While these British media groups have made sizeable investments in their Irish operations, they could relatively easily withdraw from the Irish market were losses to mount. In this regard, the British publishers might be expected to be under greater pressure than their Irish-owned competitors to deliver profits.

Irish broadcasting was rooted in state ownership and operated in a monopoly environment for over half a century after the foundation of the Irish State in 1922. For much of this period, radio was essentially a passive medium as far as political coverage was concerned. When the new national television service – Teléfis Éireann (now RTÉ) – made its first broadcast at the end of 1961, it did so as a station in public ownership. The legislation that established the new television service moved broadcasting away from direct government control, allowing it some autonomy as a semi-state entity. RTÉ first faced domestic free-to-air competition in the television market in 1998, when TV3 went on air as a single-channel service, but now operates three separate channels and is owned by Liberty Global, the international media group. (TG4, a publicly owned Irish language station, started broadcasting in 1996.) Irish TV has not wholeheartedly followed Britain and America into the age of the 24-hour news channel that breaks news as it happens and influences the broader values of the media sector (Cushion, 2015). RTÉ launched a 24-hour news channel in 2008 (McCaughren, 2017). The Irish broadcasting landscape today contains a mixture of public and private, commercial and community-licensed services operating at national, regional, and local levels. RTÉ has retained a significant market share in Ireland's television market, but, as shown in Table 2.3, audience fragmentation is an increasing reality.

The Irish radio market is equally competitive, with licensed stations at local, regional, and national levels. Some 83 per cent of those over fifteen years – almost three million people – listened every weekday to radio in 2016. RTÉ Radio 1 and the privately owned Newstalk are the main national talk-based radio stations, although Today FM – a music-based station which has the same owner as Newstalk (Communicorp) – has a talk-based current affairs programme in the evening drive-time slot. The fact that Denis O'Brien – the dominant shareholder in INM – through his company Communicorp owns Newstalk and Today FM, as well as a number of music stations, has raised concerns about cross-media ownership in the Irish media market.

While commercial television and radio stations survive on advertising revenues, RTÉ is funded by a combination of licence fee and commercial revenue. The national licence fee is currently 'top-sliced', with 93 per cent of the annual payment (€160 for each household with a TV set) ring-fenced for RTÉ and TG4. The remaining 7 per cent is allocated by tender for individual

Table 2.3 Television audience, share of total viewers (%)

Channel	2005	2010	2015
RTÉ One	27.8	24.8	19.9
TV3	13.4	12.8	8.4
RTÉ Two	11.1	9.8	6.3
UTV	5.9	4.0	7.0*
BBC One	7.1	4.7	3.8
3e	–	1.1	2.8
TG4	3.2	2.2	1.8
Channel 4	4.4	2.9	1.5
BBC Two	4.0	2.7	1.5
Sky Sports News	–	0.6	1.0
All other channels	23.1	34.4	46.0

Source: Nielsen Market Research.
*Combined figure for UTV and UTV Ireland.

public-service-type programming on all licensed stations, irrespective of their ownership profile. It is not possible, however, to fund news and current affairs programming from this 'top-sliced' fund.

Under the Broadcasting Act 2009, the Broadcasting Authority of Ireland (BAI) has statutory oversight over the two public broadcasters, RTÉ and TG4, and monitors their adherence to agreed strategy commitments in respect of programming and other key targets. Moreover, as the licensing authority for private broadcasters, the BAI monitors compliance with the various programme content commitments in licence contracts. The 2009 legislation specifically deals with news and current affairs coverage, including coverage of elections. All broadcasters, irrespective of their ownership status, are legally obliged to report and present news in an objective and impartial manner and without any expression of the broadcaster's own views. A separate regulatory regime exists for the newspaper sector, covering its print and online content, but they are free to determine their own editorial direction. In Britain, broadcast news also have a legal requirement to broadcast impartially. However, they share the media landscape with highly partisan newspapers, making it much more difficult to follow through on stories and debate from the print sector while maintaining impartiality (Cushion *et al.*, 2018).

As we have outlined, the Irish media now comprises a diverse set of actors. Differences in format and ownership should affect how politics is reported. The liberalisation of broadcasting broke open RTÉ's monopoly, first on radio and then on television. These new competitors obviously had to begin small and appear to have conformed to the existing norms of election coverage. Indeed, many of the journalists working for the new outlets had gained experience with the older broadcasters or publications.

Changes in regulation and technology have increased commercial pressures over time. We see evidence of critical impartiality in the composition of the Irish media landscape in 1969: the arrival of television spurred on less deferential coverage of politics in all media sectors, while legislation ensured adherence to balance and fairness in the broadcast sector. The media landscape changes significantly in subsequent years – more newspaper titles emerge, both domestic and Irish editions of British titles. Following legislative change in the late 1980s, the monopoly of the public broadcaster ended with the licensing of commercial, privately owned broadcasters. As the number of media organisations covering politics has expanded, so too has the number of specialist political reporters. The number of members of the Parliamentary Press Gallery was less than a dozen at the outset of our study in 1969. The number of reporters covering politics also increased from the late 1970s onwards; by 2016, the number was approximately 130.

The establishment of television in Ireland was not just the introduction of a new medium but the sudden arrival of a powerful monopoly. The closest comparison to television in the 1960s is not the series of media market shocks and regulatory shake-ups in the twentieth century – it is, of course, social media. The internet, at least initially, was not really a new medium, in that it was just a way of accessing print, audio, and video. Social media was something more akin to a new medium, so different, indeed, that it almost inevitably was governed by different norms than broadcasting or newspapers. Like the political correspondents had quickly secured their own television programme, journalists now quite swiftly moved in trying to dominate current affairs on Twitter – and did so with a considerable degree of success.

In its adaption to social media, Ireland's media is still on a path taken at the advent of the mass media. Ireland had, and has, a liberal media system. The press has been independent and largely commercial. Objectivity is valued and is implemented by a strict separation between reporting and commentary.

Our data

The historical data is drawn from the *Irish Times* and the *Irish Independent*. They were and are the papers with the highest circulation in Ireland. Moreover, they operate on different business models, providing divergent incentives on the quality and quantity of political news. The analyses of this book pertaining to the election years in the period 1969–2011 are based on these sources. For 2016, we extend the analysis to more cross-sectional data, including most newspapers operating on a nationwide basis. We also sample and transcribe broadcast data for popular television and radio programmes. The dataset consists of 1,044,822 paragraphs of text. Where possible, we only systematically exclude sports sections and let the machine learning algorithms (described below) parse the data for politically relevant content.

We analyse this data at the paragraph level, as this unit of analysis increases the reliability of our manual coding and is more conducive to automated computer coding (Le and Mikolov, 2014). While content sourced from LexisNexis appears in our data in the original format, content sourced from the Irish Newspaper Archives does not. This data is drawn from the source in PDF scans, which require optical character recognition software to convert the images into plain text. This software does not intuitively know which paragraphs are related to which articles, though it does make some shallow attempt to parse articles systematically. The data from the *Irish Independent* (1969–2011) and the *Irish Times* (1969–92) was gathered using the PDF/OCR process. For broadcast, we define a 'paragraph' in the transcribed text as being a continuous utterance of speech by a single speaker without interruption. Paragraph breaks are thus defined by interruptions and a change of speaker. There is strong contrast between print and broadcast in the amount of data. Some of this is attributable to the lower number of source days in the broadcast, but mostly it is due to print sources generating more text than transcribed audio.

To analyse the data, we induce automatic content classifiers using supervised learning. The classifiers are trained to identify three distinct sets of concepts: news about public policy and political competition (Breen *et al.*, 2015), political frames, and sentiment. The policy and political competition classifier identifies content focused on policy debate and policymaking and the 'game' of political competition, including commentary on elections, polls, parties, leaders, coalitions, and government formation. Policy is further divided into macroeconomic, microeconomic, and other policy. The political frames classifier identifies whether the election coverage is framed as being about 'stability', 'austerity', 'leadership effectiveness', or 'equality'. The data is also coded for sentiment. This classifier identifies whether sentiment is present or absent, and if present, whether the tone is positive or negative. This is presented as a three-category classification where a paragraph coded as neutral contains no sentiment, while a paragraph coded as negative or positive indicates that sentiment is present and the respective direction of the tone.

Supervised learning is a process by which an algorithm induces an automatic classifier from manually coded texts – in other words, the computer learns from humans. In the appendix on machine learning (Appendix 2), we present the results of reliability tests on manual coding and accuracy tests on automatic coding. They show that the human coders trained themselves to code the same texts in the same ways. Crucially, they show that the computer also codes texts in the same way as humans. In addition to these formal tests, this book features many examples of 'face validity', where informed observers tend to agree that the results just must be right. Here are some instances:

In 2011, an election prompted by an economic disaster, there is a sharp jump in the proportion of news on macroeconomic policy.

In 2016, consistent with the views of expert commentators, the *Irish Independent* adopts a markedly more negative attitude to Sinn Féin.

Tabloids report a lot less politics than other sources.

Election news is reported more positively in 1969 than later on.

The algorithms were not informed of any of these pieces of relevant context but still coded as expected. In summary, the huge amount of text automatically analysed in this book has been classified in the same way as human coders would have done.

We observe in the data a number of cases that lead us to trust the data. For instance, the negative sentiment in the coverage by the *Irish Independent* of Sinn Féin in 2016 and the significantly elevated framing of Fianna Fáil in relation to competency in 2011 give the overall results a reassuring face validity.

Conclusion

In this study, we present a complete analysis of election coverage, not just a sample of coverage. We cover fourteen elections from 1969 to 2016. The study is of election coverage, so we can only make general claims about political coverage. It is likely that coverage of politicians, policy, and political parties differs in election time to other periods. It is also possible that at elections journalists, newspapers, and broadcasters move into a well-worn groove, using tried and tested formula in their election coverage and, as for broadcasters, taking note of coverage guidelines issued by regulators. This might mean that broader changes in media coverage are not reflected in election coverage. However, we doubt this. Campaigning has changed significantly, and it is likely that at the very least journalists would adapt to that changing environment. The news cycle has also changed significantly; it is unlikely that journalists are condemned to replay the past in their election coverage.

In this study, the text is coded automatically but coded as if it had been done by well-trained humans. Good theories identify a range of outcomes and explanations for those outcomes. Ireland is interesting in itself and interesting to scholars of comparative political communication. In the period from 1969 to 2016, Ireland offers wide variation in relation to the major potential explanations for changes in election coverage that have been proposed by comparative media scholars. Politics has shifted from a strict Westminster system to a much more fragmented system. The economy has moved from economic basket case to economic miracle, and back again. Ireland has changed from an isolated, highly conservative society to the European liberal mainstream. The Irish media features a range of public and privately owned outlets, as well as important outposts of British newspapers. Having provided an overview of Ireland's political system, economy, social change, and media landscape, in subsequent chapters we will systematically explore whether this variation is associated with changes in election coverage.

Notes

1 Counting 'Independents 4 Change' as independents here, rather than as a party.
2 This is an adjusted number of political parties using a formula by Laakso and Taagepera (1979) that counts parties weighted by their relative strength. Broadly, if you have two large parties and one smaller party, as in Ireland in 1969, the formula will calculate it as two and a half parties. The formula is $1/\Sigma p_i^2$, where p is the proportion of seats each party receives.
3 Volatility can be measured using the Pedersen (1979) Index, which simply aggregates each party's vote gain or loss, divided by two.

3

The media and political change

This chapter assesses three broad perspectives on how the Irish media has covered political change in Ireland over almost fifty years. The first, which we call 'hypercritical infotainment', emphasises the media as a collective agent of change. According to this approach, the media shifts from passive reporting of politics to framing it as a political competition and adopting a negative tone towards politics. This, in turn, imposes a media logic on politicians, who become more interested in spin and soundbites than policymaking and party-building. Equally, citizens, bombarded by negative coverage of smooth media performers, become disenchanted with the media and politics. The second approach, which we term 'critical impartiality', emphasises the media as a collective agent of stability. Today's media perpetuates a culture that originated, as discussed in Chapter 2, in the particular conditions of the introduction of television to Ireland. Journalists became more critical and less deferential, while widely adopting political impartiality, which was a legal requirement for the national broadcaster. The third and final broad approach emphasises how 'exogenous factors' can affect election coverage. In this chapter, we concentrate on political change. It could be expected that a shift towards coalition governments and fragmented parliaments would change the tone and framing of elections, as well as placing greater emphasis on smaller parties that are potential coalition partners. We also investigate how the rise of social media campaigning has impacted on election coverage in the print and broadcast sectors.

In order to explore these ideas, we look at the distribution of coverage across political actors, the tone of that coverage, and the framing of the election campaign in terms of a policy debate or political competition (game coverage). We present two areas of analysis: First, for the fourteen elections from 1969 to 2016, we study the *Irish Times* and the *Irish Independent*. This long timeframe allows for a good test of the three hypotheses, all of which make predictions about change over time. Second, we study nine more media outlets – broadcast and print – for the 2016 general election. We cannot make direct comparisons to media coverage by these outlets under political conditions different to those of 2016. However, if we find similarities of coverage across this diverse range of media, we will be able to infer that the historical newspaper data can be tentatively generalised.

In the first section, we present observable implications of the hypercritical infotainment perspective. The political competition frame portrays elections as a competition between teams. It emphasises the strategy of parties, the strengths and weaknesses of their candidates, and their chances of eventual victory. By contrast, the policy frame sees an election as a debate about alternative plans for society. It concentrates on practical problems and ideological visions. According to the hypercritical infotainment argument, there should be an increase in the ratio of political competition to policy coverage of elections. It also predicts an increase in negativity, partly because political competition is associated with a more negative tone. Conflict is a much better story than consensus.

In the second section, we focus on the critical impartiality perspective, which suggests substantial homogeneity and continuity. Homogeneity means that different outlets adopt similar frames and similar tones and distribute coverage amongst parties in a similar way. Continuity means that such a collective approach is consistent over time. Furthermore, impartiality means that parties receive coverage proportional to their popular support and that the tone of coverage of different parties is similar.

In the third and final section, we examine exogenous factors. Shifts in the logic of the political system should influence the coverage of politics. A shift to government formation by coalition bargaining, rather than a simple electoral race between two teams, could mean a move towards the policy frame and away from political competition. The importance of coalitions should also be associated with more, and disproportionate, coverage of smaller possible coalition parties, especially 'kingmakers' that have alternative coalition partners. Close elections make the political competition frame more exciting and more relevant, again heralding a shift in that direction. The positions as well as the sizes of the parties should impact on election coverage. Therefore, the more polarised the party system, the greater the variation in the tone of the election coverage. Lastly in this section, we look at whether social media made a bigger impact on coverage during Ireland's so-called 'first social media election' compared to its predecessor.

Hypercritical infotainment

Figure 3.1 shows the framing of elections in the *Irish Times* and *Irish Independent* from 1969 to 2016. Between 1989 and 2002, we see a large increase in the probability of all categories in both newspapers, but especially in the *Irish Times*. This indicates an overall increase in political coverage. By 2016, however, the emphasis on all three policy categories and political competition has returned to a similar level to the starting point in 1969. The evidence contradicts the idea

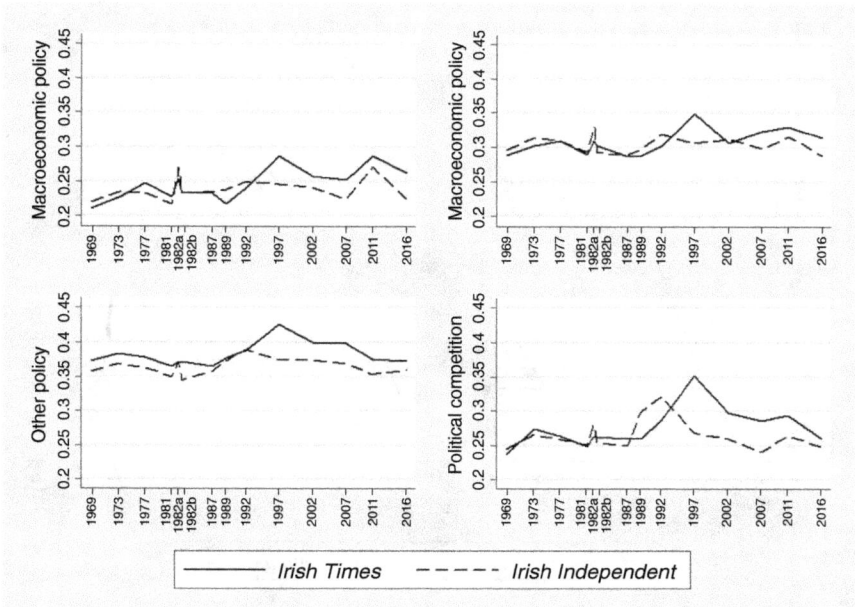

Figure 3.1 Framing of coverage, *Irish Times* and *Irish Independent* 1969–2016
Note: The graphs show the probability that a paragraph is classified in a specific category.
Since this is not a sample, we do not show standard errors.

that there has been a gradual and decisive shift away from policy and towards political competition.

Figure 3.2 shows the tone of the *Irish Times* and the *Irish Independent* across our fourteen elections. We can see that election coverage shifted towards negativity in 1973. It has shown no consistent pattern since, but has never come close to the more positive tone of 1969. This shift to negativity in 1973 is consistent with the hypercritical infotainment thesis. Indeed, we began in 1969, when RTÉ broadcasts had begun to be important and the media as a whole had adopted a less deferential attitude to politicians. Even so, the permanent drop in tone is less than half of the range of the subsequent variation. The metric suggests that the actual drop was too subtle to be a major driver of political attitudes. The long-term shift to negativity in the graph is about 0.03. One way of interpreting this is to say that there were at least 1.5 per cent more negative articles in the election coverage after 1969. Moreover, the hypercritical infotainment argument tends to assume a longer-term process of transformation of content, not one that ends in the early 1970s. There is no doubt that Irish politics became mediatised in the sense that politicians became self-conscious media actors and parties adopted explicit

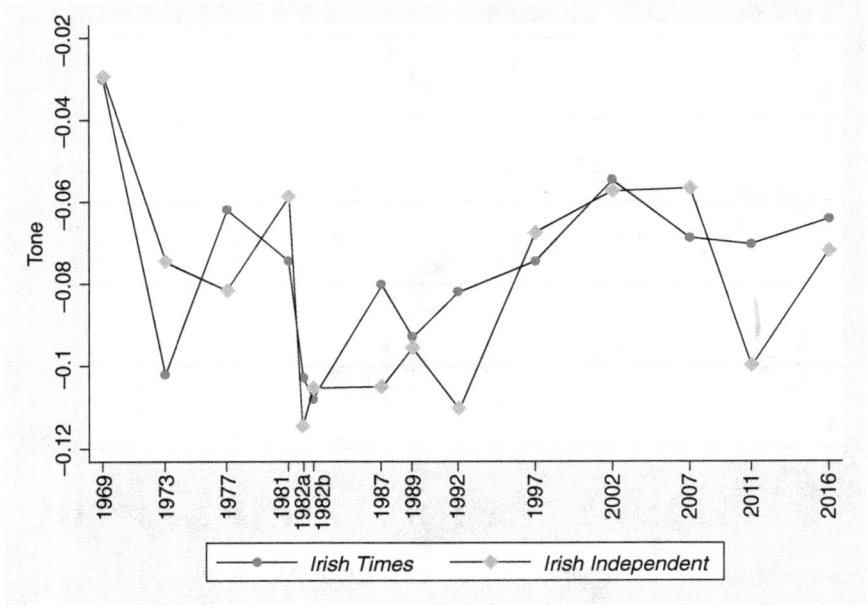

Figure 3.2 Tone of coverage, *Irish Times* and *Irish Independent* 1969–2016
Note: Tone is defined as the probability that a paragraph is positive less the probability that
it is negative. Non-Irish and non-political paragraphs are excluded. '1' indicates that the
classifier judged all content to be definitely positive, and '–1' indicates that all content was
assessed as definitely negative. Since this is not a sample, we do not show standard errors.

media management strategies. Nevertheless, this does not appear to have been
associated with more negative coverage in the *Irish Times* and *Irish Independent*.

We find no evidence of a secular shift towards political competition in Irish
election coverage and a noticeable increase in negativity between 1969 and 1973,
but no consistent pattern thereafter. So, the damaging syndrome of an increase
in political competition bringing with it more negativity, as evidenced in numerous
international studies, has not beset Ireland. However, as Figure 3.3 shows, political
competition is associated with a more negative tone. This difference is much
bigger than the overall increase in negativity noted above. The mean tone of
policy coverage is over 0.1 more positive than that of political competition,
suggesting that there are over 5 per cent more positive articles in the policy frame
than in the political competition frame. The relationship is consistent across the
two papers over time and has changed little. Our data validates this part of the
causal mechanism associated with hypercritical infotainment. This implies that
if there were a move towards political competition in Ireland, there would also
be a shift towards negativity.

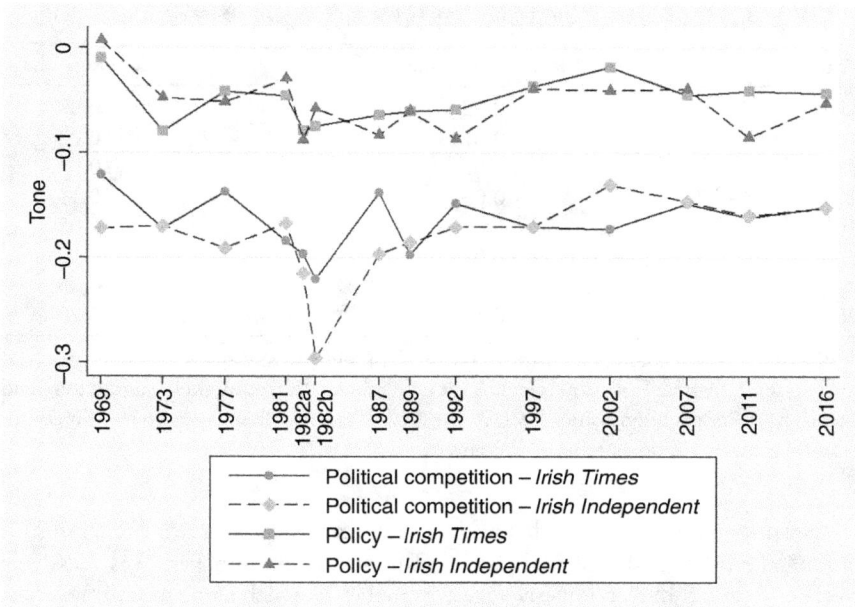

Figure 3.3 Tone by frame, *Irish Times* and *Irish Independent* 1969–2016
Note: Tone is defined as the probability that a paragraph is positive less the probability that it is negative. Non-Irish and non-political paragraphs are excluded. A paragraph is defined as political if one of the political categories exceeds the machine learning threshold for that category (0.57 for macroeconomic, 0.39 for microeconomic, 0.39 for other policy, and 0.46 for political competition). A political paragraph is defined as political competition if political competition exceeds the probability of all three policy categories. A political paragraph is defined as policy if any of the three policy categories exceeds political competition. Since this is not a sample, we do not show standard errors.

The final hypercritical infotainment hypothesis is that conflict will receive increased coverage. We know that populist parties seek to introduce conflict into a political system they see as controlled by a homogeneous elite, i.e. the so-called 'establishment'. In an Irish context, Sinn Féin fulfils this criterion and is Ireland's most controversial political party because of its links with the Provisional IRA and, more recently, anti-establishment positioning. Therefore, if the media increasingly sought to emphasise political conflict, Sinn Féin should have received a bonus in coverage.

Table 3.1 compares the party's vote share to its share of coverage in the *Irish Times* and *Irish Independent*. Sinn Féin abstained from elections until 1987 because it did not recognise the Irish Parliament as legitimate. So, its participation in that election was a story in itself. Even though it still supported the Provisional

Table 3.1 Coverage of Sinn Féin, *Irish Times* and *Irish Independent* 1969–2016

Year	Election vote share	Coverage share
1987	0.02	0.05
1989	0.01	0.03
1992	0.02	0.02
1997	0.03	0.11
2002	0.07	0.08
2007	0.07	0.10
2011	0.10	0.09
2016	0.14	0.23

Note: The coverage share is mentions of Sinn Féin and its candidates as a proportion of mentions of Fianna Fáil, Fine Gael, Labour, and the PDs and their candidates, and mentions of independent candidates, in the *Irish Times* and *Irish Independent*. Since this is not a sample, we do not show standard errors.

IRA's campaign of violence, this was an important step closer to the consensus among the other Irish political parties. The next time Sinn Féin was massively over-represented in election coverage was in 1997, which came at an important juncture in the Northern Ireland peace process. Again, the over-representation of Sinn Féin signifies coverage of the reduction of conflict, not the increase of conflict. The cessation of the IRA campaign ultimately allowed Sinn Féin to position itself as a left-wing populist party in the Republic of Ireland, and its support increased accordingly. Therefore, the four elections after 1997 are relevant to the pessimistic hypothesis that the media will prioritise conflict. This is evidently untrue for 2002, 2007, and 2011. Sinn Féin received far more coverage in 2016 than its eventual election result would suggest. However, its over-representation is less spectacular when compared to the result of 0.17 predicted by opinion polls during the campaign.

Our findings do not identify the change in framing as implied by hypercritical infotainment. We see only a minimal and one-off increase in negativity. It is theoretically interesting, but of little practical relevance in these two Irish newspapers over the last three decades, to note that political competition is associated with negativity. In the 2016 election, the papers seem to have concentrated extra coverage on the most controversial party. Overall, however, the hypercritical infotainment approach generates little insight into the history of election coverage in these two national titles.

Critical impartiality

To determine whether critical impartiality is a dominant norm in Irish election coverage, we begin by considering the distribution of election coverage in the *Irish Times* and the *Irish Independent* across political actors from 1969 to 2016.

The distribution of coverage is the most basic decision media outlets have to make in an election period. Newspapers, in particular, may have had their ideological favourites, or news about particular political parties was seen to sell more papers than coverage of their competitors. Alternatively, impartial coverage simply involves reflecting the level of popular support or existing representation enjoyed by the political parties. Ireland's political history in our period allows a good test of this hypothesis, as there have been substantial changes in the distribution of political power and the concentration of the Irish party system. From the 1970s to 1980s, Ireland was characterised by a 'two-and-a-half-party' system: the two parties being the centre-right nationalist parties – the dominant Fianna Fáil and the eternally second-placed Fine Gael – and the Labour Party constituting the 'half'. As discussed in Chapter 2, this system fragmented from the 1980s onwards.

Figure 3.4 shows the distribution of the coverage across competing political parties from 1969 to 2016 in the two titles. It uses a concentration index to summarise the distribution of coverage across parties: the higher the score, the

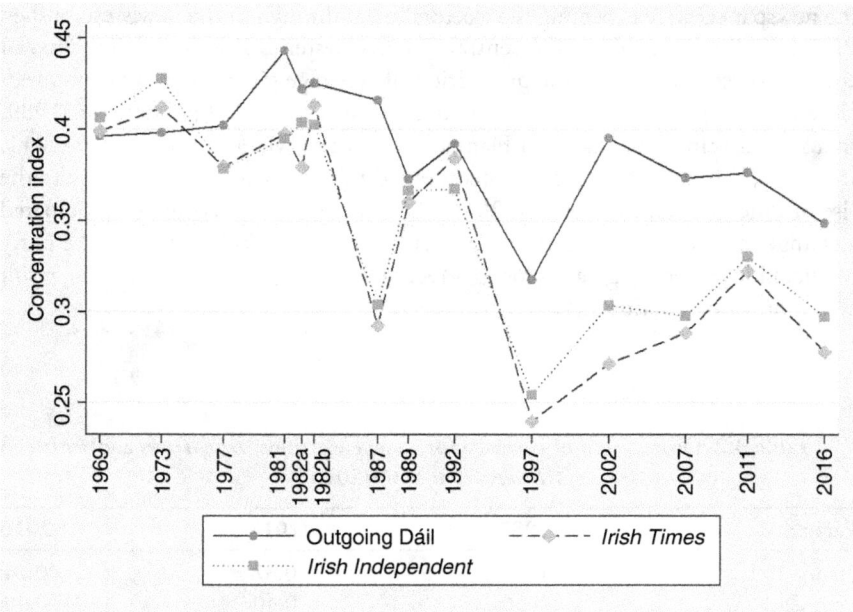

Figure 3.4 Share of coverage across parties, *Irish Times* and *Irish Independent* 1969–2016
Note: We measure concentration using the Herfindahl–Hirschman Index: the fewer the parties and the more unequal their sizes, the higher the score. The parties included are Fianna Fáil, Fine Gael, Labour, the Progressive Democrats, and Sinn Féin. The underlying data consists of counts of mentions of the parties' names and/or their candidates. Standard errors are not shown because the data is based on the whole population of articles for each election.

greater the extent to which the newspapers concentrated on fewer parties. The graph compares the newspaper coverage to the distribution of seats in the outgoing Dáil. We can see the collapse of the old two-and-a-half-party system in the 1980s with the breakthrough of the PDs. The atrophy of the PDs and the weakness of Fine Gael led to a re-concentration in the early 2000s, but thereafter the rise of Sinn Féin continued the progress of fragmentation. The graph shows that the newspapers faithfully tracked changes in the composition of the party system. The Pearson correlation coefficient (Pearson's r) between the outgoing Dáil's concentration and *Irish Times* coverage is 0.66; for the *Irish Independent*, it is 0.68. Coverage goes up and down with changes in the composition of the Dáil. In 1987, and consistently from 1997 onwards, the two papers presented a less fragmented picture than the outgoing Dáil. For 1997, 2002, and 2007 this is because the papers over-reported a small party, the PDs. Although their popular support was minimal at these elections, the PDs secured participation in governments.

In the cases of 1987, 2011, and 2016, shown in Table 3.2, it seems that the two papers were anticipating substantial change in the party system. In 1987, the newspapers were expecting the electoral breakthrough of the newly established PDs and, therefore, a less concentrated party system. This prediction was, of course, correct. Moreover, the proportion of coverage given to the PDs was very close to the opinion poll numbers and election result (11.9 per cent) in 1989. In a similar vein, the collapse of Fianna Fáil was also widely anticipated in 2011. Ironically, this collapse was so unprecedented that it became as big a story as the rise of Fine Gael and Labour. In 2016, the two papers also correctly anticipated a change in the political system. However, similarly to 2011, Labour – the party predicted to suffer the greatest losses – received coverage proportional to its result at the previous election.

Table 3.2 Distribution of coverage for change elections, *Irish Times* and *Irish Independent* 1969–2016

Party	1987	2011	2016
Fianna Fáil	0.37	0.37	0.24
Fine Gael	0.36	0.40	0.40
Labour	0.08	0.12	0.13
PDs	0.13	0.01	0.01
Sinn Féin	0.06	0.09	0.22

Note: Each cell entry is the proportion of the total mentions of all five parties and their candidates represented by the mentions of one party and its candidates for the *Irish Times* and the *Irish Independent*. Since this is not a sample, we do not show standard errors.

Until the 2016 general election, it was unimaginable that Fianna Fáil and Fine Gael could work together or that a government could be led by any other party (notwithstanding occasional calls from Labour for 'revolving taoisigh' and the like) (Collins, 2009). The relative coverage given to the two parties is, therefore, a key part of the election coverage. While remaining roughly proportional overall, perhaps the two newspapers have given more coverage to the outgoing Government, or maybe, in a Westminster spirit, they provided a little more coverage to the 'official opposition' than their seat share warranted. Figure 3.5 explores these ideas by plotting Fianna Fáil's seat advantage over Fine Gael against its advantage in election coverage in our two newspapers. It shows that the two papers have tended to track the relative size of the two parties in their election coverage, albeit less closely than for the overall party system. Pearson's r for the outgoing Dáil's ratio of Fianna Fáil to Fine Gael seats with the *Irish Times*' coverage is 0.47, and for the *Irish Independent* it is 0.41.

There are two notable exceptions: 1992 and 2007. Both titles over-represented Fianna Fáil in 1992. This was not an anticipation of a surge in support for the

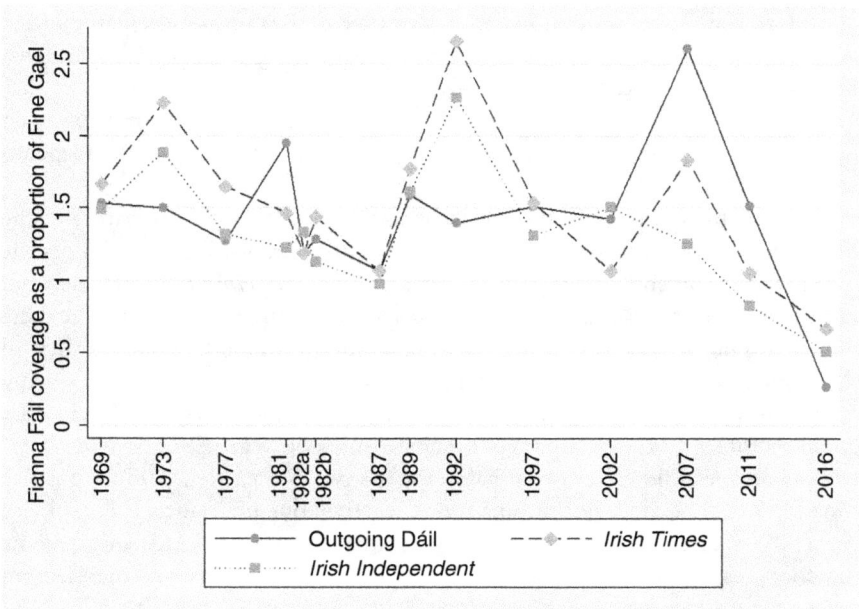

Figure 3.5 Coverage of Fianna Fáil and Fine Gael, *Irish Times* and *Irish Independent* 1969–2016

Note: The y-axis shows Fianna Fáil's Dáil seats or newspaper coverage as a proportion of Fine Gael's. Since this is not a sample, we do not show standard errors.

party. One conjecture would be that it reflected the newsworthy and acrimonious relationship between the outgoing Taoiseach and leader of Fianna Fáil, Albert Reynolds, and the leader of the junior government party, Desmond O'Malley of the PDs. The situation in 2007 is more straightforward. Fine Gael had had a bad election in 2002. The *Irish Times* did not increase its coverage of Fianna Fáil proportionally, while the *Irish Independent* actually focused more on Fine Gael, in spite of their relatively low representation in the outgoing Dáil.

We have established that the Irish party system has fragmented during the period of our study. More fundamentally, perhaps, voters have turned away from parties towards independent candidates. Independent candidates tend to be local candidates taking the approach 'you do anything you can to benefit your locality and your constituency and your district, and your TD will do anything he can to benefit your locality and your district and your constituency and, in a sense, damn everything else' (Mair, 2011). Local candidates can be difficult for national media outlets to cover as they are selling to a national market and trying to cover a national campaign. For example, from the outset of the 2011 election campaign, internal concerns were expressed at RTÉ about the proportion of coverage being given to independent candidates and those representing smaller parties. One internal memo noted, 'all programmes must work towards getting the proportion of attention given to independents and smaller parties up to acceptable levels' (Rafter, 2015). Accordingly, as Figure 3.6 illustrates, coverage of independents in the *Irish Times* and *Irish Independent* has risen as their electoral success has grown. In summary, we present strong evidence of a rigorously neutral approach by the newspapers in distributing coverage amongst political parties and independent candidates.

What matters to parties and citizens is not just whether parties feature in the media but also to what extent they are covered favourably. Figure 3.7 plots the mean tone of content for five political parties in the *Irish Times* over each election; Figure 3.8 does the same for the *Irish Independent*. The range of tone in these figures is quite wide, much wider than the figure for overall tone, and similar to that which divided tone by frame. Differences that look big in the graph are big enough to be politically meaningful. For example, an increase from –0.2 to –0.1 could be interpreted as a 5 per cent increase in positive articles.

Media tone is not a zero-sum game for the two big parties. A more positive tone for Fine Gael does not mean a more negative tone for Fianna Fáil, and vice versa. More often, the tone of coverage of the two parties heads in the same direction, especially in the *Irish Times*. The correlation between the election means for the two parties is a very high 0.78 for the *Irish Times* and a low, but still positive, 0.18 for the *Irish Independent*. There is no evidence of a trend over time, for example, of increasing hostility to parties. The minima in the *Irish Times* for the two big parties are associated with the tension and chaos of the two 1982 elections. The same dip is evident in the *Irish Independent*, although

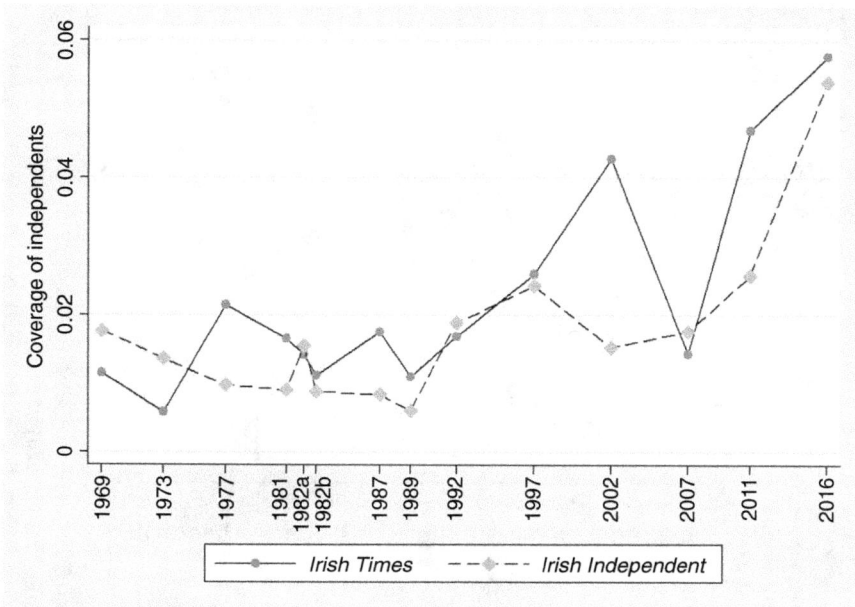

Figure 3.6 Coverage of independent candidates, *Irish Times* and *Irish Independent*
1969–2016
Note: Coverage of independents is the proportion of paragraphs mentioning 'independent'
in an Irish-focused paragraph, excluding mentions of 'Independent Fianna Fáil'. Since this
is not a sample, we do not show standard errors.

it is less dramatic. In 1997, the *Irish Independent,* very unusually, endorsed Fianna
Fáil. But we find no improvement in tone for Fianna Fáil in this election. Instead,
there is a decline. However, there is an improvement of the tone of Fianna Fáil
when compared to that of Fine Gael.

Our findings suggest that when tone is considered smaller parties are also
generally indistinguishable from their competitors. The tone of content featuring
the Labour Party and/or its candidates takes a noticeable dive in 1989 in the
Irish Times, although Labour was an opposition party at the time and not involved
in any particular scandal or controversy. There is a less dramatic dip in the *Irish
Independent's* tone towards Labour in 1987. This may indicate frustration with
their role as junior party in a coalition government that was seen to have failed
to deal with an economic crisis. The insurgent PDs suffered from an increasingly
negative tone. They took a steep dive until hitting the floor in 1992 in the *Irish
Times*, and a longer, shallower dive continuing until 1997 in the *Irish Independent*.
Like the electorate, the two newspapers decided that the PDs were not the
saviours of Ireland, but just a micro-party that some saw playing a positive role

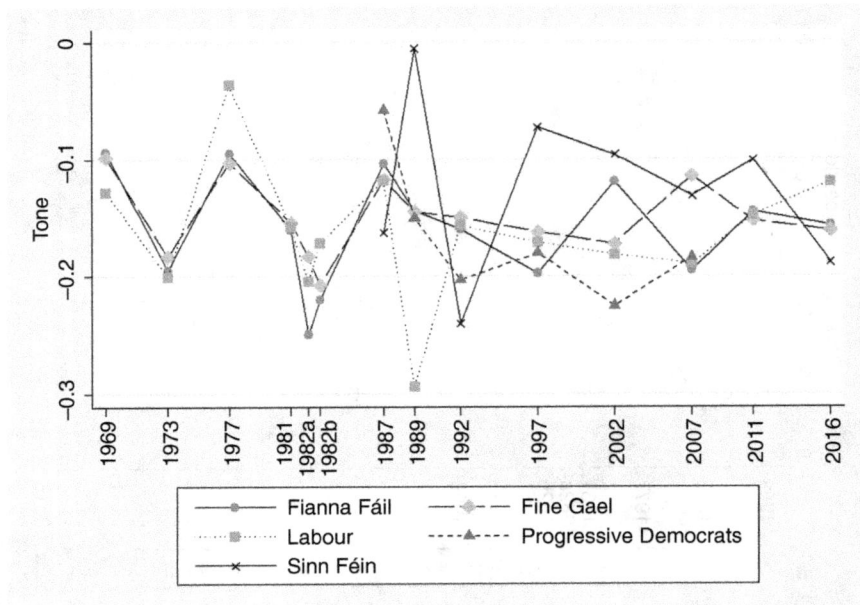

Figure 3.7 Tone, *Irish Times* 1969–2016

Note: Tone is defined as the probability that a paragraph is positive less the probability that it is negative. '1' indicates that the classifier judged all content to be definitely positive, and '–1' indicates that all content was assessed as definitely negative. Since this is not a sample, we do not show standard errors. We do not directly identify tone about a political party. We classify the tone of a paragraph that mentions a political party or one or more of its candidates.

in curbing the populism and clientelism of Fianna Fáil in government. The tone of Sinn Féin coverage jumps in a positive direction in both newspapers in 1989, perhaps representing approval of the party's entry into electoral politics. Thereafter, however, Sinn Féin is generally indistinguishable from the other parties. Both newspapers take a more negative tone to coverage of Sinn Féin in 2016. In the *Irish Independent*, this shift is very sharp and clearly separates it from the other parties. At that election, the *Irish Independent* was seen to have taken a very tough line against the party (Leahy, 2016: 91–2). It is possible that the two titles switched from encouraging the peace process in Northern Ireland to warning of Sinn Féin's threat to Ireland's political and economic consensus.

Based on our findings related to coverage and tone from 1969 to 2016, there is strong evidence of the norms of critical impartiality in reporting by both the *Irish Times* and *Irish Independent*. There was a shift towards negativity at the beginning of our period. The two newspapers take similarly impartial decisions

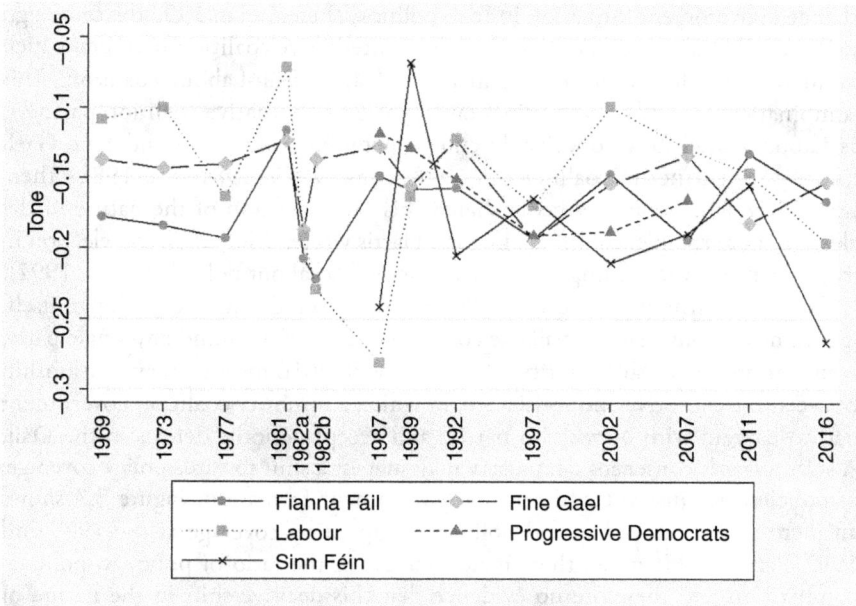

Figure 3.8 Tone, *Irish Independent* 1969–2016
Note: Tone is defined as the probability that a paragraph is positive less the probability that
it is negative. '1' indicates that the classifier judged all content to be definitely positive, and
'–1' indicates that all content was assessed as definitely negative. Since this is not a sample,
we do not show standard errors. We do not directly identify tone about a political party.
We classify the tone of a paragraph that mentions a political party or one or more
of its candidates.

in relation to the distribution of coverage amongst parties and the tone of that
coverage. We find, however, that these norms do not appear to have changed
since 1969. The one possible caveat is that 2016 may have been the beginning
of a bias against Sinn Féin. This is something we can investigate more closely in
our intensive study of the 2016 election later in this chapter.

Exogenous factors

Between 1969 and 2016, the Irish political system made a substantial shift from
the majoritarian politics of its Westminster heritage towards consensus democracy,
as more traditionally found in Northern and Central Europe. As noted in Chapter
2, there are two turning points to consider. The Fianna Fáil–PD coalition in 1989
marked Fianna Fáil's admission that it could not govern alone after five elections
in which it failed to achieve an overall majority. This decision fundamentally

changed government formation in Irish politics. Therefore, in 1992 the campaign took place in the context of a debate about alternative coalition partners, which resulted in the formation of the first ever Fianna Fáil–Labour coalition. This combination opened up a continental scenario of alternative coalition partners, as Labour could now conceivably choose between Fianna Fáil and Fine Gael, its previous partner in coalitions in 1948, 1954, 1973, 1981, and 1982. There is some evidence that the media shared this interpretation of the nature of the election. For example, columnist Eoghan Harris wrote: 'More than any election in living memory, the coming general election will be about policy' (Harris, 1992).

The other turning point came in 2016, when, even during the campaign itself, it became obvious that no available coalition option, never mind any single party, would approach a Dáil majority. The outcome in 2016 meant a new relationship between the executive and legislature, in which a minority coalition government had to bargain with opposition parties and accept periodic defeats in the Dáil. A shift towards consensus democracy may suggest a shift towards policy coverage, as policies, not just votes, determine government formation. Figure 3.3 shows an increase in both policy and political competition coverage at the 1989 and 1992 elections. However, there is no increase in the ratio of policy to political competition and therefore no evidence that this decisive shift in the nature of the political system affected framing in the newspapers.

The 2016 campaign also saw a qualitative change in the Irish political system. As widely anticipated during the campaign, the executive had lost its traditional dominance of the Irish legislature. The change from 2011 to 2016 is particularly hard to interpret in this respect, as the crisis election of 2011 had led to a decisive shift towards policy in election coverage. But there is no evidence that a change in the nature of the political system affected framing. The move towards consensus democracy changed the relative importance of political parties. In particular, small parties, including the PDs and Labour, could now potentially decide which big party (Fianna Fáil or Fine Gael) would lead the Government.

Table 3.3 compares the coverage Labour and the PDs received with their vote share. It shows that Labour did not receive a bonus in coverage when its potential as a coalition partner became more important in 1992. Neither do we see its share of coverage relative to its vote increase appreciably over the next quarter of a century. However, it is obvious that the PDs were substantially over-represented in coverage in all but their first election. This is surely due to their status as coalition partners of Fianna Fáil.

It might be that close elections are covered differently to contests where the winner is more predictable. In close elections, political competition becomes more important, so we can assume that the closer the election, the greater the emphasis on political competition. Unfortunately, closeness is difficult to measure. The main problem is the absence of a good series of opinion polls spanning our sample period from 1969. In addition, the complexity of the Irish political system

Table 3.3 Coverage of Labour and PDs, *Irish Times* and *Irish Independent* 1969–2016

	Labour		PDs	
Election	**Election vote share**	**Coverage share**	**Election vote share**	**Coverage share**
1969	0.17	0.11		
1973	0.14	0.06		
1977	0.12	0.11		
1981	0.10	0.08		
Feb. 1982	0.09	0.07		
Nov. 1982	0.09	0.08		
1987	0.07	0.08	0.12	0.13
1989	0.10	0.06	0.06	0.10
1992	0.19	0.10	0.05	0.10
1997	0.10	0.13	0.05	0.14
2002	0.11	0.09	0.04	0.10
2007	0.10	0.08	0.03	0.12
2011	0.19	0.12		
2016	0.07	0.11		

Note: The coverage share for each party is the mentions of that party and its candidates as a proportion of mentions of Fianna Fáil, Fine Gael, Labour, and the PDs and their candidates, and mentions of independent candidates, in the *Irish Times* and *Irish Independent*. Since this is not a sample, we do not show standard errors.

raises the issue of deciding which parties to include in a closeness calculation. Since, prior to 2016 at any rate, the two options continued to be Fianna Fáil, perhaps plus others, or a Fine Gael–Labour coalition, perhaps plus others, we define closeness as a difference of less than 3 per cent between Fianna Fáil's total and that of Fine Gael and Labour. For each election, we check whether the election result, and/or available polls during the campaign, comes within this threshold. We find that the elections in 1969, 1973, 1981, 1982 (February), and 1992 had a higher emphasis on political competition in the *Irish Times* but a similarly lower emphasis in the *Irish Independent*. Therefore, we do not see any evidence for a closeness effect.

Ireland has a reputation for little, or very weak, ideological differentiation between parties. Nonetheless, the language of left and right is used in debate on public policy and has also been used to analyse election manifestos of Irish political parties. The Comparative Manifestos Project has analysed the content of Irish election manifestos until 2011 and estimated the extent to which parties emphasise left- or right-wing issues. This source has several limitations, but it is the only measure of party ideology stretching across our elections. The standard deviation of party positions on this left-right scale is a plausible indicator of the ideological polarisation of the system. There were jumps in polarisation in 1973, in the trio of elections in the early 1980s, and again in 2011. These elections should mark increases in the standard deviation of tone of the two newspapers' coverage of economic policy and the standard deviation of the tone of their coverage across political parties. However, when we compared the manifesto measures to the media data, there was no such relationship. Therefore, we cannot say there is a relationship between ideological polarisation and content. Shifts in the nature of Irish governance did not change the framing of elections or the coverage of the Labour Party. However, the high profile of the smaller PDs was conditional on their presence in a coalition government. Close elections and changes in ideological polarisation do not appear to have affected the coverage of elections either. In summary, we can conclude that Irish election coverage has been very resistant to exogenous influences from the political system.

There are many ways to think about the impact of the internet on the media. Perhaps most obviously, it has undermined the revenue basis of both broadcast and print media, and this feeds into our analysis in Chapter 7. Here we investigate how social media's impact on politics has changed election coverage in the traditional media. In this sense, it is an exogenous political change – a major shift in the nature of election campaigning. The 2016 election campaign has been described as 'the first truly social media election in Ireland' given the extent to which social media platforms were 'used by candidates and parties to sell their messages, and by voters to converse about the issues' (Goodbody, 2016). Therefore, if the Irish media report reasonably accurately on election campaigns, we would expect both a substantial number of references to social media and a big increase since 2011. We identified all paragraphs mentioning 'social media', 'Facebook', 'Twitter' and 'tweet'. Thus, we do not study social media online, but rather the new media in the old media. Table 3.4 reports the total of these measures for the *Irish Times* and *Irish Independent* in 2011 and 2016. It shows that the two newspapers barely reference social media during the two election campaigns. There is indeed a big percentage increase (107 per cent in the *Times* and 32 per cent in the *Independent*), but since the numbers are so small, the increase will not have been noticed by readers. Like other changes in the nature of the political

Table 3.4 Social media mentions in the *Irish Times* and *Irish Independent*, 2011 and 2016

	Count		Proportion of total	
Year	2011	2016	2011	2016
Irish Times	91	189	0.003	0.006
Irish Independent	173	229	0.005	0.007

system, the rise of social media campaigning appears to have had very little impact on the two leading newspapers in 2011 and 2016.

General election, 2016

Having considered election coverage in the *Irish Times* and *Irish Independent* from 1969 to 2016, we now further explore our perspectives with data from nine additional media sources in 2016. Most of this section relates to critical impartiality. With a larger number of sources, we can go much further in investigating impartiality and consensus in the media. In relation to hypercritical infotainment, we examine whether political competition, negativity, and the association between the two, were more prevalent beyond the *Irish Times* and *Irish Independent*. We do not pursue the exogenous factor perspective in this section, as we cannot examine an inherently dynamic concept by looking at one point in time.

We look at framing in 2016 with two aims in mind. First, we use this data as a further test of the hypercritical infotainment thesis that political competition has come to dominate over policy discussion. Second, we look at the extent of consensus to assess the influence of the overall media system over particular media outlets. The election of 2016 was not distinctively framed when compared to our other thirteen elections. Figure 3.9 shows the macroeconomic policy frame across all sources. There is some substantial variation. There is a difference of over 0.1 between the highest scoring (RTÉ's *Morning Ireland* and *Six One*) and the lowest scoring (*Irish Daily Mail* and *Irish Daily Mirror*). This means there is a 10 per cent greater chance of a given paragraph being about economic policy in the former two broadcast programmes than in the latter two print titles. There is a clear division between broadcast and print. All of the broadcasters, whether television or radio, whether public or private, covered more economic policy than all of the newspapers in the sample. All of these differences are statistically significant at the 5 per cent level or better.

Figure 3.10 shows the equivalent graph for political competition, i.e. game coverage. TV3's *News at 5:30* is an outlier with a much stronger emphasis on political competition than the other sources. Our best estimate is 0.54, but the 95 per cent confidence interval stretches from 0.49 to 0.59. Even looking at the other ten outlets, we can see substantial diversity. Indeed, the pattern is like that of macroeconomic policy, with higher values for broadcast than for print. The difference between all broadcast outlets and all newspapers is statistically significant at the 5 per cent level, except for the difference between the *Irish Times* and *The Last Word* (Today FM). However, in relation to the somewhat more prevalent microeconomic policy and other policy, there was a relatively tight consensus amongst the eleven sources. The newspapers place less emphasis on political competition than do the broadcasters. Nonetheless, the evidence does not suggest that the election was primarily framed in terms of political competition in the

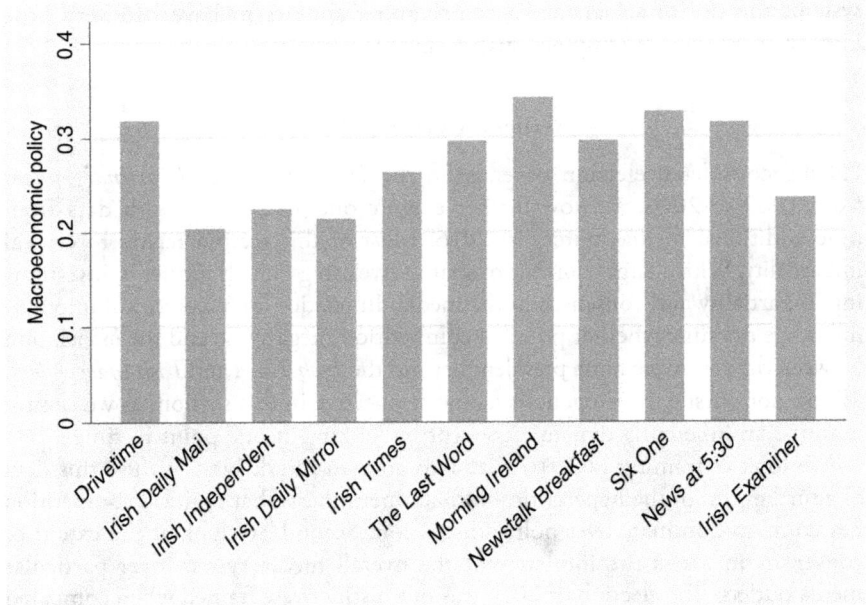

Figure 3.9 Coverage of economic policy, 2016
Note: 'Macroeconomic policy' denotes the mean probability of a paragraph about Ireland
being about macroeconomic policy. Standard errors for broadcast sources range from
0.0054 for *Newstalk Breakfast* to 0.0188 for TV3's *News at 5:30*. There are no standard
errors for the print sources as the data are not sampled.

broadcast sector. Separate calculations suggest that only on TV3 did political
competition dominate over policy coverage.[1] There is mixed evidence on whether
there was a consensus on how to frame the election. There was agreement on
the importance of microeconomic and other policy but some noticeable differences
between the broadcast and print sources in relation to the emphasis on macroeconomic policy and political competition.

Table 3.5 shows tone by source and frame for all eleven outlets in 2016. All
sources cover the election negatively. However, the three quality papers do so
more positively than all other sources. The difference in tone between the *Irish
Examiner, Times, Independent* and all others is statistically significant at 5 per
cent, while the more negative broadcast sources are statistically indistinguishable
from each other and the two other newspapers. All bar the *Irish Daily Mirror*
adopt a more negative tone for political competition than for policy. The gap is
very similar for the three self-styled quality papers: 0.12 for the *Irish Examiner*,
0.1 for the *Irish Independent*, and 0.11 for the *Irish Times*. The gap between the
tone of the two frames is noticeably lower for all other sources, ranging from

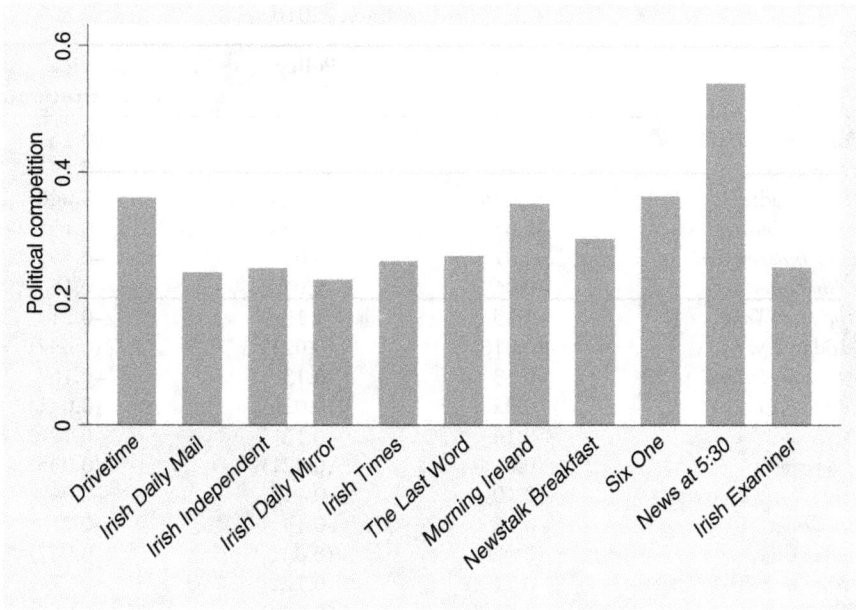

Figure 3.10 Political competition, 2016

Note: 'Macroeconomic policy' denotes the mean probability of a paragraph about Ireland being about macroeconomic policy. Standard errors for broadcast sources range from 0.0054 for *Newstalk Breakfast* to 0.0188 for TV3's *News at 5:30*. There are no standard errors for the print sources as the data are not sampled.

0.04 for *Morning Ireland* (RTÉ Radio 1) to 0.08 for *Drivetime* (RTÉ Radio 1) and *The Last Word* (Today FM). The standard errors do not enable us to state confidently that the tone for political competition is different to that for policy in relation to any individual broadcast source. However, it does seem clear that the difference in tone found in the historical and 2016 newspaper sources extends to the two broadcast sectors, albeit probably at a less dramatic level.

The intensive study of media coverage in the 2016 election campaign tends to confirm our rejection of the hypercritical infotainment perspective. Political competition does not predominate, although in our wider sample it is somewhat more important than in coverage from 1969 to 2016 in the *Irish Times* and *Irish Independent*. Similarly, the tone of the extra media sources is more negative than the two newspapers we have studied through fourteen elections. In relation to macroeconomic policy, political competition, and tone, the two newspapers tend to occupy one end of a seemingly narrow spectrum. We now go on to investigate whether there is a consensus on the impartial treatment of political parties.

Table 3.5 Tone by frame, 2016

Outlet	Overall	Policy	Political competition
Irish Daily Mail	−0.12	−0.11	−0.16
Drivetime	−0.14	−0.11	−0.19
(RTÉ Radio 1)	(0.024)	(0.029)	(0.040)
Irish Examiner	−0.05	−0.03	−0.15
Irish Independent	−0.07	−0.05	−0.15
Irish Times	−0.06	−0.04	−0.15
The Last Word	−0.15	−0.13	−0.21
(Today FM)	(0.018)	(0.021)	(0.037)
Morning Ireland	−0.13	−0.13	−0.167
(RTÉ Radio 1)	(0.022)	(0.026)	(0.045)
Newstalk Breakfast	−0.14	−0.12	−0.18
(Newstalk)	(0.018)	(0.021)	(0.035)
Irish Daily Mirror	−0.10	−0.11	−0.04
Six One	−0.16	−0.14	−0.21
(RTÉ One)	(0.026)	(0.031)	(0.047)
News at 5:30	−0.21	−0.12	−0.27
(TV3)	(0.058)	(0.097)	(0.073)

Note: Tone figures are means for 2016, excluding non-Irish and non-political news. Standard errors are given in parentheses. These standard errors account for propagation of error. They incorporate the standard errors of the two variables (positive and negative sentiment) that are used to calculate tone.

We begin with Fine Gael – the leading government party in 2016 – which for the first time was defending its position as the largest party in the Dáil. Figure 3.11 shows the amount and tone of coverage given to Fine Gael by ten of our eleven sources.[2] The mean score for all sources except *Drivetime* (RTÉ Radio 1) gave Fine Gael more than their predicted vote share would suggest (0.286 in Tom Louwerse's data for 15 February 2016, the midpoint of the campaign). Nonetheless, we cannot be statistically confident that *Six One* (RTÉ One), *The Last Word* (Today FM), and *Newstalk Breakfast* (Newstalk) did not also give less. There is a wide range among the sources, with the *Irish Examiner* probably giving a 50 per cent larger share of its coverage to Fine Gael than RTÉ's *Six One* and *Drivetime*.

The newspapers, and most of the broadcast programmes, appear quite close together on tone, although it is likely that RTÉ One's *Six One* took a particularly negative and RTÉ Radio 1's *Morning Ireland* a distinctively positive tone. The *Irish Examiner* is an outlier in terms of the proportion of coverage but is in the middle in terms of tone. In summary, the Irish media made a firm decision to

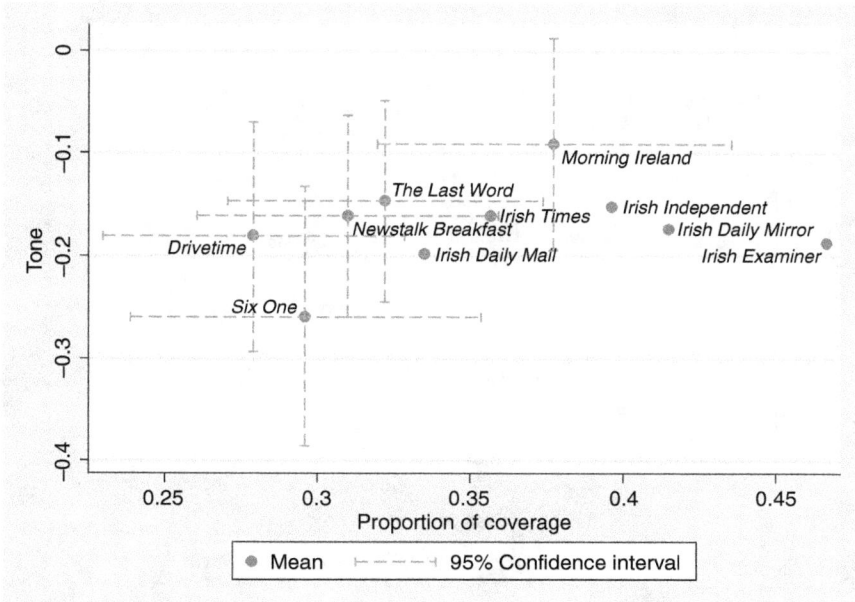

Figure 3.11 Coverage of Fine Gael, 2016

Note: Dots identify means. For newspapers, the mean is calculated from all paragraphs and, consequently, there is no standard error. For broadcast media, we sampled a number of days; the dot indicates our best estimate. The faint dotted lines indicate the 95 per cent confidence interval. This means that sampling theory suggests with 95 per cent certainty that the mean is within the interval. Since we had very few paragraphs for each party in TV3's *News at 5:30*, we do not show it on this graph. The confidence intervals account for propagation of error. They incorporate the standard errors of the two variables (positive and negative sentiment) that are used to calculate tone.

give the Government's leading party more coverage than its vote share, although the size of the bonus differed substantially. There also seems to be a consensus in relation to tone.

Figure 3.12 examines Fianna Fáil, which was looking to bounce back after the disastrous election of 2011. Fianna Fáil received more coverage than its vote share from most sources (0.205, again Louwerse's mid-campaign figure). The *Irish Daily Mirror* was the only clear exception, and *The Last Word*, *Morning Ireland*, and *Drivetime* possibly were just under this level. The greatest bonus is still quite close to the vote share. The range is also about half that of Fine Gael. While there was clearly some disagreement on the extent to which election coverage should be focused on the leading government party, the media was quite clear that the largest opposition party should be treated proportionally. It appears that

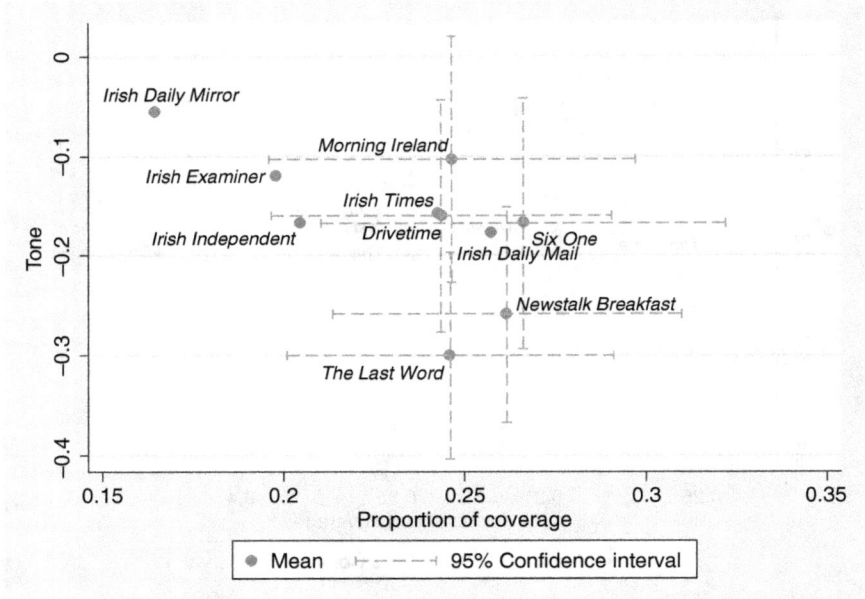

Figure 3.12 Coverage of Fianna Fáil, 2016
Note: Dots identify means. For newspapers, the mean is calculated from all paragraphs and, consequently, there is no standard error. For broadcast media, we sampled a number of days; the dot indicates our best estimate. The faint dotted lines indicate the 95 per cent confidence interval. This means that sampling theory suggests with 95 per cent certainty that the mean is within the interval. Since we had very few paragraphs for each party in TV3's *News at 5:30*, we do not show it on this graph. The confidence intervals account for propagation of error. They incorporate the standard errors of the two variables (positive and negative sentiment) that are used to calculate tone.

there was less of a consensus on the tone with which Fianna Fáil was covered: the range of our best estimates is about 50 per cent greater than the range for Fine Gael. The *Irish Daily Mirror* is a definite positive outlier, and *Newstalk Breakfast* (Newstalk) and *The Last Word* (Today FM) are likely negative outliers. However, the others are within the −0.1 to −0.2 band observed for Fine Gael. There was quite a clear consensus on roughly proportional coverage or a minor bonus in its amount for Fianna Fáil. There was also a consensus on tone, albeit with outliers more noticeable than for Fine Gael.

We undertook a similar exercise for two smaller parties, the Labour Party and Sinn Féin. Figure 3.13 shows the graph for the Labour Party. Labour enjoyed a historic success in 2011 but for years before the election had been suffering from a drastic loss of support, which a change of leader had failed to reverse. There

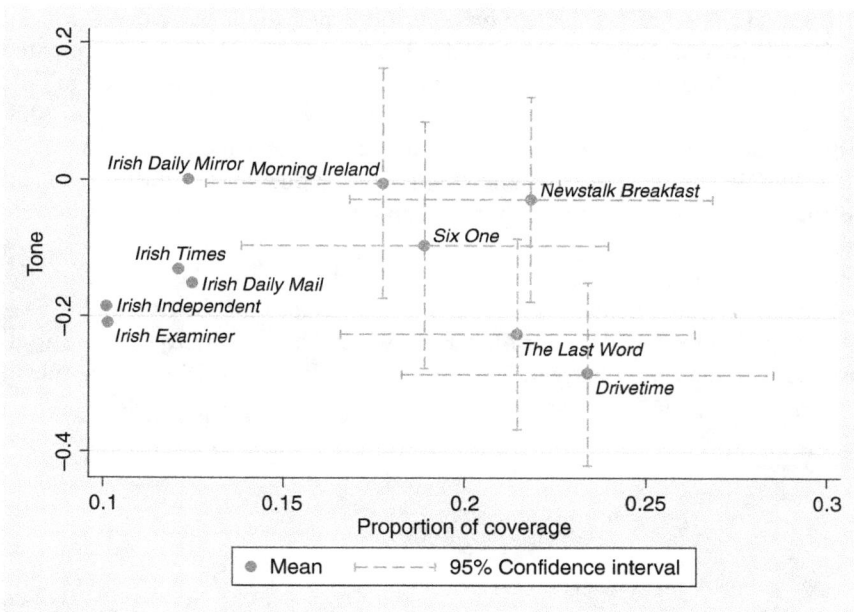

Figure 3.13 Coverage of Labour, 2016

Note: Dots identify means. For newspapers, the mean is calculated from all paragraphs and, consequently, there is no standard error. For broadcast media, we sampled a number of days; the dot indicates our best estimate. The faint dotted lines indicate the 95 per cent confidence interval. This means that sampling theory suggests with 95 per cent certainty that the mean is within the interval. Since we had very few paragraphs for each party in TV3's *News at 5:30*, we do not show it on this graph. The confidence intervals account for propagation of error. They incorporate the standard errors of the two variables (positive and negative sentiment) that are used to calculate tone.

was a consensus that the Labour Party merited much more coverage than its predicted vote share of 0.066 would imply (Louwerse, 2016). The newspapers gave it up to double that amount, while the broadcast programmes ranged between approximately three and four times that figure. To some extent, this was perhaps a governing bonus like the one received by Fine Gael. However, the desperate plight of the Labour Party and its first female leader, Joan Burton, who was in danger of losing in her own seat, was a story in its own right. The bonus in coverage is similar to Fine Gael's – so is the wide range in the amount of coverage. Three broadcast programmes – *Drivetime* (RTÉ Radio 1), *The Last Word* (Today FM), and *Newstalk Breakfast* (Newstalk) – gave Labour twice as much coverage as did the *Irish Times* and the *Irish Independent*. Labour is unusual in relation to tone: three outlets (the *Irish Daily Mirror*, RTÉ Radio 1's *Morning*

Ireland, and Newstalk's *Newstalk Breakfast*) present Labour Party coverage with a virtually neutral tone. In other words, they are remarkably positive compared to what we have seen elsewhere. This makes for a wide range compared to Fine Gael, since all the others occupy the more familiar territory of –0.1 to –0.3. There is no association between tone and coverage for Labour. We cannot say that the *Irish Daily Mirror*, for example, is pro-Labour, as it is in the lower half in the proportion of coverage given to Labour. Although there is considerable diversity, Figure 3.13 suggests that – on average and across the two dimensions of coverage and tone – Labour's miserable election cannot be blamed on the media. If anything, media coverage may have helped limit the damage.

Finally, Figure 3.14 looks at Sinn Féin, which was seeking to establish itself as the main opposition party in 2016 and was emboldened by its leading role in

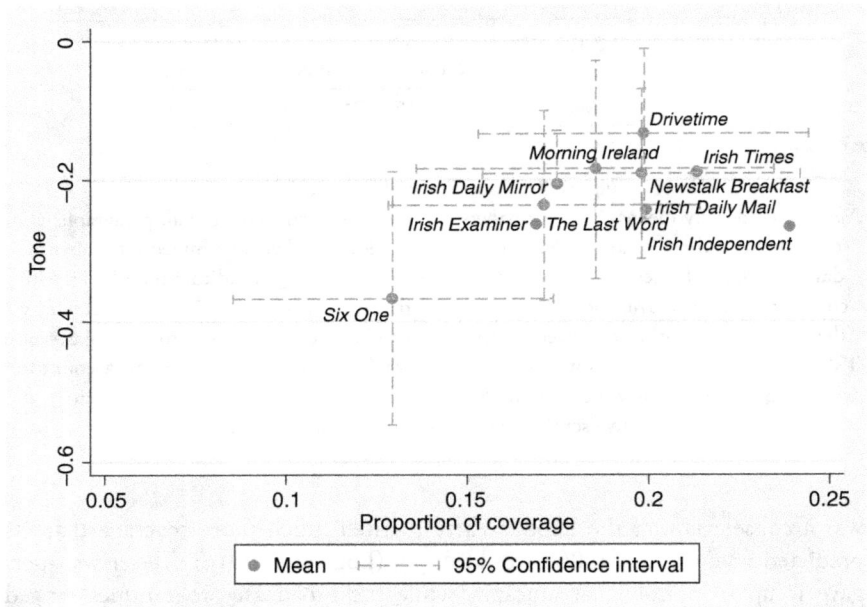

Figure 3.14 Coverage of Sinn Féin, 2016

Note: Dots identify means. For newspapers, the mean is calculated from all paragraphs and, consequently, there is no standard error. For broadcast media, we sampled a number of days; the dot indicates our best estimate. The faint dotted lines indicate the 95 per cent confidence interval. This means that sampling theory suggests with 95 per cent certainty that the mean is within the interval. Since we had very few paragraphs for each party in TV3's *News at 5:30*, we do not show it on this graph. The confidence intervals account for propagation of error. They incorporate the standard errors of the two variables (positive and negative sentiment) that are used to calculate tone.

the successful protests against the outgoing Government's attempt to introduce domestic water charges. In relation to the proportion of coverage, Sinn Féin seems to have been treated very similarly to Fianna Fáil, its rival for largest opposition party. There is a relatively tight consensus that it be given somewhat more coverage than its 0.17 poll value would have suggested. We have already seen how the two main newspapers, and especially the *Irish Independent*, adopted a more negative tone towards Sinn Féin in 2016 than they had in previous elections from 1969 onwards. This level, whatever about the change over time, also appears to represent our other sources. Sinn Féin paragraphs feature the most negative tone of all four parties for seven out of eleven sources, and it is the second most negative for three. The outlier is RTÉ Radio 1's *Drivetime*: this programme featured Sinn Féin in the most positive content. All of the newspapers present Sinn Féin as their most negative party.[3] For all of these (except the *Irish Times*) the difference between the tone of Sinn Féin coverage and that of the most positively covered party is over 0.1, which would indicate 5 per cent more positive content for that party. For the *Irish Daily Mirror*, the number is double that level. In summary, we can say that if floating voters were to read the *Irish Daily Mirror* regularly, that might well reduce their chances of voting Sinn Féin. Sinn Féin has been especially successful amongst younger voters, who tend not to read newspapers, so we doubt these differences had an effect on their election result.

The tone of the coverage of Sinn Féin is the most negative of the four parties, whether the tone is restricted to mentions of the party, its candidates, or its leader. Sinn Féin's leader – Gerry Adams – is associated with much more negative tone than the party name or its other candidates. The gap of 0.17 between Adams and the party leader with the most positive tone (Micheál Martin of Fianna Fáil) is big – much bigger than the gap of 0.11 between Sinn Féin candidates and the most positively covered candidates (again, Fianna Fáil) and the gap of 0.07 between the tone of mentions of the Sinn Féin party name and the most positively covered party name (Labour). There is a similar pattern if Sinn Féin is compared to the next most negatively covered party in each category. Adams was also associated with more negative tone than any other leader in 2011 when we just consider coverage in the *Irish Times* and *Independent*. Indeed, in that year, Sinn Féin the party and its candidates in general were not associated with a more negative tone compared to the other three parties. The negative shift in the *Irish Times* and *Irish Independent* from 2011 to 2016, therefore, runs across all three types of mentions (party, candidates, leader). This also suggests that Adams's negative media tone is associated with enduring questions about his role in, and attitude to, the IRA's violence and not ephemeral issues like his confusion about economic policy as displayed in interviews in 2016.

Despite the aforementioned efforts by RTÉ to balance out coverage, it seems that Ireland's unusually prominent independent candidates lose out in coverage in the national media in 2016. It is hard to classify and measure independents for our purposes, especially when you have an entity called the 'Independent Alliance' in the 2016 election. Nonetheless, our search for the names of independent candidates made up less than 10 per cent of mentions of parties and candidates for all media outlets, except for RTÉ One's *Six One* at 14 per cent. Of course, since the independents are individual local candidates, their story is hard to integrate with the narrative of a national election, and national media coverage is less relevant to these candidates, who can thrive on mentions on local radio, in local newspapers, online, and, above all, in face-to-face contact.

Overall, our study of 2016 extends the pattern of impartiality from the *Irish Times* and *Irish Independent* to nine other sources. The graphs for each party show a much greater range than the tight consensus between the *Irish Times* and *Irish Independent*. However, these two newspapers are never outliers. In relation to Fine Gael, Fianna Fáil, and Labour they stay in a cluster of the five newspapers. By contrast, when it comes to Sinn Féin, the broadcasters and newspapers are mixed in together. While there are outliers in some graphs, no source is a consistent outlier. There is a broad consensus on impartiality, a characteristic of a liberal media system. However, within the system, the broadcast and print sectors differ somewhat, as was also shown in relation to framing and tone.

There are some caveats. The most important one is that the tone of coverage featuring Sinn Féin appears to be more negative than for other parties. We do not want to exaggerate this. We do not measure approval or disapproval for Sinn Féin, only the tone of paragraphs featuring the party and its candidates. Moreover, the difference to the other parties is not hugely significant. When norms of impartiality fray, it can be hard to say to what extent they are under pressure from ideology or commercialism. Newspapers in the US once saw impartiality as a commercial opportunity, an obvious selling point when previously only party propaganda sheets were available. It is possible that the liberal media may be finding it hard to accept Sinn Féin as an important player in the Irish political arena because it challenges mainstream assumptions about Irish nationalism, social justice, and the efficiency of public policy. This may also be a commercial decision, reflecting the anxieties of the ageing, relatively affluent consumers of traditional broadcast and print media, or an attempt to foment controversy without offending too many viewers and readers. The second caveat is that the two government parties received a notable bonus in 2016. A government bonus is not something we generally observed in this historical study, although there was a regular bonus for the small PDs. In a fast-moving campaign, it is hard to combine news values and impartiality. The drama of the poor campaign by Labour leader Joan Burton and confrontations between Gerry Adams and victims of IRA violence were hard to resist for the media, even in a system committed to liberal impartiality.

Earlier we showed that social media made virtually no impact on the content of election coverage in the *Irish Times* and *Irish Independent*. Here we investigate whether the broader media sector marginalised social media in election coverage

Table 3.6 Mentions of social media entities by outlet, 2016 general election

Outlet	Mentions	Proportion campaign
Irish Daily Mirror	696	0.00
Irish Independent	257	0.13
Irish Times	204	0.05
Irish Examiner	166	0.15
Irish Daily Mail	111	0.04
The Last Word	25	0.14
Newstalk Breakfast	13	0.00
Morning Ireland	9	0.50
Six One	2	1.00
Drivetime	0	0.00
News at 5:30	0	0.00
Median	25	0.13

in 2016. Table 3.6 shows the number of mentions of social media and the proportion of those mentions that referred to the election campaign. Clearly, social media was not considered a significant aspect of the campaign in any outlet. The media number of mentions is strikingly low across the sector, with the partial exception of the *Irish Daily Mirror*. However, the low number of mentions of social media in a political context is universal. Indeed, there is a negative correlation between the number of social media mentions and the proportion of those mentions that are political. The *Mirror's* relatively high social media score almost exclusively refers to the world of entertainment and celebrity. The handful of stories about social media and the campaign were so colourful it would have been utterly bizarre to omit them. The most memorable of them involved politicians putting photoshopped versions of each other's campaign posters online. Of course, social media is an important part of the work of political journalists, as a source of stories and as a way of promoting the core content of outlets as well as ancillary material. Nonetheless, it leaves little trace in the actual text of articles and programmes. Remarkably, the print and broadcast sectors ignored social media as part of the election campaign in 2016. The traditional media reported only on the traditional election campaign.

Conclusion

This chapter explored three broad perspectives on Irish election coverage since 1969. Our analysis tends to reject the widespread assumption of hypercritical infotainment that media coverage has focused more on political competition, has become more negative (partly because of the overemphasis on political competition), and has concentrated on the most controversial parties. Many who take this view of the media attribute to it a decline in popular participation in, and respect for, politics. Our analysis may miss out on some elements of the hypercritical infotainment perspective that a quantitative study using other variables, or a qualitative study, might have validated. Nonetheless, our analysis should give pause to any simplistic or uncritical assumptions about the cynicism or sensationalism of media coverage of elections in Ireland. Our work comprehensively rejects the idea that changes in the Irish political system are reflected in how the media covers politics. The media reports on major changes, such as the emergence of coalition government and the fragmentation of political representation, but such changes do not appear to influence how elections are reported. Perhaps most remarkably of all, Ireland's established media did not consider the social media campaign an important aspect of the 2016 election.

We can conclude that the main reason why we have not seen the changes over time predicted by the hypercritical infotainment and exogenous factors perspectives is that Ireland's media system is guided by enduring and relatively strict norms of critical impartiality. The rejection of hypercritical infotainment and the affirmation of critical impartiality present an encouraging view of the Irish media. It seems to play a positive role in conveying political information and encouraging political debate. It is, of course, not passive. Each of our sources, and many of their individual journalists, are important actors in the Irish political system, with the power to shape outcomes. However, we have shown that they are not actors in the partisan sense. In party-political competition, they have usually restricted themselves to providing an arena instead of taking sides. Coverage of Sinn Féin in 2016 is a challenge to this position. There are many good reasons for liberal journalists to be sceptical about this party, to confront its representatives, and warn of the possible consequences of its gaining power. Nonetheless, journalists and citizens need to ask themselves if media coverage of Sinn Féin is a violation of the norm of liberal impartiality. If it is not, then those same journalists and citizens need to define the scope of the liberal consensus outside of which impartiality no longer applies.

Notes

1 These were based on the ratio of a binary policy category to a binary political competition category. A paragraph is defined as political if one of the political categories exceeds the machine learning threshold for that category (0.57 for macroeconomic, 0.39 for microeconomic, 0.39 for other policy, and 0.46 for political competition). A political paragraph is defined as political competition if political competition exceeds the probability of all three policy categories. A political paragraph is defined as policy if any of the three policy categories exceeds political competition.
2 Please note that in the following graphs the scale changes from party to party for presentational reasons.
3 These are all unweighted means for 2016.

4

The role of the economy in media coverage

In previous chapters, we have argued that Ireland's media system is characterised by norms of critical impartiality, and that these norms have survived and continue to influence media content in the information age. This chapter addresses our third broad hypothesis regarding the role of 'exogenous factors' outside the media itself. Recent scholarship in political science and political communications argues that exogenous factors such as the economy are responsible for important changes in media coverage (Soroka *et al.*, 2015). The Irish economy is an excellent case for testing the importance of exogenous factors. Since 1969, it has moved from boom to bust and back again without concern for the norms of critical impartiality or consumer demand for infotainment. If media content does not follow the economy, then it suggests that we must look at the dynamics of Ireland's media system for answers. If, on the other hand, changes in the economy are responsible for media content, then we must take seriously the role of exogenous forces.

The analysis in the chapter is divided in two parts. First, for the fourteen elections from 1969 to 2016, we study coverage in the *Irish Times* and the *Irish Independent*. We find that the economy matters; the tone of election coverage is increasingly negative in bad economic times but does not improve in good times. Furthermore, there is a strong correlation between the tone of election coverage and consumer sentiment, suggesting that past economic conditions and a current feel-good factor influence election coverage. The evidence linking the economy to the emphasis and framing of media content is mixed. The conventional wisdom is that there should be a greater emphasis on economic policy in bad times, but we find more emphasis on economic policy in both very good *and* very bad times. Second, we study nine more media outlets for the 2016 election. In doing so, we establish the importance of commercial orientation and media format in reacting to economic performance.

In the next section, we focus briefly on the media's representation of Ireland's economy in order to contextualise our study. In the subsequent section, we develop the concept of exogeneity, i.e. the idea that forces outside of the media themselves affect election coverage. The final two sections present results from a study of the *Irish Times* and the *Irish Independent* from 1969 to 2016 and then findings from a wider sample of sources for the 2016 election.

Media representation of Ireland's economy

The Irish economy has, at various times, been described as a hare, a tortoise, a tiger, and a phoenix.[1] The story of the economy used to be a classic tale of modernisation. According to the narrative, the protagonist starts out as a pre-industrial economy protected by high tariffs and heavily dependent on Britain. If the narrative followed a straight line, it would begin in 1958 with the Government's publication of 'Economic development' and 'Programme for economic expansion' (Government of Ireland, 1960). Most scholars agree that the publication of these documents marked a pivotal moment in Irish history after which the idea of economic modernisation became increasingly acceptable among political elites (Breen and Dorgan, 2013).[2]

The vision of a modernising Ireland was depicted on the cover of *Time* in 1963. The magazine featured an image of the then Taoiseach, Seán Lemass, depicted in a paternal style, ushering in new industries with the assistance of a leprechaun. The article's headline read, 'Ireland: New Spirit in the Ould Sod'. The tale of a modernising economy persisted throughout the 1960s. Its grand finale should have come in 1973 with Ireland's accession to the European Economic Community (EEC). Symbolically at least, this should have represented the moment when Ireland had taken its place in a community of modern economies and was no longer wholly dependent on its nearest neighbour. But like Homer's *Odyssey*, the real story of Ireland's economy from 1958 until the birth of the Celtic Tiger in the mid-1990s is a disjointed narrative, where there are major setbacks, and important moments in the plot happen out of sequence.

The modernisation narrative is ultimately a story about the need for change, and many feared the consequences of change. Indeed, a considerable section of Irish society cleaved to values that extolled the virtues of rural living and rejected material wealth. In 1943, Taoiseach Éamon de Valera offered a portrait of his ideal society in a St Patrick's Day radio address in which he blended aspects of nationalism, religion, and pastoral imagery to envision a society that was free from the corruption and degeneration associated with industrialisation. De Valera was not alone in holding such views. According to Garvin (2004), as late as the mid-1960s the content of Dáil Éireann debates was split between debates about whether change was desirable at all, and what the direction of change should be.

These competing visions of Ireland often came into conflict; Ireland's economic performance was disappointing and modernisation proved to be elusive (see Daly, 2016). In particular, Ireland missed out on what is known as the post-war European growth miracle. The failure was noted by Barry Eichengreen, who commented in a review of post-1945 European economies that Ireland was the 'most dramatic outlier' in terms of its poor economic performance (Eichengreen, 2008: 118–19). The vision of a modernising Ireland advanced by *Time Magazine* and some domestic political elites did not square with reality.[3]

The two oil shocks in the 1970s furthered delayed economic modernisation by at least a generation. Reckless government borrowing followed, precipitating an economic depression in the 1980s (Ahearne *et al.*, 2006) and a return to levels of emigration not seen since the 1950s. *The Economist* published an article in 1988 describing Ireland as 'Poorest of the Rich' and remarked that 'Ireland is easily the poorest country in rich north-west Europe. Its gross domestic product is a mere 64 per cent of the European Community average' (Donovan and Murphy, 2013: 15).

Not long afterwards, economic growth began to accelerate, averaging 6.4 per cent for each year from 1994 to 2008 (World Bank, 2016). Few economies have experienced such rapid growth. Donovan and Murphy (2013: 19) argue that the Irish economy changed so much that it represented an 'abrupt leap-frogging from a predominantly pre-industrial economy to a post-industrial high-tech economy'. With Ireland's economic success, the media abandoned the modernisation narrative and turned to 'rags-to-riches' news stories. *The Economist's* 2004 article 'The luck of the Irish' is typical of the Celtic Tiger era. In rags-to-riches stories, Ireland is portrayed as a poor economy that suffered through hard times but finally awakes from its long slumber of low economic growth to become one of the world's richest economies. These gains were eloquently summarised in 2006 by Taoiseach Bertie Ahern when he said, 'probably the boom times are getting even more boomer', in the context of a discussion about rising inflation.

The next chapter in media representation of the Irish economy coincided with the global financial crisis. In this era, the media witnessed the collapse of the property market, banking system, mass unemployment in the construction sector, and the return of high levels of emigration. The exuberant coverage of the Celtic Tiger era was replaced by a 'Rise and Fall' narrative. The collapse had all of the elements of Greek Tragedy: economic excess leading to hubris and, finally, national humiliation. As Ireland sought financial assistance from the so-called Troika of the International Monetary Fund (IMF), the European Commission (EC), and the European Central Bank (ECB), the dramatic collapse was illustrated by the front-page headline in the *Guardian* on 23 November 2010: '€90bn Irish Bailout Ends in Turmoil – Now Europe Fears Crisis Will Spread'. The financial crisis gave rise to widespread panic but it also provoked some deeper reflections about national sovereignty. In an editorial reflecting on Ireland's struggle for independent statehood, the *Irish Times* asked whether this was 'what the men of 1916 died for: a bailout from the German chancellor with a few shillings of sympathy from the British chancellor on the side' (Anonymous, 2010).

If the story of Ireland's economy was indeed a Greek tragedy, it would have ended in 2010 with national bankruptcy and the Troika bailout. Like all Greek tragedies, the protagonist was worse off than at the beginning and faced into an economic depression with no end in sight. In recent times, however, media representation of the economy has increasingly turned to redemption and the rebirth. In 2012, Enda Kenny became the first Taoiseach since Seán Lemass to make the cover of *Time*, with the headline 'The Celtic Comeback'. In November 2015, *The Economist* published an article entitled 'Celtic Phoenix' in response to Ireland's economic performance, as once again the economy experienced one of the fastest rates of growth in the industrialised world.

How the economy matters

Election campaigns are attractive to journalists because they provide a constantly shifting set of topics and characters (Aalberg, Strömbäck and de Vreese, 2012). The economy is an important subject in most election campaigns, but it would be a mistake to assume that it always takes precedence. In this section, we put forward four conjectures to explain how a dynamic economy may translate into differences in media content across emphasis, tone, and framing.

The first conjecture – news values – centres on how the media processes information. Across the social sciences, scholars have detected stronger reactions to negative information. In the study of voting behaviour, political scientists use the term 'economic voting' to describe the influence of economic considerations on voting behaviour. Research in this area has argued that voters respond more strongly to negative information (Kappe and Schoonvelde, 2013). Similarly, work in political communications (Soroka, 2012) and psychology (Kahneman and Tversky, 1979) has found a tendency to focus more on negative than positive information, and on losses more than on gains. These findings fit in with how the media approaches information. A dominant tendency towards negative news has been widely identified in empirical studies internationally (see Shoemaker and Cohen, 2012). The prevalence of negative news is such that it has been argued that 'negativism is often considered a basic news value' (Leung and Lee, 2015: 289). Negative news can be thought of as coverage of events and information considered 'undesirable' by the public. An economic crisis undoubtedly comes within the remit of what the media would classify as a negative but newsworthy event. The amplification of negative news is in part a function of the media's professional watchdog role in alerting the public to dangers and threats but also driven by market considerations in that conflict and controversy sell (Harcup and O'Neill, 2001; Zaller, 2003).

Against this background, we expect that media content – emphasis, tone, and framing – will respond more to bad economic news. In particular, we expect that negative economic performance is associated with more coverage of economic policy, as the media reacts to society's perception that something should be done to resolve a problem. Furthermore, we expect that the tone of the news becomes increasingly negative in a worsening economy. By contrast, we do not expect that positive economic performance is associated with a change in tone or coverage. The literature on economic voting shows little reward for good performance (Lewis-Beck and Stegmaier, 2007; Reidy *et al.*, 2017). However, there might be a threshold at which poor performance is defined as a crisis and prompts a change in media coverage of the economy. We address this important point in Chapter 8 on economic crisis and media coverage.

The second conjecture centres on economic change versus economic conditions. Scholars have found that economic change is potentially more important than the present state of the economy. For example, media coverage may not react to high unemployment so much as to a sharp change in the rate of unemployment (Soroka *et al.*, 2015). Alternatively, an election may bring more focus to an issue – like persistently high unemployment – that may have fallen out of the spotlight. Therefore, we examine the correlations between election coverage and economic conditions, and changes in economic conditions.

The third conjecture focuses on the proximity of economic change to the election. Researchers have found that economic change closer to the election is more important than earlier economic change (Soroka *et al.*, 2015). Therefore, in our data analysis, we will look at the correlation between economic change in the preceding twelve months and media content during elections.

The fourth conjecture focuses on expectations. According to Thomas Patterson (1994: 60), 'above all else, reporters are taught to search for what is new and different in events of the past twenty-four hours'. In the study of voting behaviour, political scientists use the term 'retrospective voting' to describe when voters look back at the performance of the economy and punish or reward the government accordingly. Prospective voters, on the other hand, cast their ballot depending on what they think the government will do in the future. While the media is not a monolith, its forward-looking bias should manifest in content that responds more to expectations about where the economy is going in the future than where it is now or has been in the recent past. In summary, it is likely that the economy plays a key role in election coverage, but it is important not to fall into the trap of economic determinism. Voters care about the economy, but that position explains only a portion of voting behaviour (Lewis-Beck and Stegmaier, 2007; Reidy *et al.*, 2017). Similarly, we must be alert to other explanations for changes in the emphasis, tone, and framing of media content of the economy.

Coverage in the *Irish Times* and *Irish Independent*, 1969–2016

This section presents findings from our content analysis of election coverage of the *Irish Times* and the *Irish Independent* from 1969 to 2016. Our content analysis takes the diversity of economic news reporting seriously by presenting findings related to both macroeconomic and microeconomic policy news. Macroeconomics refers to large-scale or general economic factors, e.g. the national budget and taxing, trade and monetary policy. Microeconomic policy can be described as regulation, e.g. of the labour market, companies, and financial markets.

The section is divided into three parts. The first part presents findings related to our conjecture regarding news values, i.e. whether the emphasis, tone, and framing of media content responds more to bad news than to good news. The second part presents findings related to the difference between economic change and present economic conditions, and our third conjecture on the degree of economic change since the last election. The section concludes with the third part, which presents findings related to the fourth conjecture on the role of expectations.

News values (conjecture 1)

We find a strong correlation between the economy and the tone of election coverage, and a weaker correlation between the economy and the emphasis and framing of coverage. Beginning with our findings related to the tone of coverage, Table 4.1 shows the correlation between tone and economic conditions – the present rate of unemployment and growth are strongly correlated with the tone of coverage in the *Irish Times* and *Irish Independent*. Figure 4.1 illustrates tone across our fourteen elections since 1969. The figure shows that the tone of coverage is similar across the two titles. It also shows that with the single exception of 1969, election coverage comes in different shades of negativity. Indeed, Ireland's Celtic Tiger years do not correspond with a general increase in positive tone, and some of the most negative coverage was in 1982 (Feb.) and 2011, corroborating previous findings about the emphasis of economic policy coverage in these years. There is also a negative tone in 1992 but only in the *Irish Times*.

A closer look at the 1982 (Feb.) election may help to understand why there was a more negative tone. The incumbent Fine Gael–Labour Government collapsed in January 1982 after failing to get its budget through the Dáil. The collapse happened when several independent TDs voted against the minority government

Table 4.1 Economy correlations, *Irish Times* and *Irish Independent* 1969–2016: Economic conditions

	Emphasis macro.	Emphasis macro.	Emphasis micro.	Emphasis micro.	Tone	Tone
	Times	Indep.	Times	Indep.	Times	Indep.
Unemployment	−0.34	0.44	−0.41	0.05	−0.78	−0.73
Growth	0.20	−0.37	0.36	−0.26	0.15	0.80

Note: The figures are Pearson's r, where 1 is the total positive correlation, 0 is no correlation, and −1 is the total negative correlation.

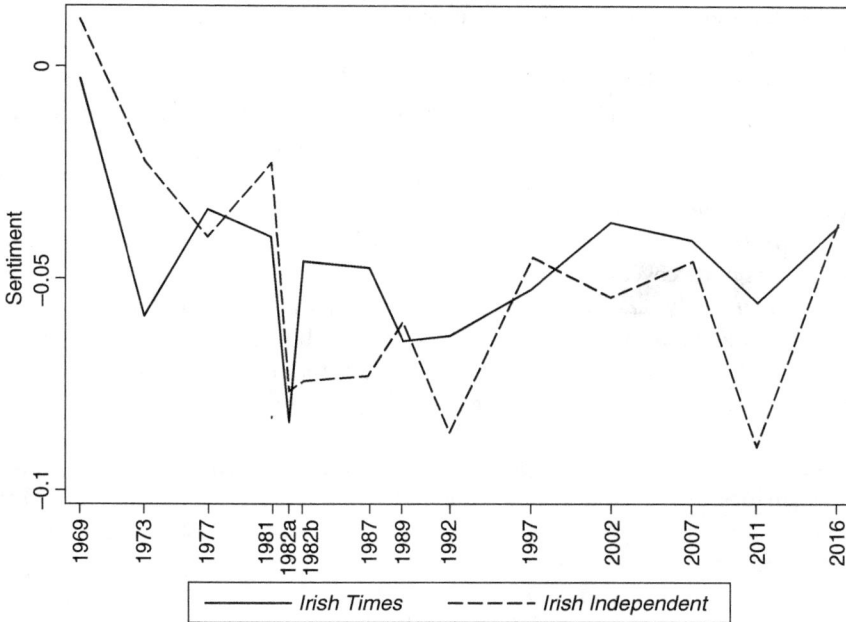

Figure 4.1 Tone of economic coverage, *Irish Times* and *Irish Independent* 1969–2016

over its proposals to put VAT on children's shoes. This controversy went on to become a central issue in the election campaign that followed, with the outgoing Taoiseach Garret FitzGerald eventually reversing the decision (Glennon, 1982).

Apart from this contentious issue, the economy cast a long shadow over the campaign in the February 1982 contest. Some indicators had improved since 1981, but the economy remained in peril and macroeconomic issues featured prominently in the news.[4] Prior to polling day, the *Irish Independent* reported on its front page that the Central Bank was advising for a harsh austerity budget regardless of the election outcome (Rapple, 1982). During the campaign, media coverage turned increasingly to whether the spending proposals of all parties were credible rather than what was on offer. It was widely understood that there was little room for an expansionary budget and that Ireland was on the brink of economic and financial collapse. The outcome of this first election in 1982 was a short-lived minority Fianna Fáil Government which lost power the following November after a Dáil confidence vote.

We now turn to the emphasis of election coverage. Table 4.1 shows the correlation between media emphasis and present economic conditions.[5] It shows that there is no clear correlation between the present rate of unemployment or economic growth and the emphasis of coverage. In other words, there is no particular trend in the media's emphasis on economic policy news, whether unemployment is high or low.

While the correlation between emphasis and present economic conditions is weak, there are individual cases worth further attention. In our sample, the elections held in 1982 (Feb.), 1997, and 2011 stand out as examples of very high levels of economic policy coverage. In 2011, there is 2.0 standard deviations more economic policy coverage in the *Irish Independent* and 1.82 more in the *Irish Times*. In 1997, a year of rapid economic growth, there is 1.82 standard deviations more coverage in the *Irish Times*, and in 1982 (Feb.) there is 1.9 more in the *Irish Independent*. In short, the emphasis of election coverage in 1982 (Feb.) and 2011 is in line with our expectations, but the emphasis of coverage in 1997 challenges the news values conjecture. Rather than noticing a greater emphasis on the economy in bad economic times, we observe greater coverage in good *and* bad times. A closer look at the 2011 and 1997 elections can help us to understand why the emphasis of coverage is greater in both cases, yet the performance of the economy is different. In the three years leading up to the 1997 campaign, the Irish economy grew at an average rate of 9.1 per cent per year.[6] Despite this period of remarkable growth, the incumbent 'Rainbow Coalition' of Fine Gael, Labour, and Democratic Left narrowly lost the election to an alternative coalition of Fianna Fáil and the PD backed by a number of independent TDs. In the campaign, economic coverage tended to focus on the booming economy, with typical headlines emphasising the good times, such as 'Borrowings halved as tax cash pours in' (Keenan, 1997). Surprise about the rapid expansion of the economy may explain why we observe more economic policy coverage on average, as there may have been more news stories heaping praise on the economy's performance.

By way of contrast, the ruinous state of the economy was the central issue during the 2011 campaign. Ireland's banking system lay in tatters following a general panic. In September 2010, depositors withdrew €18bn from domestic banks and €13bn from non-domestic banks. Overall, deposits declined by roughly €125bn from a peak of €600bn in late 2008 (O'Callaghan, 2011: 9). As funds evaporated, the ECB signalled that it would not tolerate further losses, which spooked investors and sealed the fate of the Irish economy. In November 2010, Ireland entered a long-term economic adjustment programme with Troika support. After the bailout negotiations were made public, Ireland's coalition government began to fracture. Fianna Fáil's junior coalition partner, the Green Party, indicated that it would pull out of government after the external funding programme had been secured.

The election campaign followed within three months of the November 2010 bailout. Media coverage was dominated by economic policy debates about technical issues like bailout programme design, bank system restructuring, sovereign debt, and the state of the political system. Taken together, the 2011 and 1997 election

Table 4.2 Economy correlations, *Irish Times* and *Irish Independent* 1969–2016: Policy v. game

	Emphasis macro.	Emphasis macro.	Emphasis micro.	Emphasis micro.	Emphasis game	Emphasis game
	Times	Indep.	Times	Indep.	Times	Indep.
Unemployment	−0.34	0.44	−0.41	0.05	−0.12	0.28
ΔUnempl. (1 year)	0.08	0.53	−0.10	0.63	0.27	−0.55

campaigns illustrate how economic change, both positive and negative, can feed into higher levels of economic policy coverage.

We now explore the correlation between the framing of election coverage and economic conditions. Framing refers to the media's focus on political competition and politics as a game between opposing factions. We observe more game-related news stories in editorial coverage in the *Irish Times* in electoral contests in 2011, 2007, 1973, and 1977 (and in that order of magnitude). In the *Irish Independent*, there is a large spike in 1981 and greater than average coverage in 1989. The lack of overlap between the two titles, and the clear spikes when the economy is performing well or poorly, indicate that the use of the game frame may be driven by policy, party politics, or party system fragmentation, not to mention different editorial choices among our newspapers. The lack of a clear association between the game frame and the economy is confirmed when we look at the correlations in Table 4.2. In the *Irish Times*, the correlation is weak and there is a negative association between these two variables. The association is stronger and positive in the *Irish Independent*. In summary, the level of unemployment in the month of the election is not correlated with the media's focus on political competition and politics as a game.

Economic change versus more of the same (conjectures 2 and 3)

We now explore the correlations between different types of economic change and media content. First, we describe the correlation between media content and the change in unemployment (as opposed to the level of unemployment). The purpose is to establish whether there is a stronger relationship between economic change and election coverage than present economic conditions. Then, we consider the relationship between unemployment and the tone of election coverage in the *Irish Times* and *Irish Independent*.

Table 4.3, shows that the level of unemployment is correlated with less economic policy coverage in the *Irish Times* and more in the *Irish Independent*. Similarly, the change in unemployment – i.e. the increase in unemployment since the previous year – is correlated with more coverage in the Irish Independent but

Table 4.3 Economy correlations, *Irish Times* and *Irish Independent* 1969–2016:
Change v. conditions

	Emphasis macro.	Emphasis macro.	Emphasis micro.	Emphasis micro.	Tone	Tone
	Times	Indep.	Times	Indep.	Times	Indep.
Unemployment	−0.34	0.44	−0.41	0.05	−0.78	−0.73
Unempl. (1 year)	−0.36	0.31	−0.38	−0.10	−0.78	−0.55
ΔUnempl. (1 year)	0.08	0.53	−0.10	0.63	0.01	−0.71
ΔUnempl. (election)	0.04	0.60	−0.09	0.25	−0.39	−0.82

not the Irish Times. In other words, the greater the increase in unemployment in the twelve months before the election, the more economic policy coverage is found in the *Irish Independent* but not the *Irish Times*. The stark differences between newspapers may be down to commercial pressures and editorial decision-making; these issues will be explored in Chapter 7.

There is less divergence when it comes to the tone of news coverage, which is uniformly negative and strongly correlated with high levels of unemployment. Figure 4.2 shows where Irish elections are placed in relation to both unemployment and tone. As expected, the tone of coverage during election campaigns that were marked by high unemployment, including elections in 1989, 1992, and 2011, is much more negative. Intermediate levels of unemployment, including 1997 (at the onset of the boom) and 2016 (after the crash), are associated with a somewhat less negative tone, and 2007 and 2002 (the two elections at the height of the Celtic Tiger years) are associated with a substantially less negative tone.

The 1987 election is an interesting outlier: the tone of coverage in both titles is somewhat similar to 1997 and 2016, even though unemployment was much greater in 1987 than in either 1997 or 2016. Furthermore, the economy had not grown at the same impressive rate that would prevail in 1997 and 2016, perhaps ruling out economic growth as an explanation. In all cases, there was a competition between a Fine Gael–Labour incumbent Government and Fianna Fáil as the main contender. The difference in tone may be explained by policy or electoral competition, but probably not in this instance by the economy.

Previous research has shown that economic change closer to an election is more important than earlier change. Our findings support these claims. In particular, we find that the level of unemployment at the time of the election campaign is correlated more strongly with media content than the change in unemployment since the last election. Table 4.3 shows no correlation between the change in unemployment since the last election and the emphasis of coverage, with the exception of macroeconomic policy news in the *Irish Independent*. The

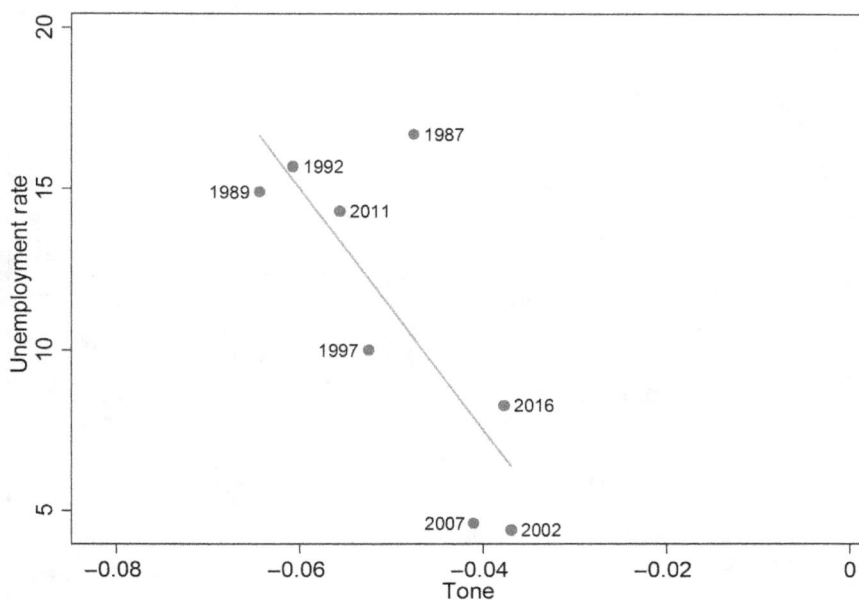

Figure 4.2 Tone and unemployment, *Irish Times* and *Irish Independent* 1987–2016
Note: Standardised unemployment rates are not available before 1987.

Table 4.4 Economy correlations, *Irish Times* and *Irish Independent*
1969–2016: Expectations

	Emphasis macro.	Emphasis macro.	Emphasis micro.	Emphasis micro.	Tone	Tone
	Times	Indep.	Times	Indep.	Times	Indep.
Consumer sentiment	0.23	–0.51	0.34	–0.45	0.37	0.88
Consumer sentiment (prior year)	0.29	–0.57	0.35	–0.34	0.63	0.91

findings regarding tone are similar, except that the correlation between tone in the *Irish Times* and the change in unemployment since the last election is smaller.

Expectations and election coverage (conjecture 4)
We now explore the relationship between expectations about where the economy is heading in the future and election coverage. To measure expectations, we use the consumer sentiment index in the month of the election campaign in order to capture the extent to which consumers have positive feelings about the future of the economy. Our findings, which are summarised in Table 4.4, show that

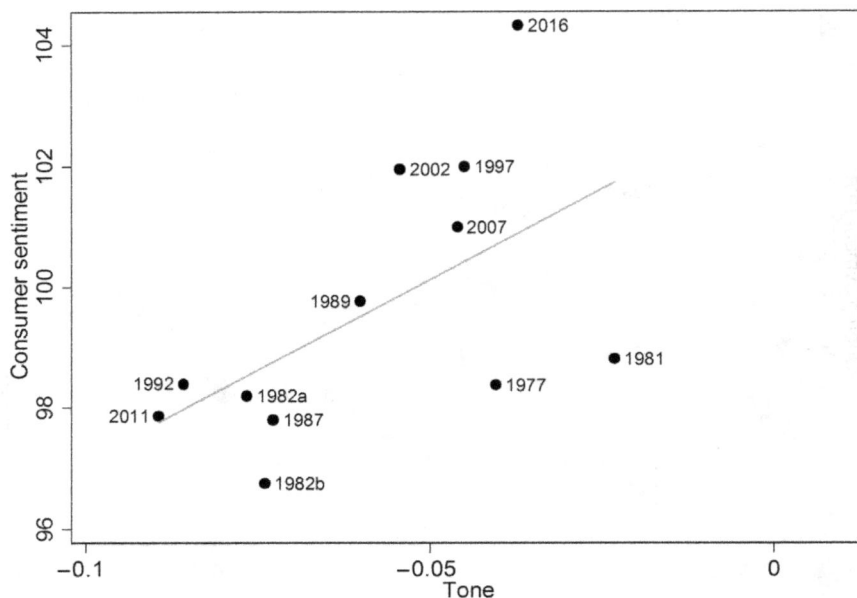

Figure 4.3 Tone and expectations, *Irish Times* and *Irish Independent* 1969–2016

there is a strong correlation between consumer sentiment and tone, especially in the *Irish Independent*.

Consumer sentiment and economic policy coverage are also correlated, but the relationship tends to vary significantly by newspaper. In particular, the association is strong and negative in the *Irish Independent*, which may shift to other types of news when people feel good about the economy. When there are great expectations, positive language is used in both newspapers, but the relationship is clearly much stronger for the *Irish Independent*. In fact, the score is so high for the *Irish Independent* that consumer sentiment almost perfectly predicts the tone of the news. Figure 4.3 illustrates how each election is positioned in terms of consumer sentiment and the tone of news coverage in the *Irish Independent*.[7] When consumer sentiment is low, we observe a very negative tone in election coverage. Indeed, there is a cluster of elections at the low end of consumer confidence, including 1982 (Feb.), 1982 (Nov.), 1987, 1992, and 2011. Interestingly, the economy had performed well during some of these elections, but consumers were not confident about the future and this is strongly reflected in the language used in media coverage of the elections in the two titles in our study.

In Figure 4.3, the elections in 1977 and 1981 are outliers where consumer sentiment is at very low levels but the tone of coverage does not follow the trend. Taking a closer look at these campaigns helps us to explain why pessimism about the future of the economy did not translate into a more negative tone. The 1977 election campaign is notable for increased policy polarisation. Fianna Fáil, the main opposition party, published a manifesto which included the abolition of taxes and promised to address unemployment. Some argue that this election marked the birth of 'auction politics' in modern Ireland. The election in 1981 is perhaps the most difficult to explain – the relatively more positive tone of coverage seems at odds with what happened on the ground, including the dire performance of the economy and the long shadow cast by the Republican hunger strike in Northern Ireland.

General election, 2016

We now study nine more media outlets for the 2016 election. We cannot make direct comparisons to media coverage by these outlets under economic conditions different to those of 2016. However, studying the similarity of coverage across this diverse range of media will help us understand whether our previous work using historical newspaper data is broadly representative of Ireland's overall media system. Indeed, in the findings below, election coverage in the *Irish Times* and the *Irish Independent* does not appear as outliers in our data, providing confidence in the findings in the previous section. However, we do find substantial variation in the emphasis and tone of coverage across our eleven media sources. In particular, the tone of coverage is the dimension of media coverage that exhibits the most variability (coefficient of variation = 0.33), followed by macroeconomic policy news (0.18) and microeconomic policy news (0.07).

What might explain the variation in coverage across the sources? Figures 4.4 and 4.5 show the emphasis on economic coverage across our eleven sources. There is a clear difference between broadcast and print, and between the public-service broadcasters and the other media. RTÉ's *Morning Ireland* and *Six One* appear in first and second place in both charts. The more commercial-oriented outlets like the *Irish Daily Mail* and *Irish Daily Mirror* cover the economy in the least detail.

Figure 4.6 illustrates the tone of election coverage across our sources. Although the tone of coverage exhibits the most variability, there appears to be no clear split on the grounds of commercial orientation or media format. Many of the newspapers tend to use a more positive tone than the broadcast media, except for the *Irish Daily Mirror*. Figure 4.7 illustrates the association between the proportion of economic news coverage and the tone of the news. TV3 and the *Irish Daily Mirror* are outliers – the tone of their election coverage is not related to their emphasis on the economy. The other sources, however, tend to use an increasingly negative tone the more they cover economic news. RTÉ's *Morning Ireland, Six One,* and *Drivetime* devote more coverage to economic news and at the same time use a more negative tone, while the *Daily Irish Mail* focuses less

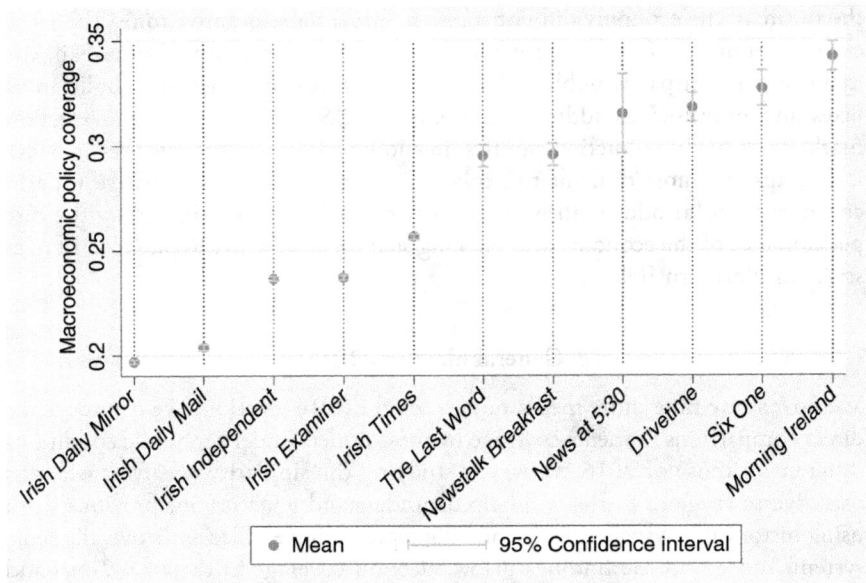

Figure 4.4 Emphasis in macroeconomic policy coverage, 2016 general election

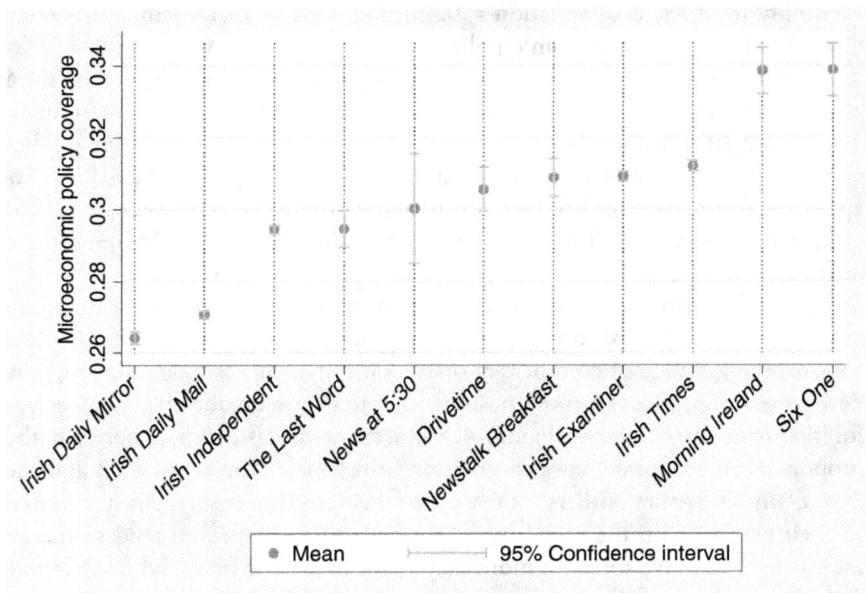

Figure 4.5 Emphasis in microeconomic policy coverage, 2016 general election

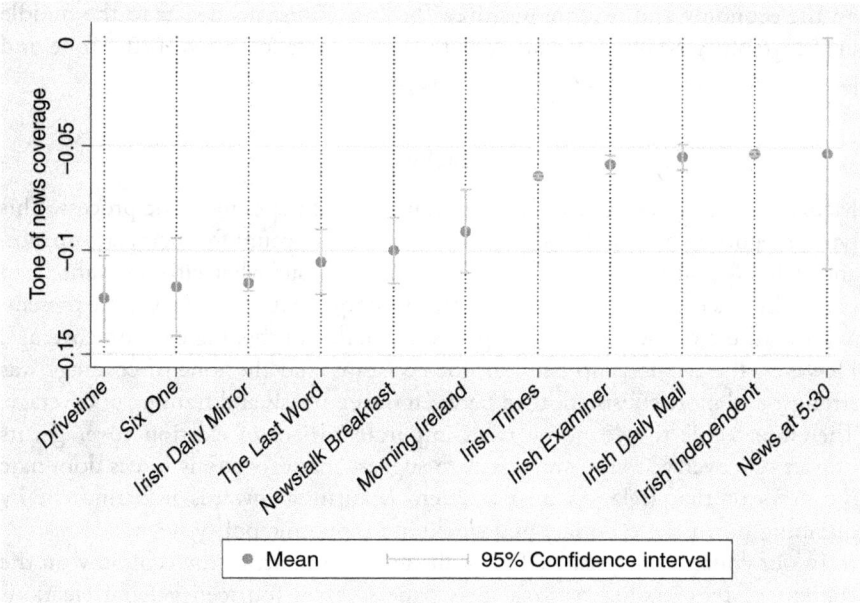

Figure 4.6 Tone of news coverage, 2016 general election

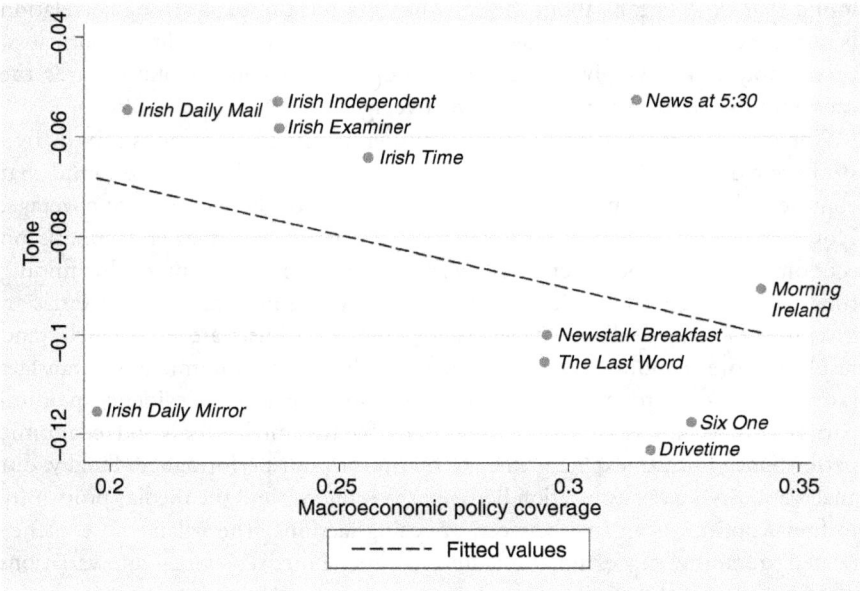

Figure 4.7 Tone and macroeconomic policy coverage, 2016 general election

on the economy and is more positive. The *Irish Times* sits nearer to the middle of the graph, possibly in an attempt to strike a balance between the tone and proportion of coverage it devotes to the economy.

Conclusion

Media coverage of elections is an important part of the democratic process. This type of reporting helps citizens to hold politicians to account for their performance, and it helps politicians, in turn, to learn more about what citizens want from policy. In this chapter, we found that the economy matters; the past, the present, and the future of the economy all played some role in shaping election coverage. However, the relationship between the economy and the tone of coverage was stronger and more consistent than between the emphasis and framing of coverage. Therefore, while the economy is an important driver of election coverage, its impact on coverage is too variegated to suggest that exogenous forces dominate the news or that Ireland's media system is turning towards infotainment by dumbing down the economy and sidelining economic policy news.

In our content analysis, we first evaluated the impact of the economy on the content of two leading national newspapers across fourteen general elections from 1969 to 2016. We found evidence of an asymmetric relationship between the tone of election coverage and the economy to the extent that tone is increasingly negative in bad economic times but does not improve in good times. We also found that expectations about the economy matter: there is a strong correlation between the tone of election coverage and consumer sentiment. Political journalists, presumably unknowingly, reflect the mood of the general public towards the economy in the tone of their election coverage.

The evidence regarding the framing and emphasis of coverage is mixed. In a study of eleven media sources during the 2016 general election, we found that commercial orientation and media format matters for the emphasis of coverage. However, in our historical newspaper study, there was a greater emphasis on economic policy in both very good *and* very bad economic times. This finding runs counter to the conventional wisdom that negative news alone drives variation in emphasis. Our findings suggest that booms and busts are newsworthy and result in more economic policy coverage, but that only economic busts translate into changes in the tone of election coverage. On the balance of evidence, political parties should not expect to be rewarded by the media for good economic performance but can expect greater criticism for poor performance. Finally, our analysis shows a weak association between the economy and the media's propensity to frame politics as a game between opposing factions. The balance of evidence related to framing suggests that it is Ireland's liberal media system – and variations of critical impartiality and/or critical infotainment – rather than exogenous factors like the economy, that is responsible for differences in the propensity to frame politics as a game.

Notes

1 Honohan and Walsh (2002) use the term 'Hare'. 'Tortoise' is used in the Honohan and Walsh article by way of comparison, and also in Lains (2006); the term Celtic Tiger is credited to Kevin Gardiner in a 1994 Morgan Stanley report.

2 For example, F. S. L. Lyons argues that 'Economic development' was 'well nigh revolutionary', and that 'It is hardly too much to say, indeed, that even today it can be seen as a watershed in the economic history of the country' (Lyons, 1971: 583, 628).

3 The historian Mary E. Daly (2016) argues that in a wider European context Ireland remained one of the poorest countries in Western Europe until the end of the twentieth century.

4 An account of economic policy in 1982 is given by the International Monetary Fund (1983).

5 The correlations between media content and unemployment should be more accurate because we have unemployment data for the month of the campaign. However, the unemployment data only covers elections from 1987 onwards. The correlations between media content and growth cover all elections except 1969.

6 This figure is calculated using the Rate of Change of Real GDP (%) statistics for 1995, 1996, and 1997 from the IMF's WEO database.

7 The relationship appears to be curvilinear; consumer sentiment varies substantially but within a narrow band.

5

Gender bias and Irish election coverage

There is a gender bias in Irish politics. Men are severely over-represented in the executive and legislature. However, there are many particular explanations for this outcome, some of which are more convincing than others. It is hard to find strong evidence that Irish voters are biased against women (McElroy, 2016). By contrast, parties are biased against women and consistently select men to run for election (Buckley and O'Connor, 2016). There is no doubt that the media plays an important role in reproducing traditional ideas about gender. While explicit references tend to advocate the reduction of gender differences, and bemoan the low representation of women in Irish politics (Melia, 2016), the framing of many issues is gendered. For example, articles about parenting overwhelmingly tend to focus on mothers. Like many of the media's limitations, this may be pragmatic rather than ideological. Journalists may implicitly assume or explicitly argue that women are more likely to consume parenting content than men. Of course, there is a circular logic to this: men are less attracted to content that appears to exclude them. This type of gendered framing of the non-political surely feeds into the political system in some way. However, gender bias in the explicit coverage of politics also occurs, of this there is no doubt. For example, many would doubt that a 67-year-old male politician would have received similar treatment from the *Irish Daily Mail* when it wrote of Tánaiste Joan Burton before the election: 'The Labour Party tweets a picture of Joan Burton reading *Hot Press*. Except she's half a century older than the average reader and the phrase painfully hip at pensionable age normally means exactly that' (Molony, 2016).

However, it is much less obvious how prevalent sexism is, what forms it takes, and to which extent it has changed over time. Attitudes to gender in Ireland have changed massively in the period covered by our study. We can test the effect of exogenous social change on the Irish media by looking at gender bias. Indeed, we can also check the extent to which the media was an agent of social change in this respect. As in the other chapters, we do not look at a small number of episodes in detail. Instead, we explore the general frequency of gender bias in Irish election coverage.

This chapter examines three potential biases and how they have evolved over time. First, we look at the relative coverage of men and women. If a candidate's name does not appear in the media, it is less likely to be present in the minds of voters or indeed political party selection conventions. Second, we look at tone. Negative coverage can damage a candidate's standing. Third, and most subtly, we investigate the context in which a candidate was mentioned. It is commonly complained that the media discusses the appearance and family of female politicians, while coverage of male politicians is restricted to their political career. This can undermine the credibility of women as political actors. We measure each of these three biases at the level of individual candidates. These biases can impact on individual careers. However, they are also important at the aggregate level. If women candidates are under-represented, presented negatively, and their status as politicians is played down, all this feeds into traditional stereotypes that will perpetuate gender bias in elective office. In addition to the extensive data we have obtained to explore these three potential biases, we have data on the gender of different types of speakers in TV news broadcasts in 2016.

In the next section, we briefly present the theory behind our measures of gender bias. Then, we look for the three biases in a historical study of the *Irish Times* and the *Irish Independent* from 1969 to 2016. The final section focuses on the 2016 election – a significant electoral contest because it was the first since the enactment of financial penalties for political parties that fail to reach a 30 per cent gender quota for their candidates.

Media coverage of gender

'Here is the News … about Men' (Gill, 2007: 114) is a nice summary of the most basic gender bias in journalism. The general under-representation of women and their particular under-representation in political coverage are frequently portrayed as virtually universal across societies and stubbornly resistant to change (Gill, 2007: 115). Since women constitute 50 per cent of the population, a media free of gender bias might be expected to dedicate 50 per cent of its coverage to women. However, the media reports a gendered world. It is often argued that male-dominated news coverage is not gender-biased but simply reflects reality.

In this study, we look at the coverage of women candidates compared to male candidates. We begin with the bias in the selection of candidates and see whether the media has reflected, boosted, or attenuated it. In electoral terms, gender is not the most important difference between election candidates; neither is political party. Incumbency matters most. Sitting TDs (in the Irish context, predominantly men) are much more likely to be elected than their challengers. In the following analysis, we will compare male and female challengers, as well as men and women candidates more generally. Otherwise, we would risk mistaking the screamingly obvious gender bias in political representation for a gender bias in the coverage of elections.

Women are not always ignored. Indeed, some become so prominent and powerful that it is impossible for competent journalists to ignore them. But gender bias may be evident in the negative tone which is applied to women politicians. Female leaders can appear to be attacked because of their gender. Two well-known examples are Julia Gillard, the former Prime Minister of Australia (Johnson, 2015), and US presidential candidate Hillary Rodham Clinton. Indeed, it has been argued that coverage of Clinton was positive when placed in the stereotypically female role of the wronged, powerless wife, but negative when framed in the context of the powerful, ambitious politician (Parry-Giles, 2000: 209). We compare the tone of paragraphs featuring female candidates to that of paragraphs featuring male candidates.

Probably the most studied aspect of gender, the media, and politics is the framing of women politicians. Too often this reflects a deep-rooted assumption that femininity and politics are antithetical (Sreberny and van Zoonen, 2000: 1–2). While the policies and electability of male politicians are discussed, female politicians endure analysis of their appearance and family life. Explicitly or implicitly, this suggests that it is hard to combine the supposedly male role of politician with the traditionally female roles of dressing attractively and being a good mother. Stereotypes of women and politics are diverse and complex (Fowler and Lawless, 2009: 521). We do not study any particular stereotype. Instead, we focus on the fundamental antithesis between women and politics by comparing the extent to which the coverage of men and women candidates is non-political. This is an encompassing approach, both within and across elections. Women's presence in political journalism and punditry has become a subject of increasing research and public campaigns in recent years (Ross and Padovani, 2017). In the latter regard, we present data for the two television news programmes included in this study.

Coverage of men and women candidates, 1969–2016

In this section, we investigate the three types of bias in a historical study of fourteen elections in Ireland's two best-selling newspapers. Figure 5.1 compares the *Irish Times's* and *Irish Independent's* coverage of candidates from 1969 to 2016. We calculate the average proportion of all candidate mentions represented by women over the campaign. We also present the proportion of female candidates for a given election. The two newspapers track the proportion of women candidates presenting for election: in only a couple of instances across the twenty-eight measures (two newspapers by fourteen elections) does coverage go down when the proportion of candidates goes up, or vice versa. Interestingly, the two newspapers cleave much closer to each other than either does to the actual proportion of

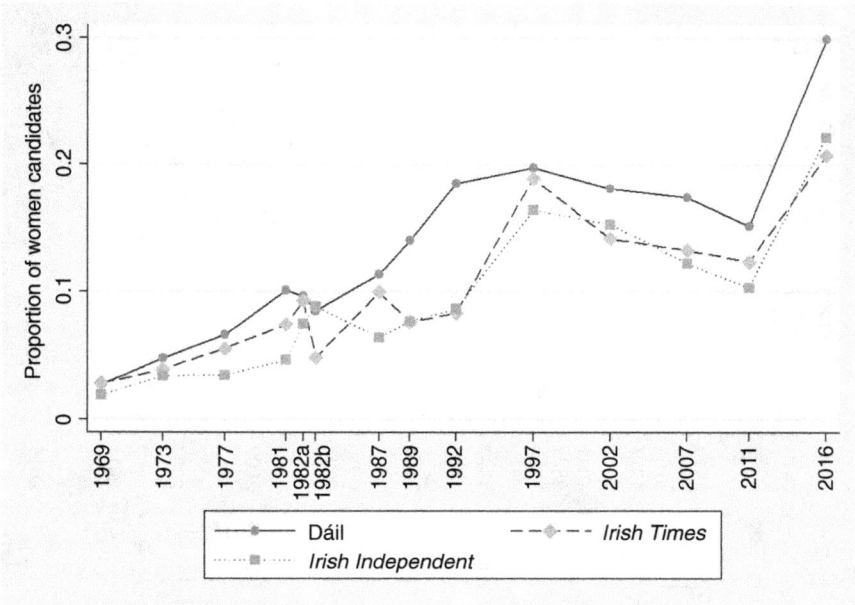

Figure 5.1 Coverage of women candidates, *Irish Times* and *Irish Independent* 1969–2016
Note: The 1987 figure for the proportion of women candidates is adjusted downwards
because one candidate stood in thirteen constituencies.

women candidates. Nevertheless, the data shows a bias against these candidates. In no election do they receive more coverage than their share of the candidates. In almost all, they receive less. However, we need to check whether this pattern is driven by different rates of incumbency between male and female candidates.

Figure 5.2 illustrates the coverage of women challengers in the two papers compared to the proportion of women candidate challengers. Like previously, changes in the proportion of women challengers affect the proportion of coverage given to these candidates. Also similar to the previous graph, the two newspapers tend to follow each other more closely than they follow the proportion of actual candidates. However, differences between the two graphs are more important. There has not been a general bias in newspaper coverage against women challengers. Indeed, more often than not, women challengers have been somewhat over-represented. After 1989, women challengers are over-represented by the *Irish Independent* in every election – until 2016. In the *Irish Times*, the run of over-representation begins in 1997 and also ends in 2016. Both newspapers' coverage is well short of the proportion of candidates in 2016. The 1997 campaign stands out in that both newspapers, and especially the *Irish Independent*, substantially over-represented women challengers.

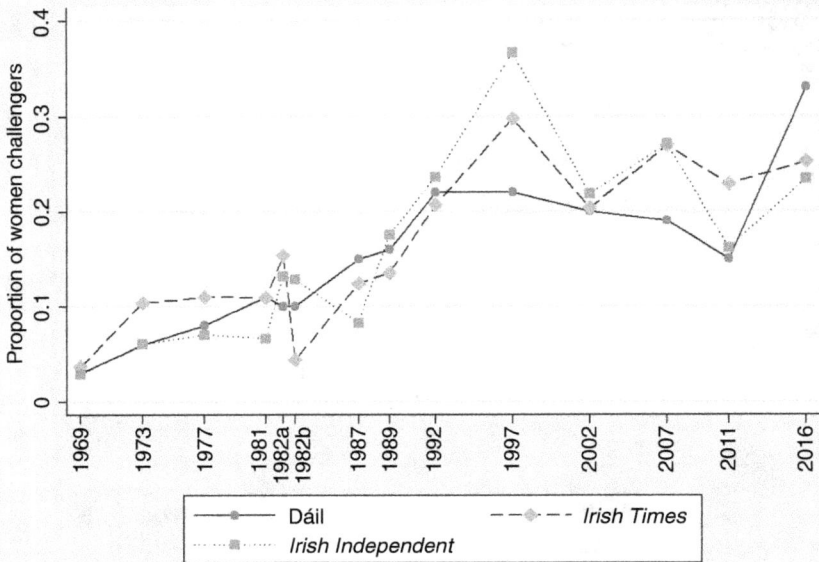

Figure 5.2 Coverage of women challengers, *Irish Times* and *Irish Independent* 1969–2016
Note: The 1987 figure for the proportion of women candidates is adjusted downwards
because one candidate stood in thirteen constituencies.

There was a substantial over-representation of challengers in the *Irish Times* in
1973 and 1977. This does not appear to represent their novelty value in a political
system where women were almost invisible. Female challengers on average had
an advantage in the 1973 campaign. Over half of the paragraphs mentioning
women candidates featured Máirín de Burca, then joint Secretary of (Official)
Sinn Féin. De Burca was a very dynamic activist and politician, at least as well
known for her feminism as for her socialism and republicanism. There was no
mention of her gender in the coverage. Rather, she was mentioned mostly in
terms of policy (divorce and housing) and political competition (complaints
about the ban on TV and radio coverage of her party and slurs from Fianna Fáil).

From 1997 to 2011, there is an over-representation of women challengers in
both titles, sometimes a large over-representation. It is tempting to think this
reflected a new, more modern Ireland. In particular, Ireland had a female head
of state for all of this period: Mary Robinson (1990–97) and Mary McAleese
(1997–2011). So, women holding senior political office became normal, as did
advocacy of gender equality. However, the proportion of women candidates
peaked at 20 per cent in 1997. The introduction of gender quotas for 2016 was
a recognition that the expected organic change had not occurred. The proportion

of women candidates increased in response to the new law that imposed financial penalties on parties that did not reach a quota of a minimum 30 per cent for both genders. Surprisingly, neither the *Irish Times* nor the *Irish Independent* appears to have responded accordingly. There is a big increase in the proportion of coverage given to female candidates, but it did not keep pace with the almost doubling of women candidates. This most recent election must, therefore, count as the most surprising, and disappointing, of the fourteen included in this study.

Tone and coverage of candidates

Even if women candidates receive roughly proportional coverage, they may be presented in a more negative context. In the latter regard, we examined the tone of paragraphs featuring female candidates compared to those featuring male candidates in coverage from 1969 to 2016 in both national titles. Tone is the probability of a positive paragraph minus the probability that the paragraph is negative. We calculated the tone of paragraphs that featured a majority of male candidates versus paragraphs that featured a majority of female candidates. We then subtracted the male figure from the female figure. Figure 5.3 shows the bias in tone in favour of women challengers in the *Irish Times* and *Irish Independent* across fourteen elections since 1969. A positive figure is a bias towards women; a negative figure is a bias towards men.

We see that women candidates have featured in more positive paragraphs than men candidates: in twenty-four data points, there is a tone bias in favour of women and in only four a bias against them. Tone bias is quite volatile in the early years, presumably because of the small number of women candidates. Nonetheless, there does appear to have been a reduction in the relative positivity of the paragraphs in which female candidates have featured. From 1989 onwards, there has been no tone bias of over 0.1 in favour of women candidates. Interestingly, this appears to coincide with a shift towards over-representation of women challengers. Possibly, this reflects a more mature and modern approach to women and electoral politics. If, as tentatively suggested earlier, women in politics had become normal, there was no need for a different tone to the coverage of male candidates.

In the early years, the bias in favour of women candidates may have been a sort of 'positive discrimination'. For example, in 1969 the *Irish Times* ran a series on the 'New Contenders', with a particular emphasis on women. The piece on Joan Gallagher in Sligo was almost entirely uncritical, lauding the candidate's qualifications and personality and quoting at length her policy ideas and ideological perspective. Nonetheless, some of the writer's attempts to be positive were clearly gendered. She is a 'good-looking, dynamic reformer ... her voice carries well ... and she likes a good laugh' (Anonymous, 1969). Similarly, in 1973 a profile of the Dublin North-Central constituency describes the male candidates in rather

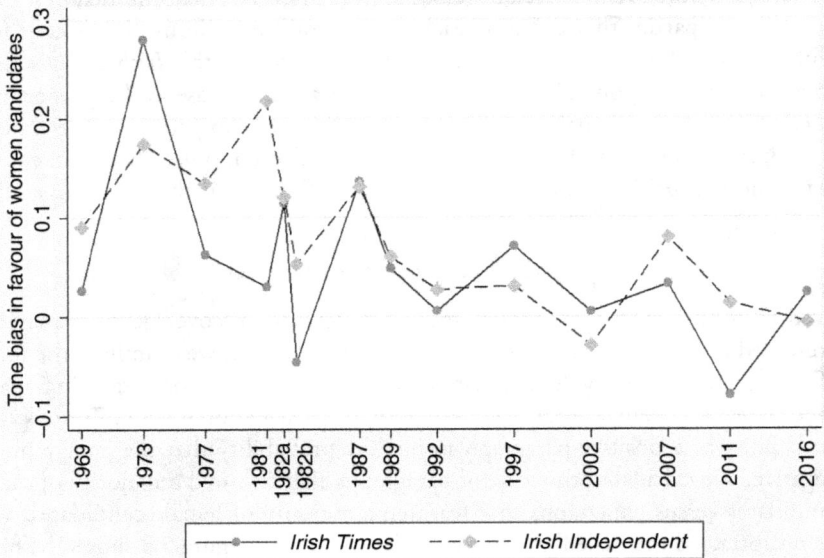

Figure 5.3 Tone bias and women candidates, *Irish Times* and *Irish Independent* 1969–2016
Note: Tone is defined as the probability that a paragraph is positive less the probability that
it is negative. Tone bias subtracts the mean tone for paragraphs featuring male candidates
from the mean tone for paragraphs featuring female candidates.

dry terms, but Máirín de Burca had 'an imaginative tactical genius for overturning
bureaucracy' and Nóirín Butler had a 'quick mind' (Grogan, 1973). The *Irish
Independent* seems to have adopted a similar tone, although it could be far less
subtle. An article on Peigin Doyle of Official Sinn Féin, the youngest candidate
in 1973, notes her 'rosy cheeks, long dark hair, and gold rimmed spectacles' and
ends with, 'A nice girl … pity she got mixed up in politics' (McCarthy, 1973).
This is a spectacularly explicit expression of the antithesis between femininity
and politics. Nonetheless, the candidate gets an opportunity to explain her
viewpoint and a sympathetic portrayal. The coverage of a much older, new female
candidate at the same election, Alice Glenn of Fine Gael, is treated in a much
more straightforward manner, with little condescension and no references to her
appearance (MacGoris, 1973). This is perhaps an example of how gender bias
interacts in a complex manner with other biases, such as ageism.

The 1992 campaign was the first in which both newspapers adopted an overall
relatively neutral tone in their coverage of male versus female candidates. In the
Irish Independent, the absence of long, soft profiles of women is notable. Instead,
there was a dry policy-focused report on Mary Harney's (PDs) plans for the

Office of Public Works (O'Brien, 1992). Other articles tended to refer to female candidates collectively and perhaps reflected an ambivalence about women in politics. In the *Irish Independent*, Miriam Lord, albeit writing in a satirical vein, referred to two Fianna Fáil candidates as 'farmerettes' (Lord, 1992a). Another article describes a failed attempt by Taoiseach Albert Reynolds to gain some feminist credibility. He was to present Fianna Fáil's women candidates at the statue of the famous feminist and nationalist Constance Markievicz but humiliated his candidates by arriving very late (MacCormaic, 1992). While the overall tone advantage disappeared in more recent elections, positive coverage was still found. As in the 1970s, a long colourful profile provided positive coverage for women candidates in 2007. In the *Irish Times*, Róisín Ingle does comment on the appearance of Deirdre Clune (Fine Gael) but also notes that her teenage son is 'tall, dark and charming' (Ingle, 2007). Another piece in the same series, 'On the Canvass', provides less colourful, but even better, coverage for Mary Lou McDonald of Sinn Féin. The description of her adept handling of a racist is particularly striking (Humphries, 2007). In contrast to the 1970s, these two challengers were hardly outsiders: Clune was a member of a leading Fine Gael family and McDonald already a Member of the European Parliament.

Our analysis of tone indicates that it may have been an advantage for female candidates in the past. However, in the modern era, in which the candidacy of female politicians is unremarkable in itself, the two newspapers perhaps no longer see a need to give women especially positive coverage. Some of the positive coverage is sexist and may have undermined the candidates' credibility as politicians. This question is addressed systematically in the next section of this chapter.

Framing of candidates, 1969–2016

Even if women are described positively as people, they may not be taken seriously as politicians. Indeed, we have already provided some colourful examples from past campaign coverage. In this section, we test the extent to which there is a general bias against women politicians that frames them non-politically. Therefore, for our last measure of potential gender bias, we calculate the probability of the classification of a paragraph featuring a majority of women candidates as non-political. We do the same for paragraphs with a majority of men candidates. Then we subtract the male probability from the female probability. Positive figures indicate that women challengers are more likely to be framed non-politically than men challengers. A score of one would indicate that all female paragraphs are definitely non-political and all male paragraphs are definitely political. As we can see in Figure 5.4, there appears to have been a framing bias against women in the earlier elections. A coefficient of 0.1 is a substantial difference. For example, it could mean that 20 per cent of paragraphs about women were non-political, but only 10 per cent about men. Since 1977, the tendency towards non-political

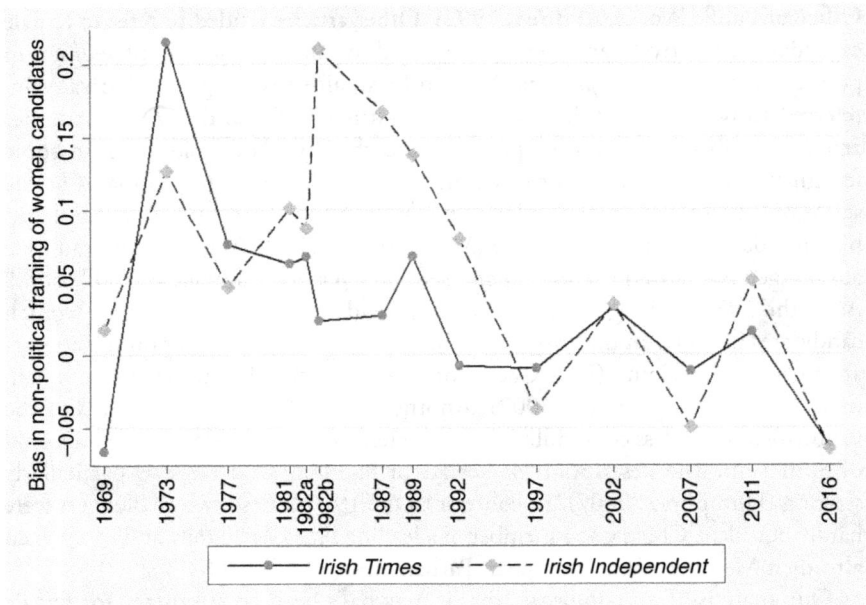

Figure 5.4 Framing of women candidates, *Irish Times* and *Irish Independent* 1969–2016
Note: A paragraph is classified as 'Other' if none of the categories reach a threshold
probability of 0.57 for 'Macroeconomic', 0.39 for 'Microeconomic', 0.39 for 'Other
policy', and 0.46 for 'Political competition'. The data underlying the graph subtracts
election means for women candidates from election means for men candidates.

framing of women in the *Irish Times* has been within 0.1 of that of men. However,
it is not until 1992 that the same can be said of the *Irish Independent*. For the
last twenty-five years, this measure indicates broad neutrality between male and
female candidates in respect of this very general and pertinent frame. Once again,
we see evidence of the eradication of differences in coverage across genders in
the two newspapers. Moreover, again the modernisation appears to happen in
the 1990s. However, for the first time we see a sustained difference between the
two newspapers: for four elections (1982 (Nov.), 1987, 1989, and 1992) we see
a much larger framing bias in the *Irish Independent* than in the *Irish Times*. It
appears that the *Irish Independent* was slower than the *Irish Times* in equalising
the proportion of political coverage across male and female candidates.

Quota election, 2016

The general election of 2016 was held under a new system according to which
parties would lose half of their public funding for a whole parliamentary term

if they nominated less than 30 per cent of their general election candidates in either gender. Like many reforms in Irish politics, this innovation was somewhat surprising. It was not a vote-winner and was unpopular with many politicians (Keenan and McElroy, 2016), especially Fianna Fáil's TDs, who were all male, when the legislation was introduced in 2012. Ultimately, the Government accepted that the gender imbalance was a problem and that the parties were unable or unwilling to overcome selection bias without a financial incentive. Therefore, it is particularly interesting to investigate our three measures of gender bias for a range of media outlets in respect of the 2016 election.

We proceed in the same order as we did in the historical study. Figure 5.5 shows the proportion of candidate mentions accounted for by women.[1] Like the *Irish Times* and the *Irish Independent*, all outlets, except TV3's *News at 5:30*, fall short of the 30 per cent rate of female candidate coverage. Most register a figure around 20 per cent, which is similar to the *Irish Times* and *Irish Independent*. The lowest is *Drivetime* (RTÉ Radio 1) with a score not far above 10 per cent. The difference between our best estimate and the quota level is only statistically significant (at the 5 per cent level) for RTÉ Radio 1's *Drivetime* and *Morning*

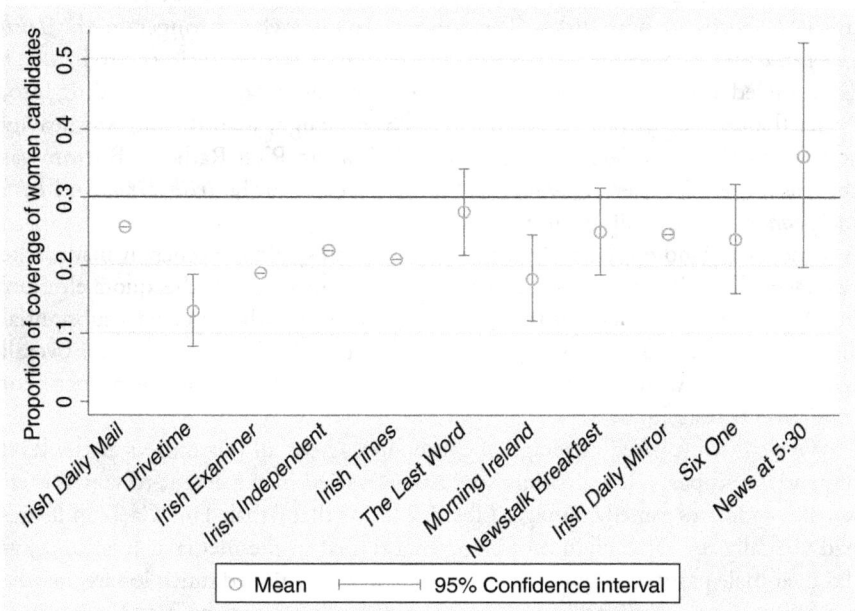

Figure 5.5 Coverage of women candidates, 2016 general election
Note: Confidence intervals are shown for broadcast programmes only, as they were sampled. We have used all text for each newspaper. For broadcast programmes, the circle indicates our best estimate.

Ireland. We cannot confidently state that any other individual broadcast outlet was below the party candidate quota rate. However, it is safe to say that the broadcast sector as a whole, just like the newspapers, failed to keep up with the increase in the proportion of women candidates. Interestingly, two RTÉ radio programmes register the lowest proportions, while the broadcast programme with the greatest coverage of female candidates is *The Last Word* on the privately owned Today FM.

Overall, we found an under-representation of women candidates in election news coverage when we would least expect it – in 2016. We re-examined our data of the *Irish Times* and *Irish Independent* from 1969 to 2016 to see if some other factor was driving this under-representation of women in 2016. In contrast to 2011, when all the leaders of the biggest parties were male, in 2016 the Labour Party was led by Joan Burton. Table 5.1 shows the relative coverage of the leaders of the four biggest parties in 2011 and in 2016. In the *Irish Times* in 2011, some 30 per cent of content mentioning any of these four leaders included the Labour Party's Eamon Gilmore, whereas the score with Joan Burton in 2016 was only 18 per cent. The contrast is somewhat stronger in the *Irish Independent*: 30 per cent versus 16 per cent. Moreover, Gilmore was the second most reported leader in 2011 in both newspapers, whereas Burton was the least reported of the four in 2016, again in both titles. The contrast is somewhat stronger in the *Irish Independent*: 30 per cent versus 16 per cent. It is worth noting that in 2011 Gilmore led a much more popular party and was almost definitely heading into, rather than out of, government. In the 2016 campaign, Joan Burton was heavily covered in all the outlets except *Morning Ireland* on RTÉ Radio 1. Burton was the least covered leader on *Morning Ireland* as well as in the *Irish Times* and *Irish Independent*. But overall, Burton was hardly under-represented in election coverage. A tendency to ignore a female leader cannot help to explain the generally inadequate coverage of female candidates across the media in our study for the 'quota election' in 2016. Indeed, the fact that there was a female leader, who received a substantial amount of coverage, makes it even more remarkable that there was an overall failure to cover women candidates equally in 2016 in light of the 30 per cent candidate threshold.

We also investigated coverage of candidates across all our outlets at the level of gender and party. It is possible that parties varied in the extent to which their female candidates gained coverage. Table 5.2 shows that female Fine Gael candidates had virtually the same chance of being mentioned in the media at least once, as did their male party colleagues. However, they were mentioned much less frequently: male Fine Gael candidates received on average 2.5 times as many mentions. Fianna Fáil women candidates were over 12 per cent less likely to be mentioned at all than a male candidate from the same party. A female Fianna Fáil candidate received on average only 30 per cent of the mentions of their male equivalents. Sinn Féin women had a very similar probability of being mentioned and percentage

Table 5.1 Coverage of party leaders in 2011 and 2016

Outlet	Year	Fianna Fáil (Martin)	Fine Gael (Kenny)	Sinn Féin (Adams)	Labour (Gilmore)	Labour (Burton)
Irish Times	2011	0.11	0.46	0.13	0.30	
	2016	0.28	0.30	0.25		0.18
Irish Independent	2011	0.06	0.50	0.15	0.30	
	2016	0.20	0.35	0.29		0.16
Irish Daily Mail	2016	0.20	0.30	0.28		0.21
Drivetime (RTÉ Radio 1)	2016	0.41 (0.07)	0.19 (0.05)	0.15 (0.05)		0.26 (0.06)
Irish Examiner	2016	0.17	0.41	0.23		0.19
The Last Word (Today FM)	2016	0.23 (0.04)	0.36 (0.05)	0.12 (0.04)		0.30 (0.05)
Morning Ireland (RTÉ Radio 1)	2016	0.22 (0.05)	0.27 (0.06)	0.37 (0.06)		0.13 (0.04)
Newst. Breakfast (Newstalk)	2016	0.13 (0.04)	0.37 (0.07)	0.18 (0.06)		0.31 (0.07)
Irish Daily Mirror	2016	0.16 (0.03)	0.37 (0.03)	0.27 (0.03)		0.21 (0.03)
Six One (RTÉ One)	2016	0.28 (0.07)	0.28 (0.07)	0.16 (0.05)		0.27 (0.07)
News at 5:30 (TV3)	2016	0.34 (0.09)	0.17 (0.07)	0.11 (0.06)		0.38 (0.09)

Note: This table reports the proportion of paragraphs mentioning the leaders of the four big parties in a given year accounted by any one of those leaders. This excludes smaller parties. Standard errors are provided in parentheses where applicable.

Table 5.2 Gender bias in overall coverage of candidates by party,
2016 general election

Party	Any mention	Total mentions
Fine Gael	0.92	0.38
Fianna Fáil	0.87	0.29
Sinn Féin	0.86	0.29
Labour	0.84	1.71

Note: 'Any mention' is the probability of a female candidate being mentioned by our eleven sources as a proportion of the probability of a male candidate being mentioned. 'Total mentions' refers to the number of mentions of a female candidate as a proportion of the number of mentions of a male candidate.

of mentions as did Fianna Fáil women. Finally, Labour women candidates were marginally less likely to receive any coverage than those from other parties, but on average, due to their leader Joan Burton, they accounted for 1.75 times as many mentions.

Coverage of Fianna Fáil's candidates is remarkably undistinctive in 2016. The Fianna Fáil front bench in 2016 was entirely male (all the party's TDs were male). At the previous election in 2011, the party contested with the same leader and a front bench in which four out of twenty members were women. Two of those women were senior members in 2011: Mary Hanafin was deputy leader and Mary Coughlan Tánaiste. In 2011, the party leader, Micheál Martin, had broken with convention by appointing Averil Power, who held no elected office, to his front bench. By 2016, Power had left Fianna Fáil and Martin oversaw a front bench composed wholly of TDs, even though he could have picked from women senators or councillors. This does not appear to have been reflected in media coverage of the party.

The continuing surge of independent politicians was one of the important features of the 2016 general election. A minority government, and whether independents could support a minority administration or participate in cabinet, was heavily debated. Independents faced different incentives to parties and were not subject to a gender quota. Therefore, it is possible that the gender bias in coverage in 2016 may have been a side effect of a decision to afford space to the independents. However, this did not happen. The proportion of candidate mentions accounted for by independents ranged from 6.3 per cent on *Morning Ireland* to 26 per cent on *Six One* – both RTÉ programmes. The proportion of mentions of female candidates amongst independents ranged from zero on TV3's *News at 5:30* and RTÉ Radio 1's *Morning Ireland* to 27 per cent on Today FM's *The Last Word*. Female candidate mentions were markedly lower for the independents than for the parties. Nonetheless, due to the under-reporting of independents, they do not account for the failure of the media to keep up with the proportion of women candidates. In summary, we are left with the simple conclusion that the Irish media sector simply failed to adjust to the large increase in women candidates in 2016.

The 2016 data also provides an opportunity to see if the pattern of tone towards female candidates in the *Irish Times* and *Irish Independent* is reflected across a wider range of media. In the historical analysis of the newspapers, there was a bias in favour of female candidates in the 1970s and 1980s, followed by a broadly neutral tone thereafter. Figure 5.6 presents tone bias towards female candidates in 2016. It shows a strong consensus on the adoption of neutrality in relation to men and women candidates. Five of the six broadcast programmes are statistically indistinguishable from zero, or perfect neutrality. These five are also statistically indistinguishable from the five newspapers. The exception is TV3's *News at 5:30*. Although its 95 per cent confidence interval is well below zero and clear of all the newspapers, we do not conclude definitively that there

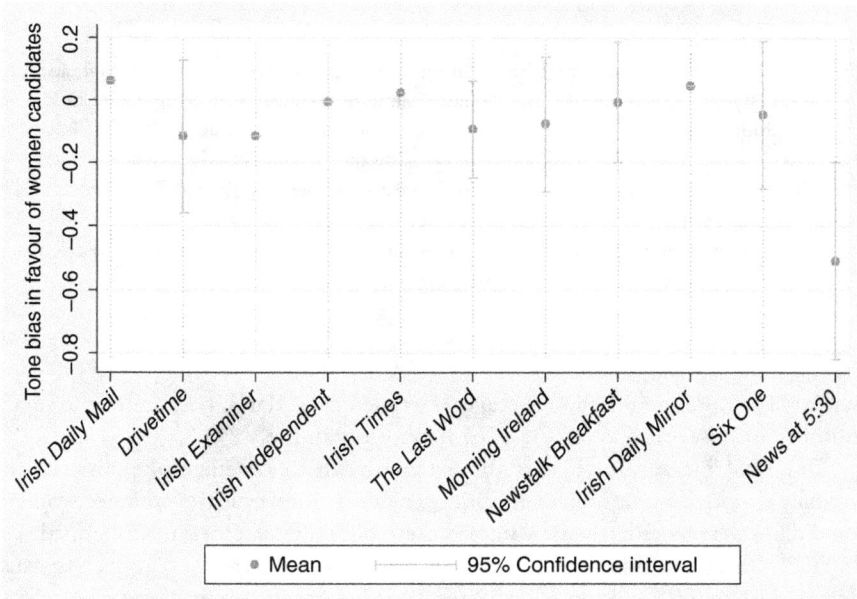

Figure 5.6 Tone bias towards women candidates, 2016 general election
Note: Tone is defined as the probability that a paragraph is positive less the probability that it is negative. Tone bias subtracts the mean tone for paragraphs featuring male candidates from the mean tone for paragraphs featuring female candidates. The confidence intervals account for propagation of error. They incorporate the standard errors of the two variables (positive and negative sentiment) that are used to calculate tone.

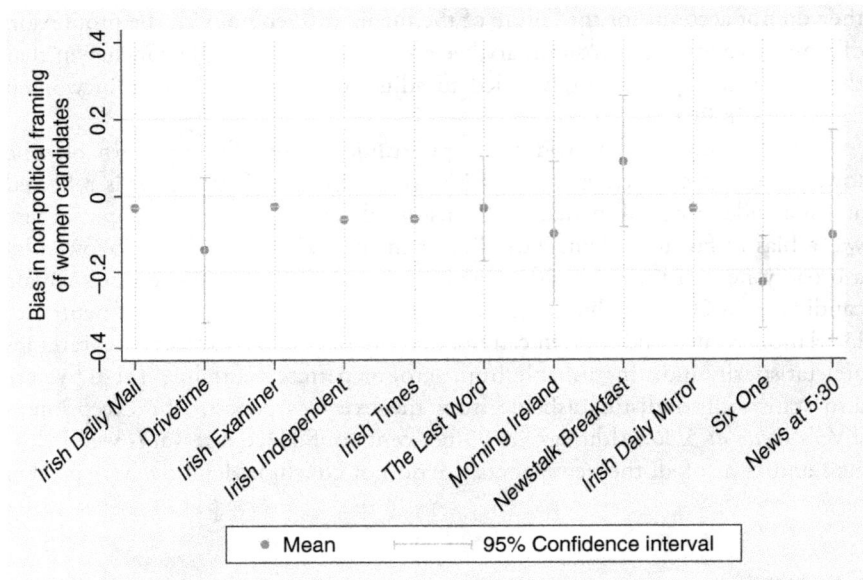

Figure 5.7 Bias towards non-political framing of women candidates, 2016 general election
Note: A paragraph is classified as 'Other' if none of the categories reach a threshold
probability of 0.57 for 'Macroeconomic', 0.39 for 'Microeconomic', 0.39 for 'Other
policy', and 0.46 for 'Political competition'. The data underlying the graph subtracts
election means for women candidates from means for men candidates. The confidence
intervals account for propagation of error. They incorporate the standard errors of the two
variables (the likelihood of political framing of men and women) that are used to calculate
framing bias.

was a more negative tone in coverage of women candidates, because of the small
number of observations for the TV3 news programme.

Our final measure of bias is the extent to which coverage of politicians is
actually devoted to the subject of politics. Figure 5.7 investigates whether women
candidates were more likely to be framed non-politically than their male competitors
in 2016. It suggests that this did not happen, and again there is a strong consensus
across the media. Only on RTÉ One's *Six One* does there appear to be a bias
towards non-political framing of women.

Finally, we have data on the gender of different speakers on the two TV
programmes. We coded whether the speaker was a journalist, a politician, or
other speaker, and their gender. The overall figures are shown in Table 5.3. There
is gender equality amongst journalists but a three to one gender bias amongst
politicians and others speakers.

Table 5.3 Speaking time by different actors on television news, 2016 general election

Actors	RTÉ One *Six One*	TV3 *News at 5:30*
Female journalist	0.300 (0.014)	0.490 (0.037)
Male journalist	0.350 (0.015)	0.170 (0.028)
Female politician	0.060 (0.007)	0.090 (0.022)
Male politician	0.170 (0.012)	0.140 (0.026)
Other female	0.020 (0.004)	0.056 (0.017)
Other male	0.095 (0.009)	0.044 (0.015)

Note: Standard errors are given in parentheses. These figures are very reminiscent of another study on the gender of voices in the Irish media (Ross, Ging and Barlow, 2017: 226).

On both RTÉ One's *Six One* and TV3's *News at 5:30,* almost exactly two-thirds of all speaking time was by journalists. On *Six One*, 53 per cent of all speaking time was by male journalists, while female journalists accounted for 74 per cent on TV3. On RTÉ One, 74 per cent of speaking politicians were males, and on TV3, 60 per cent were males. It is important to remember that this is different from the mentions of candidates' and leaders' names that we discussed previously in this chapter. The inclusion of female politicians' voices on RTÉ One's *Six One* is somewhat better than its mentioning of female candidates' names but is still short of the 30 per cent quota mark. On TV3, the two figures are quite similar. Finally, 82 per cent of other voices were male on RTÉ One, but 55 per cent were female on TV3.

Overall, we find that these two television news programmes were able to live up to gender equality ideals in their allocation of time to journalists but fell short in their coverage of other speakers of different genders. For RTÉ One, it is possible that the more obvious the category and the greater control management had, the better *Six One* did: gender equality for presenters; somewhat more male politicians' voices than the candidate pool; and overwhelmingly male speakers in terms of other participants. The TV3 sample is small, especially for other voices, but it does pass all three gender equality tests. Women dominate the journalists' role and the few other participants, but in selecting politicians to talk, TV3 broadly reproduces the 30 per cent quota. We do not believe that the gender equality found in the presentation of the news on Irish television extends to the rest of the Irish media.

Conclusion

In terms of the amount of coverage given to female candidates, Ireland's two most popular newspapers have tended to 'reflect reality' in their reporting on election campaigns from 1969 to 2016. Generally, challengers received no more or less coverage because of their gender. Neither the *Irish Times* nor the *Irish Independent* increased or reduced the heavy bias towards men in the selection of candidates from 1969 to 2016. By contrast, we see important changes in tone and framing. Women candidates were covered in a more positive tone until the 1990s. Especially in the early period, some of the positivity may have been chauvinist condescension (at least by today's standards). We do not know how much. While women may have had an advantage in tone, they appear to have suffered from non-political framing in the *Irish Independent* until 1997. Since the latter contest, there has not been an important difference in the extent to which men and women candidates are framed politically or non-politically. So, we have some good news.

By the start of the new millennium, these two national daily newspapers had adopted gender neutrality in respect of the amount of coverage, its tone, and the fundamental framing of women as politicians. This is surely the result of exogenous social change. Ours is not the first general study of political candidates to find an absence of gender bias in the media. A large and systematic study of local newspapers in two House of Representatives elections in the United States also found no general bias in any respect (Hayes and Lawless, 2016). The authors conclude that the source of the under-representation of women in the US legislature is not media or voter bias but the absence of female candidates – which is, in turn, at least partly the result of a belief in the gender bias amongst ambitious women and potential political and financial supporters (Hayes and Lawless, 2016: 10). It may be that we have a similar situation in Ireland. Of course, we are not saying that there is no sexism in the media coverage of Irish elections. Clearly, there is. Crucially, it is possible for occasional sexism to exist while we can confirm the absence of systematically sexist media coverage of elections.

Our findings also contain some bad news. In 2016, women candidates received a greater proportion of coverage in the *Irish Times* and *Irish Independent* than at any previous election. Nonetheless, as our analysis of challengers in 2016 shows, this was the first time that there was a clear gender bias in the coverage of challengers in both newspapers. More concerning still, this pattern is reproduced across other newspapers, as well as television and radio programmes. The quota legislation was a basic success in that parties radically increased the proportion of female candidates they put forward. If this seems modest, parties in France have taken financial penalties instead of meeting their legislative quota, which is admittedly much higher, at 50 per cent (Murray, 2010). But it was surely unanticipated that Ireland's quota would be the catalyst for a reduction in the coverage received by individual women candidates. We do not know why the media failed to keep up with the increase in female candidates. Elsewhere in this book, we have argued that much of the nature of Irish election coverage can be explained by the Irish media's longstanding commitment to the norms of a liberal media system. Perhaps the media had locked in norms and routines that could deliver generally gender-neutral coverage of elections where less than 20 per cent of candidates were women. If so, current debates about how to increase the visibility of women in current affairs and journalism should be extended to how to guarantee the equal coverage of male and female candidates in future general elections.

Note

1 Sources for proportions of female candidates: for 1969 and 1973, calculated from Ted Nealon (1974: 119); for 1977–2007, calculated from John Coakley and Michael Gallagher (2010: 266); for 2011, calculated from Claire McGing (2011); for 2016, calculated from Paul Melia (2016).

6

Party leaders and personalisation of politics

The focus of elections can vary from discussions of alternative policy offerings to a discussion of the election as a game or horserace. But just because election news is not discussing policy, it does not mean it is framed on the electoral game. Elections are often as much about choosing leaders as policies. Party leaders are the most prominent characters in parliamentary elections. The leader is important because it is frequently the leader who becomes Taoiseach, Tánaiste, or a senior member of the cabinet. It is these people who make decisions, and throughout the period of our study from 1969 to 2016 they dominate the policy process. Leaders matter after elections, so it makes sense that media outlets would focus on party leaders during an election campaign.

Political leaders can matter independently of a party. They can connect directly with voters, sometimes giving life to a party. In the Netherlands, a place with strongly institutionalised parties, a deeply stratified society, and a highly proportional electoral system, Pim Fortuyn emerged as a major political figure in the early 2000s almost without any institutionalised party (Lijst Pim Fortuyn), literally on the force of his personality. That it can happen in circumstances that are hardly conducive to personalisation shows that this is potentially a significant force in politics. More recently, in France, Emmanuel Macron became President of the Republic via a new political movement, *En Marche!* (On The Move!), set up to serve his personal political ambitions. The party deliberately had the same initials as Macron. The party performed remarkably well in parliamentary elections, mainly due to the personal popularity of Macron, and acts as a vehicle to serve Macron's presidency. Donald Trump, Beppe Grillo, and others show that this is not a rare phenomenon explicable only in terms of very unusual circumstance at particular times.

Ireland has not been immune to political leaders dominating their parties and its message. Fianna Fáil is widely thought to have been set up as a vehicle for the ambitions of Éamon de Valera (O'Malley and McGraw, 2017: 6). Much of the early campaigning was through mass meetings where de Valera could speak directly to the people. He set up and controlled a newspaper for this purpose, and although Fianna Fáil became a highly professional and institutionalised party, much of the messaging was based on appeals to the efficacy of the leader – his image appears on many of the party's early posters.

That Fianna Fáil became the dominant party of the State shows that leader popularity can translate into electoral support for the parties they lead. For example, reflecting on Fine Gael's heavy defeat in the 1977 election, its leader, Liam Cosgrave, referred to his Fianna Fáil counterpart, Jack Lynch, as the most popular Irish politician since Daniel O'Connell (a nineteenth-century leader of Irish nationalism sometimes referred to as 'The uncrowned King of Ireland'). More recently, Fianna Fáil's electoral success in 1997 and 2002, and the Labour Party's surge in support in 1992 and 2011 were in part due to the popularity of these parties' respective leaders: Bertie Ahern, Dick Spring, and Eamon Gilmore. Given the changing electoral dynamics of recent decades – where voters are less anchored to one political party – electoral volatility is increasing (Quinlan, 2016), and with policy differences becoming less obvious and less obviously important, the expectation that leaders are not only important but more important today is very plausible.

Commentators bought into this prevailing narrative with respect to the 2016 Irish general election. Many in the media attributed Fianna Fáil's electoral recovery to its leader, Micheál Martin. For example, one political correspondent (Leahy, 2016: 93) observed that 'its posters told the tale: big Micheál, small FF. A party leader hasn't been as influential in a campaign since 1997.' Similarly, there was a sense that Fine Gael's problem was a leadership one, with Taoiseach Enda Kenny's uninspiring campaign performance denting the party's support (Leahy, 2016). After the election, much discussion related to how, and when, Kenny would be replaced as leader of Fine Gael, with real fears of an election with him *in situ* as leader: 'Kenny rescued his party from annihilation in 2002 and led them to a stunning victory in 2011. He has proved himself to be an able leader … But he is now standing an isolated weakened figure' (McConnell, 2016). It is uncontroversial to suggest that the leader is seen by many in the media to be important.

In reaction to this centrality of the leader, we might expect to see that the media regards it as its duty to subject the leader to more exposure and close examination. This may manifest itself negatively in increasingly critical exposure. This chapter examines the changing media coverage of leaders. We consider a number of this study's three approaches: whether the changing media market has caused a move towards hypercritical infotainment; whether the exogenous political, social, and economic factors, as well as the parties' own campaign strategies have influenced or changed coverage; or whether the media system's norms of impartiality and proportionality have been resilient to the many commercial and technological pressures. An increase in media coverage focus on the leader and her or his personality in election campaigns would be consistent with, but not necessarily indicative of, infotainment. It is sometimes thought that leaders engage in performative politics, and that this type of politics has increased over time, and with it there is an increase in this type of coverage over time, though the expanding literature actually finds little empirical evidence. Another aspect of the hypercritical approach is what is called the personalisation thesis: that the media also focuses on aspects of a leader that were hitherto private. So, as well as covering leaders more, media coverage is thought to be increasingly interested in the private lives of leaders. These two phenomena, presidentialisation and personalisation, could take place because of exogenous effects of the political system. Decreased policy diversity gives the media fewer ways to distinguish the parties. In fact, as we saw in Chapter 2, policy diversity has increased since the 1970s and is probably higher in 2011 and 2016 than at any time in Ireland's recent political history. Nor can we easily observe a shift in power to the party leader within parties or at the level of political institutions. The Irish party leader has usually been the dominant political player, as has the Taoiseach within the Irish Government. That leaves mediatisation as the driver. We use the longitudinal data from our study to test whether these hypothesised phenomena occur in Ireland. We also consider how social media might be used as a way to connect directly with voters, unmediated by the press and broadcast media. This new technology might also contribute to a growing personalisation. First, however, we discuss these different dimensions of personalisation and develop hypotheses to test them.

Presidentialisation and personalisation

When leaders are covered in the media, this is regarded as reflective of the presidentialisation and personalisation hypotheses. Presidentialisation is the idea that increasing institutional power, electoral focus, and party control are centred on the party leader (Webb and Poguntke, 2013). It 'implies a movement over time away from collective to personalised government, movement away from a pattern of governmental and electoral politics dominated by the political party towards one where the party leader becomes a more autonomous political force' (Mughan, 2000: 7). It makes sense in that, with the decline in parties as social-centric institutions, they have become 'hollowed out' and are likely to be dominated by their leaders (Mair 2011). Costa-Lobo and Curtice (2015) has shown that leaders should matter more for those without party identification. So, we should see more 'leadership', and this should be reflected in the media coverage of elections.

Whether parliamentary regimes are becoming presidential in their substance is questionable. The empirical evidence for the presidentialisation hypothesis is weak, and much depends on impressionistic evidence that relates to the style of campaigning, such as the use of leaders on posters in place of or prioritised over party logos and names (Farrell and Webb, 2000). But the hypothesis itself emanates from a causal mechanism related to the media, among other factors (see Garzia,

2014: 7). The (relatively) new technology of television meant that individuals would be the focus of coverage rather than abstract political ideas. The media logic meant that leader debates became a crucial media event in campaigns and hence a crucial event in campaigns. The increasing focus on the individual leader makes leaders, and in particular prime ministers, important electoral assets (or liabilities) for parties. This, it is thought, has the effect of transferring power to the leaders. If there is little evidence of this increased focus on the leader in the media, it has implications for the vote choice literature, for the 'leaders matter' hypothesis, and for where political power is situated.

Balmas *et al.* (2014) describe personalisation in three dimensions: institutional, media, and behaviour. Where institutional personalisation refers to the power that leaders have, media personalisation is the increased focus on leaders by media, and behavioural is that political activity is more individual, and less collective. So, there is more emphasis on the leader than the party. Langer (2007) describes the personalisation of politics in terms of three other dimensions. The first is the presidentialisation of power, where power is concentrated in the individual at the top of the party or the government. The second is a leadership focus, i.e. 'increased emphasis on leaders' personality traits and skills directly related to their competence for governing', and the third is the politicisation of the private persona, where we learn about the leaders not in terms of their ideology or public statements, but them as human beings (Langer, 2007: 373). A question is raised about the authenticity of the political leader. Politics requires a public performance, but we then might question whether this is an act or if the public face is reflective of the leader's private desires and impulses. Personalisation could matter to the consumer of media if it tells them who the *real* Micheál Martin or Leo Varadkar is.

Personalisation, arguably, focuses on the style of campaigning, style of coverage, and the focus on leaders' personalities or sometimes even idiosyncrasies. For instance, there was a surprising focus on Ed Miliband's ability to eat a bacon sandwich when he was pictured awkwardly chewing it during the 2014 UK local elections. This was not new. Gerald Ford had found the same problem in 1976 when he was pictured awkwardly eating tamales without removing the husks of the corn. When asked about what lessons he learned from losing the election, he answered, 'One is – never underestimate your opponent, and two always shuck the tamale' (Safire, 1976). With some leaders, such as Silvio Berlusconi, the persona becomes the message.

Personalisation might be causally prior to presidentialisation. Personalisation can happen despite few or no institutional changes. So, while the power of the Canadian Prime Minister is the same as it was forty years ago, what is perhaps novel is the intense media and public fascination with Justin Trudeau, his family, his physique, and his sartorial choices, the so-called Trudeaumania. That is, until we consider that the term Trudeaumania was coined almost fifty years earlier for his father, Pierre Trudeau, when the public and media were fascinated by him, his good looks, and his celebrity relationships. It might be that in the context of an institutionally very powerful prime ministerial office (a form of presidentialisation) it is inevitable that there will be increased focus on the person holding that office (personalisation). Causality might also run the other way.

In this chapter, we concentrate on two distinctions in personalisation. First, what has at times been described as 'leadership stretch' (Foley, 2000), i.e. the increased concentration of coverage on the leader to the neglect of the collective, perhaps cabinet or front-bench party colleagues. Second, that which refers to the personalised nature of the coverage, which looks beyond policy to the private life and personal qualities of the leader.

The empirical evidence for the personalisation thesis, and the assumed trend over time in numerous studies (Kriesi, 2012; Zeh and Hopmann, 2013; Balmas et al., 2014), is, 'if present at all, weaker than is generally assumed' (Holtz-Bacha et al., 2014: 157). There appears to be strong cross-country variation, though this may be a result of methodological differences rather than institutional differences, regime type, and electoral systems, as Kriesi (2012) argues, though even these explanations are doubtful.

In this longitudinal study, we can test whether the broad personalisation hypothesis holds in Ireland. Given the long time-coverage in our study, if personalisation is a function of time, we should expect to be able to observe it. Election campaigns may not be ideal venues to test these theories, because elections tend to be noted for specific events, canvassing, leader tours, leader debates, etc. We might then expect to see more emphasis on leaders in these times than in everyday parliamentary politics. As such, if we do not see leadership concentration in election campaigns, then this is strong evidence against it existing at all. We might expect to see more emphasis on the character of leaders in elections, especially as the position of leader is seen as more important. Conversely elections tend not to lend themselves to coverage of the private lives, because in campaigns leaders are in full public view. But there are also attempts to add colour to reporting by getting into the private life of politicians and into discussions of their dress, their manner, and how they react under the pressure of a campaign.

Thus, we have two sets of hypotheses related to the two approaches to personalisation, leadership concentration, and emphasis on the non-political. First, coverage in election campaigns becomes more personalised over time. The ratio of references to names and titles increases over time. Second, leadership concentration (ratio of mentions of formal leaders to other senior figures) has grown over time.

Regarding the first part of this hypothesis, we expect to see that leaders are referred to by their institutional title, e.g. the leader of Fine Gael, rather than Liam Cosgrave, in the elections of 1969, 1973, and 1977, whereas it becomes more common to refer to the individual leader as time progresses. Again, the ratio of references to institutions and to protagonists' names might also change, so there could be a decreased reference to the party compared to the leader's name. If personalisation has happened, the first name might also be more commonly used. This would indicate a greater familiarity with the subject. But it is unclear if this is the result of any media logic or just an increasing familiarity and informality within society. We test the extent to which the singular figure of party leader has become more important compared to the collective group of the front-bench team. We question whether this is likely to have empirical support, and it must surely also depend on the extent to which a party puts an emphasis on the leader, judging that he or she is an asset. If there is a secular trend to coverage of the leader figure, this would support an aspect of the personalisation thesis.

The second dimension of personalisation refers to how media coverage of leaders might have changed. It could have become less policy-related and more personal. It might have become more focused on the suitability of the individuals as potential leaders of the country, and so might also be more likely to express an opinion (negative or positive) on that leader. First, coverage of leaders should increasingly be related to non-policy, non-game aspects, i.e. discuss their personal lives or other non-public aspects. Second, content covering leaders would put increased emphasis on how 'effective' specific leaders are. Third, content covering leaders would show increased levels of sentiment.

Extent of personalisation, 1969–2016

In this section, we use the data from media coverage of elections in the *Irish Times* and *Irish Independent* from 1969 to 2016 to test these hypotheses. The first set of hypotheses refers to personalisation of campaigns over time. Figure 6.1 shows the ratio of paragraph mentions of the Taoiseach by name to mentions by title, and the ratio of references to the leaders' party and to the leaders themselves. The higher the line, the more mentions by title.

Party names and positional titles tend to receive much more coverage than leaders' names. The results (not shown) at least demonstrate that the data passes some basic face validity tests. For instance, the word 'Tánaiste' shows a tenfold increase in coverage in 1997. This is because the office became more formalised and powerful after the 1992 election, when the Labour Party leader, Dick Spring, insisted that he be given institutional backup that would match that of the Taoiseach. We can also see that when the more media-shy Liam Cosgrave was Taoiseach in 1977, there was less coverage, both in name and title, than when Jack Lynch held the office in 1973. Equally, election coverage of the Taoiseach was noticeably lower in 2011, when Brian Cowen had resigned as Fianna Fáil leader and was not contesting the election but remained as Taoiseach.

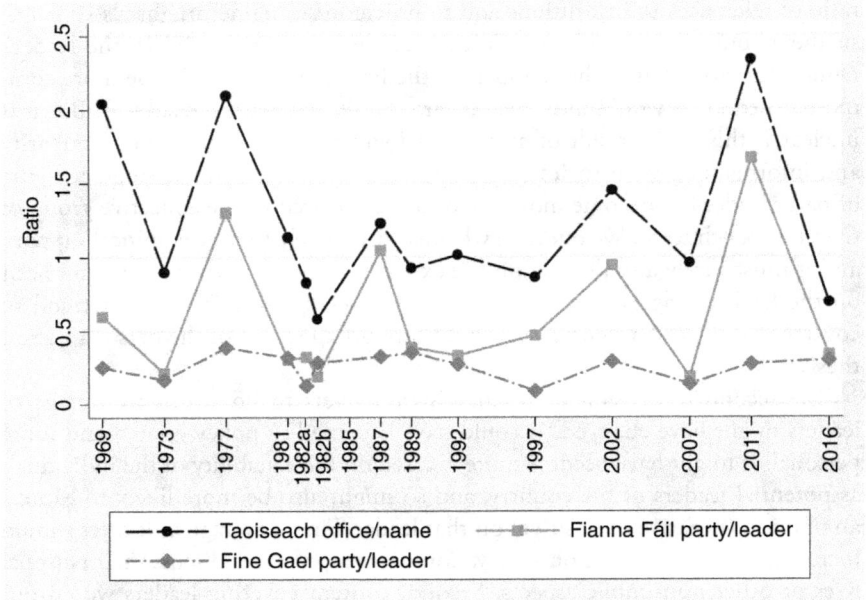

Figure 6.1 Ratio of coverage of institution to individual, *Irish Times* and *Irish Independent* 1969–2016

The proportion of coverage between (position or party) title and person shows no pattern. There is no clear temporal trend, though Fine Gael is obviously different to Fianna Fáil. Election coverage of Fine Gael is much more likely to emphasise the party than the leader. This is quite consistent, even when it had a dominant leader in Garret FitzGerald. We do see that mentions of Fianna Fáil as a party drop dramatically in 2016, as the emphasis is on Micheál Martin as leader and not on the brand Fianna Fáil. The proportionate emphasis of the Taoiseach's title is much greater in 1977, when Cosgrave is incumbent, than in the elections in the early 1980s, with Haughey and FitzGerald jostling for power. So, while individual movements are explicable, on the basis of this evidence we would be inclined to reject this aspect of the personalisation hypotheses.

Another measure of the same phenomenon is the proportion of coverage of the party leaders compared to other senior politicians. In Figure 6.2, the line gives the proportion of coverage of the top thirty named election candidates that is taken by the leaders of the three main parties, Fianna Fáil, Fine Gael, and Labour. Over time, we can see a rise in coverage of the three main party leaders at each election. This measure, in fact, underestimates the increase in coverage of leaders because since 1982 there have been more parties. The rise in coverage occurs despite the increased focus on other party leaders, such as Mary Harney

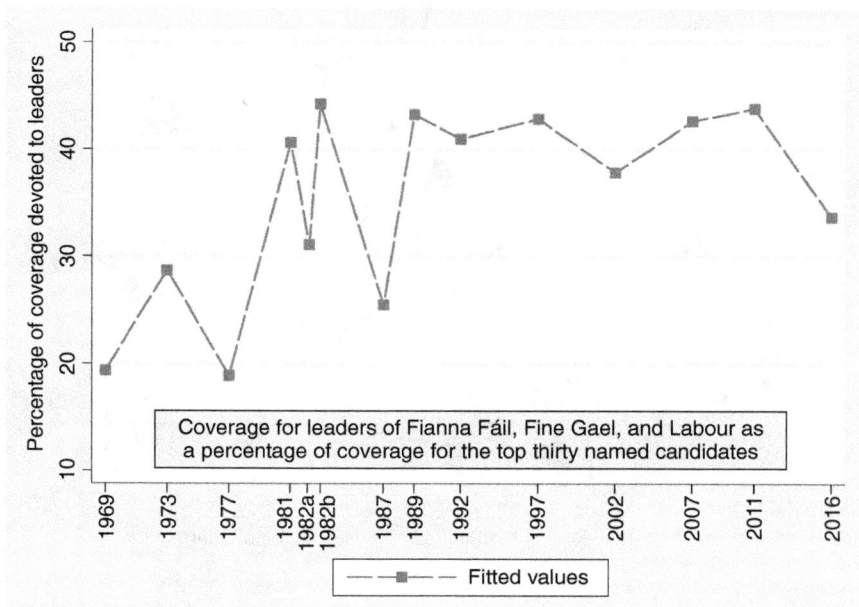

Figure 6.2 Proportion of coverage of leaders to top thirty named candidates, *Irish Times* and *Irish Independent* 1969–2016

(PDs), Proinsias de Rossa (Democratic Left), and Gerry Adams (Sinn Féin). If leader coverage is not increasing compared to the emphasis on their parties, it is certainly increasing as a proportion of emphasis on individual politicians.

We can also evaluate this feature by party. Figure 6.3 shows the ratio between the party leader and the other top three most mentioned party figures for each of the three main parties. One thing to note is that the formal party leader is not always the most mentioned figure from each party. For example, for Fianna Fáil in 1969 and Fine Gael in 1977, though the leader was the Taoiseach, other figures (in these cases, Charles Haughey and Garret FitzGerald) were mentioned more often in media coverage.

There is a clear upward trend in leadership concentration in Fianna Fáil and Fine Gael. This is not uniform, and there appears to be a greater deal of variation now than previously, but this variation is explicable in terms of party strategy. For instance, we know that Fine Gael made a deliberate effort to present Enda Kenny as the leader of a team of senior figures in 2011, whereas in 2007 he was a more singular figure. There was an increase in coverage of Micheál Martin in 2016 compared to the next most reported Fianna Fáil figure. This is again consistent with the party strategy to emphasise Martin as the party's main electoral asset. So, while we see the increase in leadership concentration, it is not uniform, and

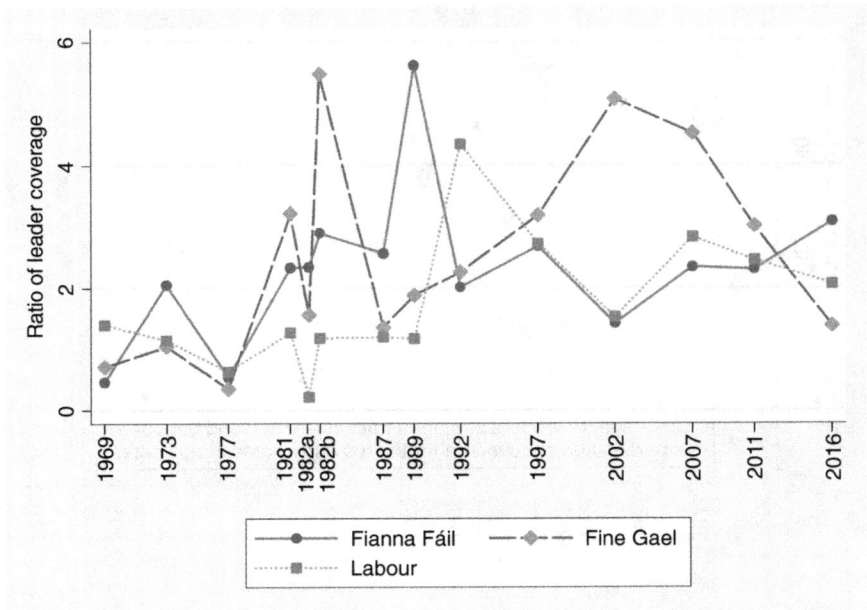

Figure 6.3 Ratio of coverage of each party leader to top three named politicians in their party, *Irish Times* and *Irish Independent* 1969–2016

it may not be the result of any media logic; rather, this increase, and the increased variation, is better explained by decisions taken by the parties.

In explaining this finding, it could be that the variation is due to whether a party is in government or in opposition. If the leader is the Taoiseach, his other party colleagues will be ministers and so may receive a greater degree of coverage as a result. In testing this idea (see Figure 6.4), we would expect the opposition line to be higher than the government line. In fact, they track each other until about 1992. Thereafter, the opposition line is clearly and significantly higher than the government line.

Taking the expanded dataset available for the 2016 election, we can compare journalistic modes to see if television or radio is more likely to cover the leader rather than the party. Table 6.1 reports the ratio of leader mentions to party mentions in the three different outlet types. The mode of communication is important, because journalists will make decisions on what is more appealing given the type of outlet. Coverage of a telegenic party leader might be more likely on TV than in the press or on the radio. We can see that broadcast media tend to be more diffuse in their coverage of political figures in 2016 for what were to become the three largest parties, Fianna Fáil, Fine Gael, and Sinn Féin. The Fianna Fáil coverage in the national newspapers and on TV in 2016 shows a higher concentration on the party leader, Micheál Martin, probably because

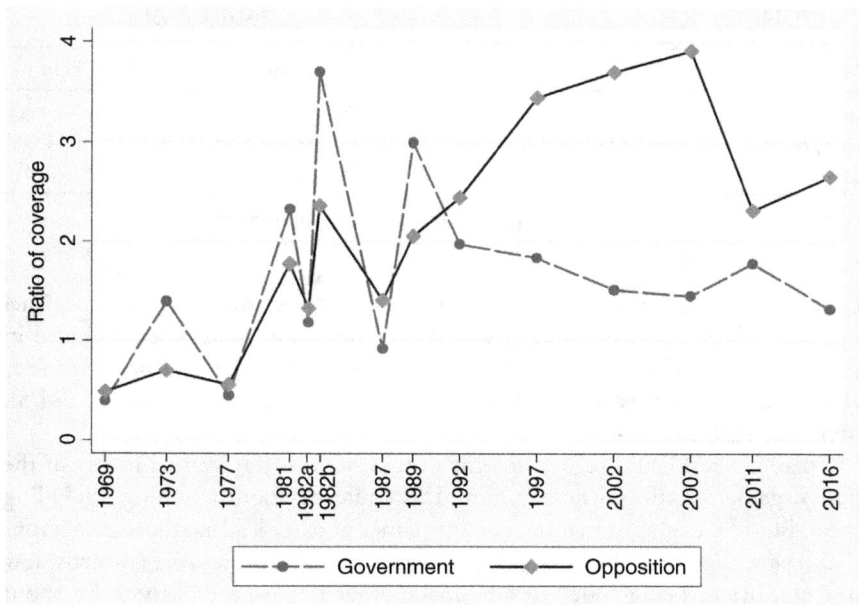

Figure 6.4 Proportion of coverage of Taoiseach/opposition leader to top three named politicians in their party, *Irish Times* and *Irish Independent* 1969–2016

Fianna Fáil intended this. The ratio of leader coverage to party coverage of the incumbent Taoiseach and Fine Gael leader, Enda Kenny, is lower than for all other parties across all three media. This is likely to be the result of a party strategy. Another notable result from the data reported in Table 6.1 is that TV tends to be more leader-focused than either radio or print. Generally, we see that leadership concentration is more likely now than in the past, but it is highly variable, and the press seems to react to the agenda of the parties in focusing on the leader at times when the leader is seen as an asset, but giving more focus to others in the party at other times.

Our second set of hypotheses focused on how the leader is covered. We have a number of expectations: one is that there is an increased focus on the personal lives of the leaders, another is that coverage about the competence or effectiveness of leaders will be increasing. The content is classified to assign probabilities that a paragraph would be coded by a human as relating to some aspect of policy, or other types of framing. These are then linked to the named entity recognition software to enable us to see if certain frames are associated with certain leaders, or leaders in general. So, content could frame a leader in terms of her or his effectiveness. This may not be a direct assessment of the leader by the media outlet, but could be, and commonly is, a report of someone else's assessment,

Table 6.1 Ratio of leader coverage to party coverage, 2016 general election

Media	Fianna Fáil	Fine Gael	Labour	Sinn Féin
Print	0.78	0.26	0.53	0.64
Radio	0.45 (0.30, 0.33)	0.39 (0.00, 0.80)	0.78 (0.19, 1.38)	0.58 (0.00, 1.38)
TV	1.13 (0.00, 2.30)	0.65 (0.15, 1.16)	1.4 (0.00, 3.16)	1.2 (0.48, 2.19)

Note: Confidence intervals for broadcasts are given in parentheses.

even a self-assessment. For example, in the 1989 election, a senior Fine Gael member offered an assessment of the Fianna Fáil leader's character, reported in the *Irish Independent* as: 'Michael Noonan had indicated this on both *Morning Ireland* and on *Saturday View* Charles Haughey is a chancer, a bully, and an opportunist' (Holt, 1989).

There is a residual category in which the content is not framed in any of the policy, game, or effectiveness frames. This could be about anything, including sport, but in paragraphs that include the names of party leaders, those paragraphs that have a high probability of being coded as a residual (or, more correctly, low probabilities of being coded in any of the other frames) are likely to be about some non-political aspect of the leader's personal life. What we see is that this category represents ephemera of the election campaign. For instance, coverage of Haughey and FitzGerald in the early 1980s included these two reports: 'Ever thought of judging politicians at their face value? Literally anyone with a knowledge of the ancient art of physiognomy might deduce that Charles Haughey is commanding and inclined to arrogance' (O'Neill, 1981), and 'Garret FitzGerald is no Shakin' Stevens, but he did his best on the public platform outside Dooley's hotel in Birr when he danced to the music of 'This Ole House' with petite show band singer Dawn Hetherington of the Avons' (Collins, 1981).

The data in Figure 6.5 below shows the likelihood of being coded for non-political where a paragraph features a leader of each party. The probabilities are consistently low, indicating that the coverage of leaders is more likely to be on policy or game coverage. These probabilities show no temporal pattern, suggesting that the personalisation hypothesis is incorrect. There is variation, and again this is explicable, but more in terms of what else the papers in question are covering. So, the decrease in coverage of non-political matters on Fianna Fáil's leader in 2011 might be because there was so much else to cover.

This type of coverage might be thought to have increased since leader debates were introduced. For instance, we see some coverage on the clothes the leaders wore:

> Sporting a salmon pink shirt and matching tie Mr Spring was flanked by his high profile comrades Ruairi Quinn and Barry Desmond both of whom opted for blood red ties. (O'Regan, 1987)

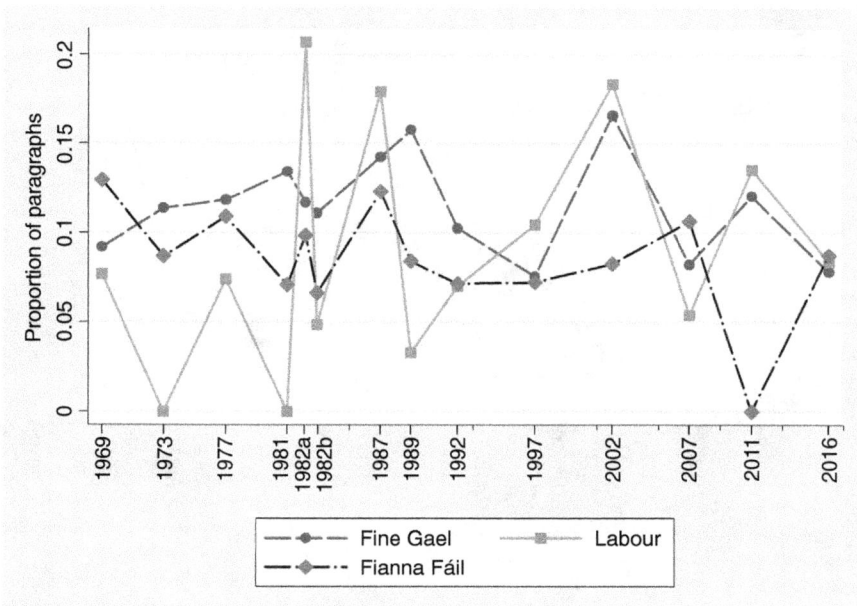

Figure 6.5 Likelihood of coverage of each party leader focusing on non-political factors, *Irish Times* and *Irish Independent* 1969–2016

John Bruton opted for a darker shade of navy double-breasted with an interesting but almost invisible red stripe running through the fabric but the Fine Gael leader came into his own with his choice of tie which was pink with navy stripes. (Lord, 1992b)

On TV3 he was wearing a flash Armani type number such as you normally associated with Ruairi Quinn. The tie too was a trendy lime coloured affair redolent of Hugo Boss or Calvin Klein. (De Bréadún, 2002)

In fact, much of the non-political coverage in these two national newspapers from 1969 to 2016 is not personal in nature but reports of the 'hoopla' surrounding an election campaign. In particular, there are many reports of campaign events, the size of the crowd, how the leader travelled, and so forth. There is little evidence of an increased focus on the personal in these data, though the classifier was not designed to find this; so, this failure to reject the null hypothesis may not be fatal to the hypothesis.

We are also interested in the type of coverage of leaders. If there is a greater focus on leaders, we might also expect that the distinguishing feature of the leaders, their competence, might correlate with their coverage. Figure 6.6 shows

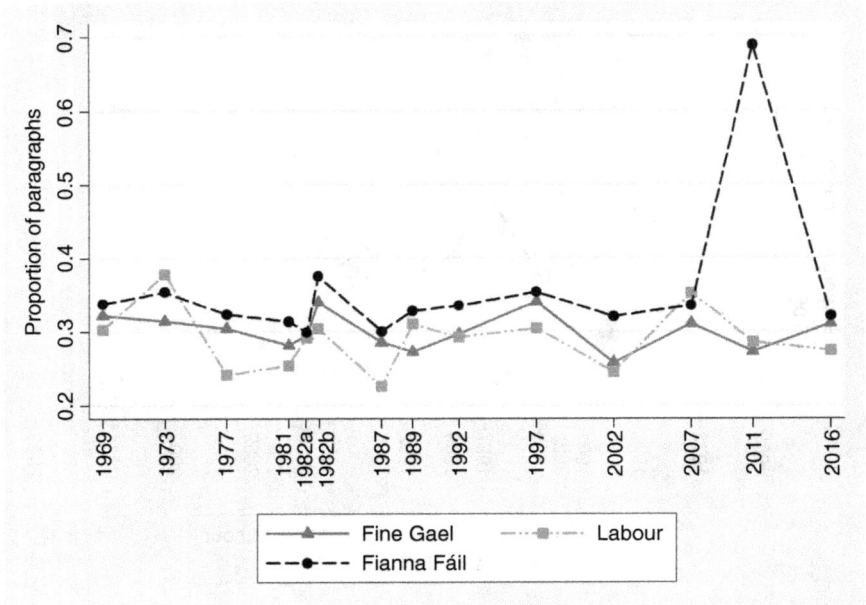

Figure 6.6 Effectiveness framing in mentions of party leaders, *Irish Times* and *Irish Independent* 1969–2016

the likelihood of a paragraph mentioning each party's leader being coded with the effectiveness frame (discussed above). Text is coded as such when there is a reference to strong leadership, political authority, and effective government. There is face validity for this measure in the increase one observes for 2011, when the then Taoiseach, Brian Cowen (whom we leave in, although he had recently been replaced as leader), was widely criticised for his ineffectiveness. The findings, however, are remarkably consistent over time. Accordingly, we can conclude that while leaders are often covered in terms of their effectiveness, this is neither a new nor a growing phenomenon.

In terms of the sentiment of the election coverage, it assumed that reporting has become less deferential over time. Especially, if there is a decrease in policy debate and an increased focus on the leader, we would expect the coverage to contain more sentiment. In terms of tone, the data (not shown) is negative, with the exception of 1969, which may have been an election where the media transitioned from old-fashioned to more modern, aggressive coverage. Since then, there has been no trend over time. The media reacts to certain leaders in perhaps predictable ways. Fianna Fáil's leaders are rarely covered in a positive light, though 2016 was an exception to this. Generally, leaders in opposition are covered more

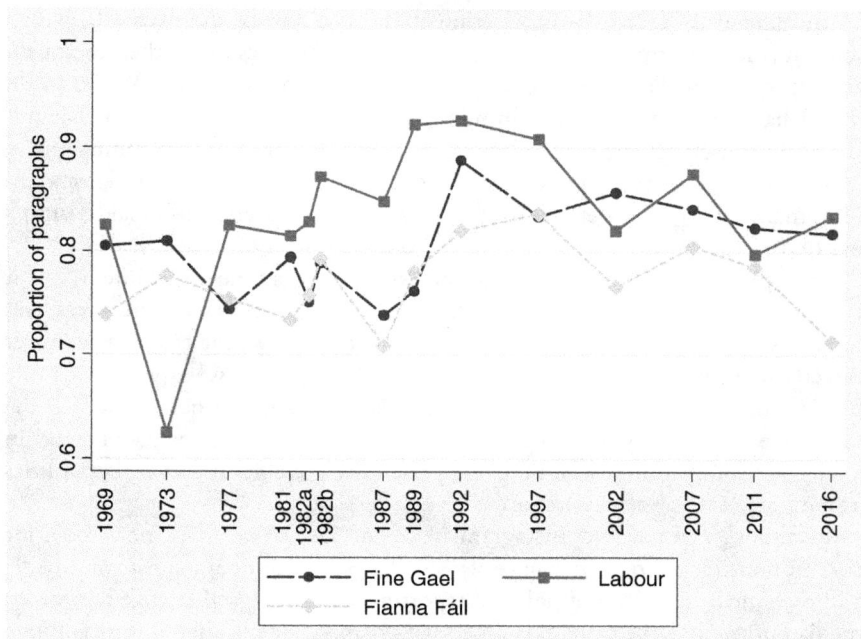

Figure 6.7 Total sentiment in coverage of each party leader, *Irish Times* and *Irish Independent* 1969–2016

positively than those in government. Charles Haughey in the early 1980s was covered especially negatively, which is unsurprising given the contested nature of his leadership of Fianna Fáil. We also see that the coverage of Bertie Ahern in 2007 was far more negative than earlier coverage, most likely due to the revelations about his personal finances, which was a continual presence in the 2007 campaign.

We could also assume that if there is an increased focus on the leaders, and the leaders are assessed as potential Taoisigh, that there will be more sentiment over time. The amount of sentiment related to the coverage of each party leader is quite high but has not obviously changed over time. Figure 6.7 shows that, if anything, there is more neutral coverage of some leaders, but there are no clear trends.

Impact of social media

The extent to which digital platforms have been normalised in Irish campaigns was captured by one commentator who described the 2016 election campaign as 'the first truly social media election in Ireland', given the extent to which social media platforms were 'used by candidates and parties to sell their messages, and by voters to converse about the issues' (Goodbody, 2016). While social media has also emerged as a communication tool in Irish elections, it has not yet been utilised on the scale of Barack Obama's US presidential campaigns in 2008 and 2012, been as targeted (and effective) as was seen in the Brexit referendum (Shipman, 2017), or generated anything like the controversy of Donald Trump's use of Twitter.

Trump's use of social media might be extreme in its tone and content, but it is not unusual for politicians to attempt to bypass parties or the press and broadcast media to directly reach the public. It also allows the public to connect directly with politicians and engage in debate in ways that were previously only possible through face-to-face canvassing. This enables the principal (be that the candidate or the party leader) to connect directly with far more people, and in a far more sophisticated way, than was previously possible. It also makes politics a more interactive spectator sport.

Facebook, Twitter, and Instagram have not just emerged as new tools for communicating politics, they have also challenged traditional mainstream media and redefined the nature of political reporting. Technological change has forced media outlets, like the print and broadcast organisations studied in this volume, to reassess the way they produce content for their listeners, viewers, and readers. These audiences have reduced by traditional measures – television viewing numbers and newspaper sales circulation – but they have expanded enormously when digital 'clicks' on related websites are included. Nevertheless, the response to revenue losses driven by technological upheaval – and advertising revenues ceded to new online platforms – has meant reductions in editorial budgets and job losses at many traditional media outlets.

By the 2016 Irish general election, most parties and individual candidates had active social media accounts. Candidates and political leaders use the medium to maintain contact with voters on local and national issues. Some politicians release weekly video blogs to communicate with voters, and during campaigns they usually post selfies with canvassers proclaiming how well they are being received on the doorstep. Perhaps for this reason, it is not surprising that we can observe from systematic analysis that the established media by and large ignores social media, even if journalists are active on media such as Twitter to promote their own material. We would expect more discussion of social media if this was the site of real developments in the campaign. But also, for the benefit of media consumers who are not engaged in social media, the established media has an opportunity to help those people feel more informed about an aspect of modern life, and modern political life, from which they might feel somewhat removed. Therefore, we would have expected more systematic discussion of how the campaign was developing on social media. In the absence of evidence suggesting systematic discussion of social media developments, the question arises: 'What does it take for social media aspects of the campaign to merit mention on established media?' Here we discuss four aspects of social media activity by campaigning parties and politicians that were significant enough to 'make the news'. The anecdotes presented here are the exceptions that prove the rule. What they demonstrate overall is that news organisations are not trawling social media looking for election campaign stories.

The most disseminated social media story formed around an advertisement run by the Labour Party in several newspapers and one radio programme. It featured the visages of high-profile opposition members, including Gerry Adams, Lucinda Creighton, Paul Murphy, Shane Ross, and Micheál Martin, photoshopped onto the bodies of the music group One Direction, with the witticism 'No Direction' as the headline. The Twitter reaction to the ad was so noteworthy that four media outlets found cause to comment on it. RTÉ Radio 1's *Morning Ireland* said that it 'got plenty of reaction' (RTÉ, 2016). The ad triggered an online discussion and taunting between the politicians themselves, which was also widely reported. Renua's Lucinda Creighton was quoted in the *Irish Examiner* (McEnroe, 2016) with a Twitter comment criticising the Labour Party for being so 'out of touch they don't know there are only four members of One Direction'. Paul Murphy of the Socialist Party took the opportunity to receive some media attention by analogising Lucinda Creighton, who had left Fine Gael three years previously, with the member of One Direction who had left the boy band. He then proceeded to tweet his own picture of Fine Gael leader Enda Kenny and Labour leader Joan Burton photoshopped onto the band Status Quo (Lenihan, 2016). One election candidate, Gary Gannon of the Social Democrats, commented on the whole affair sarcastically tweeting 'I see Irish political discourse is reaching new levels of maturity' (McEnroe, 2016).

Twitter presents itself as a personalised microblogging site and emphasises the individualism of the experience. If a Twitter account presents itself as being an individual, users assume tweets emanating from that account are the opinions of the person concerned. The bio sections of most user accounts provide a disclaimer that all tweets are the person's own views and not those of her or his organisation. If the account user is a high-profile individual like a prime minister or president, the account will indicate in the bio that tweets from the individual her- or himself are signed with initials – otherwise, the tweet was sent by the individual's staff. When several Fine Gael ministers sent tweets with similar wordings, some media felt this was worthy of comment the following day, questioning whether the social media accounts of Fine Gael ministers were being centrally managed. Three ministers, Heather Humphreys, Frances Fitzgerald, and Charlie Flanagan, sent tweets during a televised leaders' debate, criticising Fianna Fáil's record on the economy with similar phrasing and character substitution (e.g. the '=' character) for more efficient character usage. Junior Minister Damien English was also sending similar content (*The Last Word*, Today FM, 16 February 2016; *Irish Examiner*, 17 February 2016).

The third most referenced use of social media was solely focused on the *Irish Independent* (24 February 2016). Curiously, on the eve of the election, the latter newspaper re-ran a story that had been released prior to the start of the campaign (31 January 2016). This story focused on a Sinn Féin candidate, Chris Andrews, who had previously been a member of Fianna Fáil. He had left the latter party when it emerged that in 2012 he had operated an 'anonymous' Twitter account to attack political opponents, other members of his own party, and other politicians linked with political 'dynasties', despite he himself being a member of one of Ireland's most notable political dynasties. The husband of one of his victims used professional investigative techniques to track the account, eventually identifying Andrews. Fianna Fáil received a report, and Andrews quit the party, later to join and stand for Sinn Féin. Although this was not breaking news at the tail end of the 2016 general election campaign, the *Irish Independent* still found it appropriate to remind voters of the incident.

The *Irish Daily Mail* lived up to the tabloid stereotype by stereotyping female politicians. The paper ran a story about Fine Gael TD Mary Mitchell O'Connor and her difficulties in upholding a sense of style by wearing high heels while keeping pace with the demands of canvassing in a general election (Anonymous, 2016). The headline ran, '"I'm flat out from now, but not in killer heels" vows FG's Mary'. It is apparently noteworthy that 'trend-setting TD' Mitchell O'Connor 'took to twitter to alert constituents that she will be now canvassing for votes in a more sensible option (flat shoes)'. In doing so, the *Irish Daily Mail* felt that she would be 'sacrificing' fashion for comfort. The same title doubled down on latent sexism by querying whether the Labour Party leader Joan Burton was desperate for votes in the last two days of the campaign by 'tweeting a picture of herself reading *Hot Press* magazine, except she's half a century older than the average reader' (Molony, 2016). Characterising older women in a negative light as being 'past it', while older men are considered positively as 'experienced', is a consistent feature of latent sexism.

The striking aspect of these stories is their substantial lack of depth. While social media no doubt generates much heat, one would expect that it generates some light. However, the established media does not seem particularly interested in substantive online developments but more so in the most heated exchanges it would otherwise seem odd to ignore. Perhaps the established media does not want to highlight the fact that social media is better equipped to break news, and references new media begrudgingly, or perhaps it takes a cautious approach to news breaking on social media given the high risk of inaccurate reporting inherent in leaning on the same.

Conclusion

Leaders are important political actors and central to parties' campaigns. Therefore, it is unsurprising that they are a focus of the media's election coverage. The personalisation hypothesis, consistent with the hypercritical approach, suggests that both the coverage of leaders has increased and the nature of that coverage has changed. We find few trends over time. On some measures, there is greater leadership concentration – so leaders are the focus of the coverage to the neglect of other senior party figures. According to the data, media coverage of leaders has not obviously become more personal, more negative, or less policy-focused. In our findings, we can identify a clear logic to exceptional data points; often, however, the logic is one where the media is reacting to party strategies or the type of leader *in situ*. The media does not appear to be obviously driving the type of coverage, rather the media reacts to exogenous factors, such as the parties' desire to promote their leader. This does not mean that the media is not important. Parties' decisions to promote certain leaders, and indeed their choice of leaders, may be related to their ability to sustain positive media coverage. The 'tango dance' between politics and the media might be a hidden power struggle. But if Irish media has moved to hypercritical infotainment – and there is little evidence in our study for this – on the basis of this data it is not a power struggle that a hypercritical media appears to be winning.

There is an increase in coverage of leaders as a proportion of the attention given to named politicians. So, while the nature of the attention on political leaders shows no real change, including no increase in the personalisation of coverage, there is a greater concentration of coverage on the singular leader of the party as opposed to the collective leadership team. This evidence provides the necessary premise that supports those who argue that leaders matter more to voter behaviour.

In our study of two national newspapers from 1969 to 2016, the focus on leaders is somewhat driven by exogenous changes. For instance, we can see that the focus on the leader is greater for opposition parties. This is probably because opposition leaders' parties push this, whereas in government the institutional importance of other leading figures who are ministers maintains a broader focus across the party. We can also see – again consistent with the exogenous approach – that in special circumstances election coverage changes; so, the spike in the evaluation of the effectiveness of Brian Cowen in 2011 is entirely explicable by the context.

Our results are consistent with other empirical studies. Though the hypothesis is intuitively appealing, there are simply few secular trends in personalisation. It should not surprise us, however. If we look at the posters from early elections in Ireland, the parties often focused on their party leaders, or the leaders of other parties. Much of the bitterness in post-civil-war campaigns was entirely focused on the leaders. For example, Fine Gael singled out Éamon de Valera for abuse, but, similarly, de Valera was an important electoral asset for many years and the primary focus of Fianna Fáil's election campaigns, whether in person, on the radio, or in the press. It seems a fair conclusion to note that the desire to focus on leaders and senior party figures is neither new nor focused on specific types of regimes.

7

Commercialism and election coverage

The professional work of journalists has been expressed in numerous codes or principles, all of which note a public-service or social responsibility of journalism (McQuail, 2003; Kovach and Rosenstiel, 2007). This suggests the existence of substantial autonomy – in theory, if not in practice – from commercial pressures. The objective of profit maximisation is often seen as lessening the contribution that media can make in adhering to these principles and facilitating quality democratic debate (Dahlgren and Sparks, 1991; Curran, 2011). Private ownership does offer at least the potential of freedom from political control, whether via the State or political parties. Indeed, isolating the effect of commercialisation on media coverage of politics is regarded as very difficult (Hallin and Mancini, 2004: 279). Ireland has, however, some advantages as a case study in tackling this question. The absence of strident party-political loyalties eliminates one possible confounding explanation for patterns of political coverage. In addition, the ease of entry and exit for British media organisations in the Irish market offers outlets that may be subject to potentially greater commercial pressures than 'domestic' outlets.

In this chapter, we examine four major possible effects of commercialisation on election coverage. First, since most people are not interested in politics, the more commercial an outlet the less it would be expected to cover politics. Second, commercialisation is posited to affect how the media frames politics. Commercial pressures should increase the tendency to frame politics as political competition – 'game' coverage – rather than a policy debate. Elections framed as competition offer similar entertainment to sport: winners, losers, favourites, no-hopers, unassailable leads, and improbable comebacks. Policy reportage, by contrast, is dry, complicated, and finds it more difficult to attract audience attention. Coverage of policy debates is also costlier as this type of reporting involves time and research. The latter cost consideration may well have increased in recent time given heightened pressure on editorial budgets across all media outlets. Third, emotion sells – the adage 'if it doesn't bleed, it doesn't lead' has a ring of truth in the editorial section. In that regard, the more commercial an outlet, the less likely it will be to use neutral language in reporting politics and elections. Finally, and related to the latter point, readers, listeners, and viewers are attracted to 'bad' news. 'Good' news is more difficult to sell. We would, therefore, expect that commercial media outlets would use more negative language in their coverage. These hypotheses all take the form of contrasts between different media outlets at a given point in time. If we accept that commercial pressure on the whole media sector has increased in recent times, then we should find evidence of more policy coverage in media outlets less driven towards profit maximisation alongside an increased emphasis on political competition, less neutral language, and more negativity across all media types.

In the following sections, we first review the commercial position of the Irish media in general, paying particular attention to the media organisations included in this study. Second, we focus on coverage of general elections since 1969 in two national daily newspapers, the *Irish Independent* and the *Irish Times*. Third, we use content analysis data from the 2016 general election to explore the impact of commercialisation on eleven media sources in print and broadcast formats. In the latter discussion, we pay particular attention to coverage of the 2016 election in the Irish editions of British newspapers. Many of our findings do not conform to established ideas about commercialism identified in other international studies and challenge how the idea of commercialisation is considered in discussions of the media's role in reporting on elections.

Irish media market

The Irish media is characterised by privately owned, profit-oriented newspapers, broadcasters, and online outlets operating alongside a publicly owned broadcaster jointly funded by a mandatory license fee and also commercial revenues. As such, the industry – irrespective of ownership type – is highly competitive, with all media outlets chasing audiences and advertising revenues. The range of media offerings now available to the Irish public clearly illustrates the international nature of the media market in Ireland. Indeed, it is now possible for an Irish citizen to go through an average day of viewing, listening, and web browsing about Irish politics without directly using any Irish media outlet.

The leading national daily and Sunday newspaper titles remain dependent on commercial revenue (from copy sales, digital subscriptions, and advertising); none is in receipt of public funding. Like other sectors of the Irish economy, these media companies benefited during the pre-2008 boom period, with a dramatic increase in dependence on advertising (Rafter, 2017). The industry-wide impact of the internet and the collapse of the Irish economy from 2008 onwards pushed many media outlets in Ireland into loss-making positions, while a number of newspapers and radio stations ceased operation. Table 7.1 documents recent newspaper print sales for the five titles included in our content analysis study.

Table 7.1 Sample newspaper circulation, 1990–2016

Title	Jan.–Dec. 1990	Jan.–Dec. 1999	Jan.–Jun. 2009	Jan.–Jun. 2014	Jan.–Jun. 2016
Irish Independent	152,000	166,000	152,204	112,383	102,537
Irish Times	94,000	113,000	114,488	80,332	72,011
Irish Examiner	57,000	61,000	50,346	35,026	30,964
*Irish Daily Mail**	4,000	6,000	52,144	50,032	46,578
Irish Daily Mirror	60,000	62,000	64,194	50,263	38,294

Sources: Data for 2009–16 from News Brands Ireland (newsbrandsireland.ie); data for 1990 and 1999 from Barrett (2000).
*An Irish edition of the *Daily Mail* was introduced in 2006.

The State-owned public broadcaster, Raidió Telefís Éireann (RTÉ), enjoyed a monopoly on domestic broadcasting for most of the early years covered by this study. A television service was introduced in the 1960s – alongside an existing radio service – underpinned by new legislation, which provided independence from direct political control over day-to-day operations and editorial decision-making. A second RTÉ television channel was introduced in 1978. Most of the population existed in this 'two-channel land', although cable providers offered mainly urban viewers subscriber access to a selection of British channels. In the late 1980s, the domestic television and radio market was effectively deregulated. Today, the Irish broadcasting landscape is truly global and contains a mixture of public and private, commercial and community-licensed services operating at national, regional, and local levels, while the Irish audience also has access to a multitude of international television channels via digital and streamed services.

RTÉ now faces domestic competition in the television market from a number of free-to-air operators, most notably the Liberty-Global-owned TV3, which operates three separate channels. The Irish-language station TG4, a publicly owned television service, has been broadcasting since 1996. These free-to-air Irish stations exist in a highly competitive television market where the majority of households subscribe to a digital or satellite service from providers such as Sky and Virgin Media. There is also the increased popularity of online and streaming options, including Netflix, which was reported in 2017 to have 250,000 Irish subscribers, ranking Ireland only behind the US and Canada for subscription numbers globally. RTÉ has maintained clear dominance over TV3 but, as discussed in Chapter 2, these domestic stations have been losing audience share in the vast broadcast landscape available to Irish viewers.

The Irish radio market is as competitive as its newspaper and television counterparts, primarily due to the number of licensed stations at local, regional, and national levels. RTÉ Radio 1 and the privately owned Newstalk are the main

Table 7.2 Radio listenership, share of adults 15 + (7 a.m.–7 p.m.)

Channel	2010	2012	2014	2016
RTÉ Radio 1	22.7	22.8	21.5	23.8
RTÉ 2FM	8.2	7.2	6.5	5.8
RTÉ lyric fm	1.7	1.6	1.9	2.0
Today FM	9.3	9.4	8.7	7.5
Newstalk	4.0	4.4	6.4	6.0
All regional/local	53.6	54.1	54.3	54.5

Source: BAI – Broadcasting Authority of Ireland (research by Ipsos MBRI).

national talk-based radio stations. Both RTÉ and its privately owned counterparts have suffered financially on account of the post-2008 economic collapse, in the case of RTÉ leading to an almost €20m deficit for 2016. Table 7.2 shows the dominance of RTÉ's radio services over national private-sector competitors. Two contrasts with television are worthy of note: first, the audience share of our sample stations is stable; second, the radio market is dominated by local, not international, stations.

Overall, in many segments of the Irish national media market we find intense competition with great attention paid to advertising revenues, circulation, and audience numbers. Commercial pressure has undoubtedly increased over time, and the 'commercial' impact varies little between the main national media outlets, irrespective of their ownership-type – including the publicly owned RTÉ, the *Irish Times* under a trust ownership structure, public (stock market) companies such as the Independent News and Media titles, private companies, including the *Irish Examiner* and the Communicorp radio stations, as well as foreign-owned newspapers selling in the Irish market, including the *Irish Daily Mail* and the *Irish Daily Mirror*.

The *Irish Times* and *Irish Independent*, 1969–2016

If commercialism matters in the Irish media market, we should see specific differences in election coverage between the *Irish Independent* and *Irish Times* over the fourteen elections since 1969. Based on its trust ownership structure (similar to the *Guardian* newspaper in the UK), the *Irish Times* is theoretically not driven by the same overt need to maximise profits as the *Irish Independent*, which for the majority of the period under review has been in the control of a stock-market-listed company. We would, therefore, expect the more commercial *Irish Independent* to emphasise political competition over policy, use less neutral language, and adopt a more negative tone. In our analysis of the coverage of these two leading national newspapers since 1969 we can also explore whether

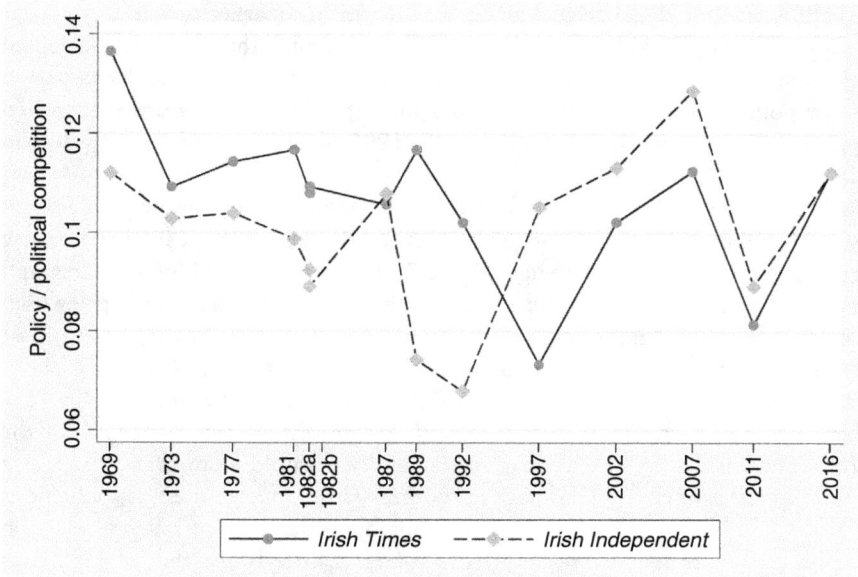

Figure 7.1 Emphasis on policy over political competition, *Irish Times* and *Irish Independent* 1969–2016
Note: This is the election mean of the daily means of the probability of a paragraph being in at least one of the policy categories less the probability of it being political competition.

increasing commercial pressure over time has pushed both newspapers in the direction of political competition, less neutrality, and greater negativity.

We first investigate how the framing of elections has changed over time in the Irish case and whether the *Irish Times* and *Irish Independent* differ in their editorial coverage. In this regard, we subtract the probability of editorial text being about political competition from the probability that it is about policy. Positive numbers suggest that policy coverage predominates over political competition. Our findings show that for all general elections since 1969 – and for both newspapers – policy coverage dominates (Figure 7.1).

The most policy-oriented coverage (0.134) occurred in the *Irish Times* in 1969 and the least (0.068) in the *Irish Independent* in 1992. The two papers generally provide a highly similar mix of policy and political competition, except for 1989, 1992, and 1997. In 1989 and 1992, the *Irish Independent* shifted towards political competition, while the *Irish Times* did not. In 1997, the *Irish Independent* returned to its historic balance of policy and political competition, while the *Irish Times* moved towards political competition. There is no evidence here to support the idea that the more commercial *Irish Independent* emphasised political competition at the expense of policy more than the *Irish Times* did in its election coverage.

There is also no evidence to suggest that increasing market pressure over time has gradually changed the framing of elections. Although the most policy-oriented election coverage in the *Irish Times* was found in 1969, the *Irish Independent's* most policy-oriented coverage was in 2007. The *Irish Independent* emphasised political competition over policy most in 1992, while the *Irish Times* did so in 1997.

We next examined the neutrality of language in election coverage in Ireland since 1969. By 'neutrality of language' we mean the absence of positive or negative connotations in editorial coverage. Figure 7.2 shows the probability of a paragraph being neutral in the *Irish Times* and in the *Irish Independent*. Both titles used their most neutral language in 1969, the election campaign at the outset of our study and a finding which would keep with our assessment in Chapter 1 about deference being a characteristic of earlier election/political news coverage. The least neutral general election for the *Irish Independent* was in 1992 and for the *Irish Times* it was in 1997. From our analysis, it would seem that 1992 was a turning point for election coverage in the *Irish Times*. Indeed, there are reductions in neutrality in both 1992 and 1997, but by 2002 the neutrality of election reportage in the *Irish Times* returns to a level a little below that of 1992 and

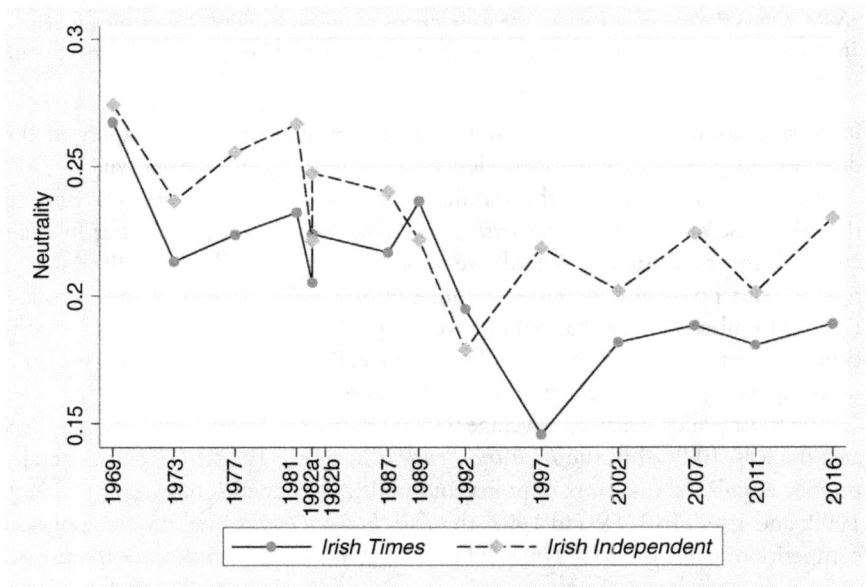

Figure 7.2 Neutrality in coverage, *Irish Times* and *Irish Independent* 1969–2016
Note: This is the election mean of the daily means of the probability of a paragraph being neutral.

thereafter remains remarkably consistent. The evolution of election coverage in the *Irish Independent* is subtler in this respect. The newspaper, like its main national rival, also registers a fall in neutrality in 1992 (when Albert Reynolds was leader of Fianna Fáil and as Taoiseach 'caused' a premature election due to disputes with the PDs, his minor coalition partner), but unlike the *Irish Times*, the *Irish Independent* recovers in 1997. The data provides no support for the idea that the *Irish Independent* should use more emotive language in its coverage based on commercial considerations. If anything, our findings suggest that the language in election coverage in the *Irish Independent* is actually more neutral than that of the *Irish Times*. The data does suggest declining neutrality over time, especially in the *Irish Times*. It should be stressed, however, that this is a tentative conclusion.

Finally, we look at the tone of coverage in the *Irish Independent* and *Irish Times* at all general elections since 1969. We define tone as the probability of coverage being positive less the probability of it being negative. In Figure 7.3, positive scores indicate positive language, while negative scores denote negative language. For both newspapers, their most positive language was used in 1969. Indeed, the *Irish Independent's* coverage of the 1969 general election was the only

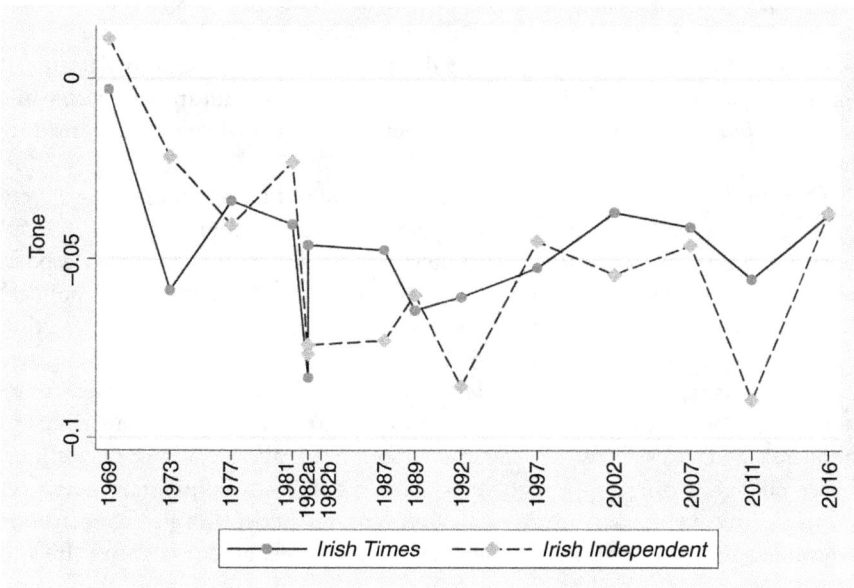

Figure 7.3 Tone in coverage, *Irish Times* and *Irish Independent* 1969–2016
Note: This is the election mean of the daily means of the probability of a paragraph being positive less the probability of it being negative.

instance of language in the fourteen electoral contests under consideration that was predominantly positive. The most negative coverage in the *Irish Times* was in February 1982, an election caused by the collapse of Garret FitzGerald's first Fine Gael–Labour coalition over the introduction of an austerity budget and also the first head-to-head contest between FitzGerald and Charles Haughey, his counterpart in Fianna Fáil. The *Irish Independent's* most negative election coverage was in 2011, an electoral contest dominated by the dramatic collapse in Ireland's economy. Indeed, coverage in the *Irish Independent* in 2011 was also the most negative example in our entire dataset.

Once again, our analysis does not confirm the idea that the more commercial-oriented *Irish Independent* covers elections more negatively than the trust-owned *Irish Times*. There is no consistent difference between the two newspapers, although the *Irish Independent* is a little more positive in 1969 and in 1973, and more negative in the four elections post-1997. Since 1987, the *Irish Independent's* tone has changed more from election to election, but it is not obvious that this is motivated by a more commercial strategy. The data does suggest that coverage of Irish elections gradually became more negative in the 1970s and early 1980s but has remained relatively similar in more recent contests.

Both newspapers in this study are privately owned, although their ownership structure places a different emphasis on profit maximisation, with the trust-owned *Irish Times* considered less driven by obligations to deliver the shareholder value required of the *Irish Independent*. Both newspapers are national in their reach but have different readership profiles: the *Irish Times* self-consciously positions itself as a 'paper of record' aiming at a more affluent and educated market, while the *Irish Independent* targets a broader section of the Irish newspaper reading public.

Our findings suggest that these differences have not mattered in terms of very broad framing and sentiment of the general election coverage since 1969. Of course, commercial situations and strategies may have influenced other aspects of election coverage. We do not find a shift away from policy and towards political competition over time, but we do see a change in the sentiment of election coverage. Since 1969, election reporting has become less neutral and more negative in both newspapers. This shift ended in the late 1980s, following which there has been a more or less stable proportion of neutral language and a surplus of negative language over positive language in both newspapers' coverage of elections. These changes do not appear to reflect direct and overt commercial pressures motivated by events such as the post-2008 economic crisis. Rather, they may be a response to, or part of, a more general social change, as 'conservative' Ireland revised its attitude to authority in general and politics in particular. In this regard, it may be the case that exogenous factors lying outside the media – as discussed in Chapter 1 – may be overriding influencers in determining election news coverage

Commercialism and coverage – 2016 general election

In our analysis of the 2016 general election, we focus on eleven media outlets, including the *Irish Times* and the *Irish Independent*. This wider study provides greater variation in the commercial situation of media outlets in Ireland, ranging from a public broadcaster to Irish editions of British newspapers. However, this wider sample also introduces variation in format. In this regard, the medium may affect the message more than the ownership of the medium. In the sample for 2016, we have direct competition between public and private broadcasters in the morning and evening radio talk programmes and also in the early evening television schedules. The situation is less straightforward in the newspaper market, where all the media outlets are privately owned and, to varying degrees, profit-oriented. Our study includes 'domestic' newspapers that have traditionally been seen as 'quality' broadsheets, including the *Irish Times*, *Irish Examiner*, and *Irish Independent*, although the latter title adopted a compact/tabloid format in 2004 while retaining a mid-market readership focus. The *Irish Daily Mail* – a publication of DMG Media (previously, Associated Newspapers) – targets a lower mid-market readership with a localised edition of its parent British title. In a similar vein, as an Irish edition of a British newspaper, the *Irish Daily Mirror* is positioned firmly in the tabloid segment of the market, with a strong emphasis on sport and entertainment/celebrity coverage.

Table 7.3 summarises the variations of commercial situation and format in our sample of broadcasters and newspaper titles for 2016. For these media outlets, we also have data on the proportion each of them dedicated to policy and game. This data turns out to be vital to our interpretation of differences in framing and sentiment.

Table 7.4 shows the results of regression analyses using all eleven media sources. The first model looks at variation in the proportion of coverage dedicated to politics and policy. The intercept effectively identifies the *Irish Times*, which is not a broadcaster, not a profit maximiser (as a trust), and not a tabloid. Our findings show that radio allocates a smaller share of content to politics than the *Irish Times*, but television allocates more. Commercial sources give less space to politics than the *Irish Times*, and the British newspapers provide the least.

The second model examines whether sources frame politics as political competition. Radio is much more likely than the *Irish Times* to cover political competition, and television even more so. Commercial sources on average take a more policy-focused approach. Most interestingly, the two low- to mid-market British newspapers are the closest to the policy-heavy perspective of the *Irish Times*.

The third model investigates the use of non-neutral language in the political coverage of our sources. Radio is more likely to use positive or negative language than the *Irish Times*. The results for television were too inconsistent across a relatively small amount of data to draw any meaningful conclusion. Commercial

Table 7.3 Media outlets included in 2016 content analysis

Outlets	Owner	Ownership type	Revenue
Newstalk *Newstalk Breakfast*	Communicorp	Irish – private	Advertising
RTÉ Radio 1 *Morning Ireland*	State	Irish – public	Licence fee & advertising
Today FM *The Last Word*	Communicorp	Irish – private	Advertising
RTÉ Radio 1 *Drivetime*	State	Irish – public	Advertising
TV3 *News at 5:30*	Virgin Media Ireland/Liberty Global	UK – publicly quoted	Advertising
RTÉ One *Six One*	State	Irish – public	Licence fee & advertising
Irish Times	Irish Times	Irish – private trust	Circulation & advertising
Irish Independent	Independent News & Media	Irish – publicly quoted	Circulation & advertising
Irish Examiner	Landmark	Irish – private	Circulation & advertising
Irish Daily Mail	DMG Trust	UK – publicly quoted	Circulation & advertising
Irish Daily Mirror	Trinity Mirror	UK – publicly quoted	Circulation & advertising

Table 7.4 Political coverage by format and commercialism, 2016 general election

	Model 1 Coverage	Model 2 Frame	Model 3 Emotion	Model 4 Tone
(Intercept)	1.66** (0.01)	0.38** (0.01)	0.14** (0.02)	1.31** (0.01)
Radio	1.44** (0.02)	1.42** (0.03)	0.86** (0.04)	1.07* (0.01)
TV	2.12** (0.07)	1.97** (0.07)	0.93 (0.10)	1.03 (0.03)
Profit-seeking	0.68** (0.01)	0.78** (0.02)	1.37** (0.02)	1.01 (0.01)
British	0.44** (0.01)	0.47** (0.02)	2.00** (0.02)	1.29** (0.01)
Log likelihood	−129,188.7	−50,507.9	−44,253.2	−55,151.0
N	190,225	98,183	98,183	81,505

Note: Standard errors in parentheses; * $p < 0.1$, ** $p < 0.01$.

sources used far more non-neutral language than the *Irish Times* or radio. Predict-ably, the British publications are the most likely to use negative and positive language.

Finally, our fourth model compares the tone of language in election coverage in 2016. It predicts the probability of a paragraph being negative less the probability of it being positive. The results are weak, suggesting that our variables do not capture variation in the positivity or negativity of paragraphs. The model suggests that the *Irish Times* and the British papers are more negative than the other sources, but does not manage to distinguish amongst basic differences of format and ownership.

In terms of findings, the models produce an intriguing mixture of the expected and the unexpected. Format and ownership explain variations in the proportion of political coverage in some unsurprising ways. However, the framing results from the 2016 campaign coverage challenge assumptions about the influence of ownership on election news content. Profit-seeking sources tend to emphasise policy more than non-commercial sources. Most surprisingly, tabloid titles also opt for policy-focused coverage. In respect of the use of neutral language, the results are in line with the theory and the findings in other studies. In general, commercial-oriented media outlets and tabloid media are more likely to use emotional language, whether positive or negative. However, in this study they do not appear to be consistently more negative than other sources.

In order to interpret these results, we look at the relationship between char-acteristics of content (the dependent variables of the models). In particular, the meaning of the framing measure becomes clearer if considered in the context of the proportion of election coverage in the various sources. Figure 7.4 plots the mean position of each source – the proportion of political content (horizontal/x-axis) and the mean probability of policy less the mean probability of game (vertical/y-axis). The conclusion that tabloids adopt a policy frame in their election coverage could have been misconstrued as a claim that these newspapers were somehow more serious than our other media outlets with their relative tendency to report the trivia of political competition. However, Figure 7.4 makes clear that the dominant frame depends on the proportion of political coverage. The more dedicated a media outlet is to covering politics, the more likely it is to frame politics as a competition rather than a policy debate. The broadcast sources are less diverse than newspaper titles. Indeed, it is difficult to determine whether a broadcast news programme is the best comparator to a newspaper. Broadcast programmes are more limited in length/duration than newspapers and less specialised in the coverage of politics. It seems they only have so much time for policy coverage once they have reported the basic developments in political competition during the day's campaigning. Quality newspapers have space to cover both policy and political competition in some detail, as well as providing extensive content on sport, lifestyle, business, and so on. During an election

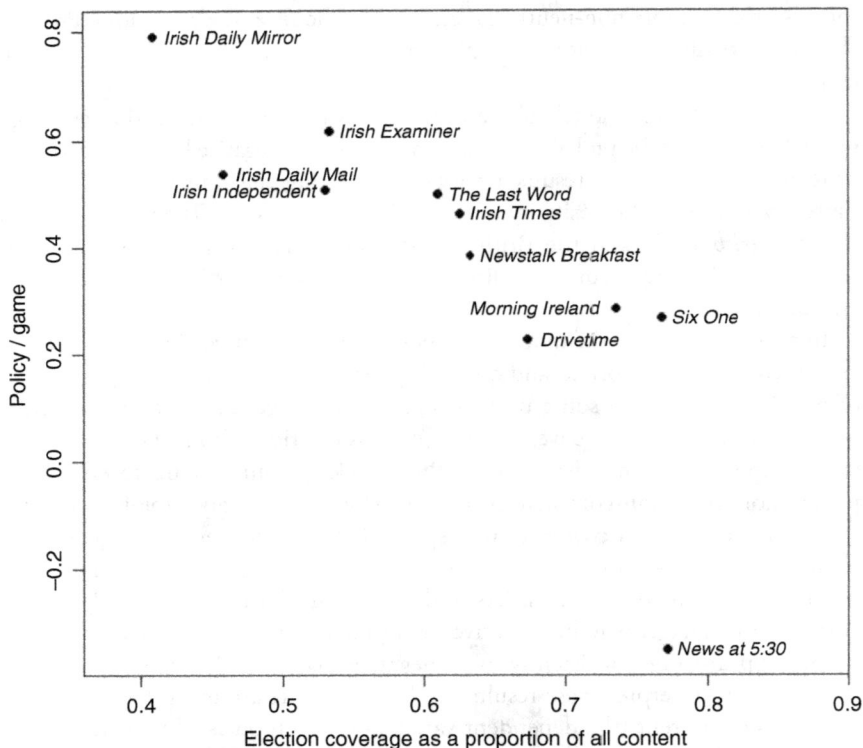

Figure 7.4 Framing and political coverage, 2016 general election
Note: The positions on this graph do not map directly onto the figures in the regression table, in which results are combined and sources account for very different numbers of observations.

campaign, politics does not predominate in the tabloids, although their limited coverage does concentrate on policy over political competition.

In contradiction to most international studies, we have shown that policy focus is the default method of framing politics in Irish media coverage. Organisations only put more emphasis on game framing when they are willing to dedicate more space to covering politics in general. In terms of the Irish editions of British titles, we suspect that the policy focus of these newspapers is largely a consequence of their populism. They regard all the parties equally negatively (O'Reilly, 2016a). An eloquent version of this classic populist thesis was published in the *Irish Daily Mail* just before the 2016 election, when the author quoted the end of Orwell's *Animal Farm* to illustrate his point: 'The creatures outside looked from pig to man, and from man to pig, and from pig to man again: but already it was impossible to say which was which' (Orwell quoted in Hamilton, 2004).

In this populist discourse, the parties are indistinguishable because they have not managed, or plausibly proposed, to resolve the problems that matter to the public. However, policy stories can also be human-interest stories. For example, the state of the health service can be illustrated through the personal experiences of ordinary people or journalists (Dee, 2016). During the 2016 election campaign, a dramatic murder at a boxing weigh-in at a Dublin hotel – part of an ongoing criminal feud between drugs gangs – pushed crime to the top of the news agenda. This event allowed newspaper titles, in particular, to add some political invective to one of their favourite subjects:

> As befits a woman who looks like she belongs at a cake sale or striding the fairways on Ladies' Day at her local golf club, Frances Fitzgerald was slow out of the blocks with any kind of meaningful response. And when she did eventually throw in her tuppenceworth, it all sounded rather contradictory. On the one hand, she insisted that An Garda Síochána is a properly resourced police force. But, on the other, she announced €5million in emergency funding and a new 55-member permanent armed response unit for the capital. (O'Reilly, 2016b)

Whether one party is leading in the polls or not matters a great deal to political elites competing for governmental office. It matters less to the wider public. A focus on policy is good for democracy in the sense that the 'game' of politics only matters insofar as it represents important policy choices and differences in performance across the parties. It is bad for democracy in that it tends to elide the differences between the parties and the important policy consequences of voters' choices.

Conclusion

The degree to which the media frames political news coverage as a strategic game, or 'horse-race', rather than focusing on policy debates is seen as a factor of media commercialisation (Strömbäck and Van Aelst, 2010). Reportage that stresses opinion polls, individuals, and winners/losers is consistent with definitions of newsworthiness and delivers classic journalistic requirements for drama, conflict, and controversy (Galtung and Ruge, 1965; Lawrence, 2000; Harcup and O'Neill, 2001). The literature in the game/policy framing area, however, tends to incorporate the assumption that public-service media has a stronger obligation to provide news that is in the public interest than purely commercial media do. Private media, in particular, is expected to represent politics as a game, with consideration of policy sidelined in its coverage. Under an excessive editorial commitment to game-oriented coverage, democratic society loses out because citizens – who receive their political knowledge increasingly through the media – are less well informed about major policy issues.

Several previous studies of media coverage of Irish general elections have highlighted a drift in reportage in the Celtic Tiger years, particularly a decline in campaign coverage of substantive policy issues between the 2002 and 2007 general elections in all parts of the newspaper market, but with a subsequent reversal in orientation to become significantly more policy-focused in the crisis election of 2011 (McMenamin *et al.*, 2013). In Ireland's diverse national newspaper market, considerable variation was reported not just in how the 2011 election was covered but also in the way in which the election was framed, consistent with the idea that different commercial situations lead to a different framing of politics (McMenamin *et al.*, 2013).

In our wider study of all election news in the *Irish Independent* and the *Irish Times* from 1969 to 2016, we conclude that commercialism does not explain differences in coverage between these two titles, in part because they have been remarkably similar in terms of their overall framing and sentiment of election reporting. Specifically, we found that these two newspapers adopted a somewhat less neutral and more negative tone since the 1989 general election. This outcome, however, appears to be driven as much by general social and cultural change in Ireland as by specific media market pressure.

In examining the impact of commercialisation on the broadcast sector, numerous international studies have focused on the difference in programming between public broadcasters and their market-oriented commercial counterparts (Barnett and Gaber, 2001; Aalberg *et al.*, 2012). A study of broadcast coverage during the 2011 general election in Ireland challenged the idea that public-service news contained more substantive coverage than equivalent output on private broadcasters in all instances (Rafter *et al.*, 2014). The latter analysis showed that the Irish case conformed to wider expectations in relation to television coverage, but the results for radio programmes challenged the idea that public-service election news contained more substantive coverage than equivalent output on private broadcasters in all instances, with the suggestion that policy-oriented private programming may react to factors such as a culture of public-service broadcasting as well as regulatory interventionism.

In terms of the 2016 general election, we found important similar differences among various media outlets. These differences cannot easily be explained by existing theories that posit the importance of commercialism in determining election news coverage. Our media sources can be grouped into three clusters by broad format. First, broadcast programmes (regardless of whether public or private, television or radio) tend to allocate most of their coverage to politics during an election campaign and divide this coverage roughly equally between policy and political competition. In particular, we found that broadcasters were very diverse in relation to sentiment during the 2016 contest. Second, we found that quality newspapers tend to give a clear preponderance to policy over political competition in their election coverage. In the context of the generally subtle variation in tone, the quality newspapers are relatively positive. Third, in our analysis of the *Irish Daily Mirror* and *Irish Daily Mail* we found that these two Irish editions of British titles gave less than half of their editorial news space to politics during the 2016 general election and also put less emphasis on coverage of policy. These findings may reflect the populist editorial approach of these two titles, with coverage, in the main, defined by human-interest stories.

8

Economy and crisis coverage

Economic and financial crises are an increasingly common feature of contemporary capitalism but their implications for the media coverage of elections has received less attention. When does poor economic performance become a crisis, and what are the implications of a crisis for media coverage? The explanation, we argue, lies in the particular context in which an election takes place. According to Charles Kindleberger (Kindleberger and O'Keefe, 2001), a financial crisis consists of three phases – mania, panic, and crash. In the first phase, asset prices skyrocket, driven by a strong belief and increasing euphoria about the asset's future price. In the second phase, prices fall and consumers panic, fearing that prices will ultimately collapse. Unfortunately, these fears are self-fulfilling and the rush to sell brings the market crashing down in the third phase. We argue that the media reacts to this particular context by changing the emphasis and framing its coverage to reflect greater demand for crisis-relevant information. Furthermore, in this context, media content is delivered in an increasingly negative tone, reflecting higher levels of uncertainty and crisis-induced anxiety.

We test these propositions in relation to the rise and fall of Ireland's Celtic Tiger, a period of exceptional economic growth that ended with an economic and financial crisis in 2008. We study the *Irish Times* and the *Irish Independent* to understand how the economic crisis shaped campaign coverage across elections in 2002, 2007, 2011, and 2016. Together, these elections provide us with episodes of mania, panic, and recovery. Fuelled by property mania, the 2002 and 2007 elections were unusually contented campaigns by the standards of most Irish elections. By contrast, the 2011 election came in the midst of an economic meltdown and was mired in crisis. We find a large increase in policy-focused journalism during this election. Furthermore, we detect an increasingly negative tone across both newspapers, in line with the greater uncertainty and anxiety in the country during the crisis. Media coverage of the 2016 post-crisis campaign was not a simple return to pre-crisis ways. Both national titles reverted to normal tones but the troubling legacy of the crisis is clearly visible in their pages, as the *Irish Times* continued to urge caution – and focused on emphasising and framing issues in terms of policy challenges – while the *Irish Independent* reverted to its pre-crisis focus on framing the election as a game rather than a policy debate. In the next section of this chapter, we provide a short history of the role of the media in Ireland's economic crisis in order to contextualise our study. The following section describes in more detail the link between crises, elections, and media content, while subsequent sections are focused on our results.

The Celtic Tiger and the media

As Ireland became one of the richest and most globalised countries in the world, the Irish public understandably thought they had left behind a long history of economic stagnation. The economy was booming, unemployment had fallen to close to 4 per cent, and the country boasted a highly educated population and vibrant global intellectual and cultural links. Ireland, traditionally a country of emigration, saw its population rise through a combination of high immigration and high fertility rates. What seemed like rapid progress during the late 1990s and early 2000s raised expectations considerably; perhaps too much, too soon.

By the mid-2000s, Ireland was firmly in the grip of property mania. The widespread obsession with buying and selling property was driven by cheap money – low European Central Bank interest rates and easy access to foreign capital. As money washed through the banks and into the hands of property developers and home buyers, Irish house prices skyrocketed. The more prices increased, the greater was the demand for property. House prices almost doubled from 2002 to 2008 and the construction sector grew rapidly. Moreover, construction cranes not only dominated Dublin's low-rise skyline, but new housing estates and apartment complexes began to appear in the most unlikely places in rural Ireland. At the same time, banks became more willing and eager to issue loans. New lending by the largest financial institutions, the Allied Irish Banks and Bank of Ireland, doubled in just three years, between 2003 and 2006.[1] In 2005, the Bank of Ireland, the oldest and widely considered the most conservative bank in the country, began offering 100 per cent loans to first-time buyers.

When house prices finally peaked in 2007, the market crashed. Banks stopped lending and the number of transactions collapsed from 151,000 at the top of the market in 2006 to almost 25,000 in 2010 – a decline of 83 per cent. The very weak regulation of the banks became apparent in late 2007, as the implications of the international 'credit crunch' were felt by the Irish financial sector. The situation came to a head in September 2008, when Irish banks could not access any more money on the financial markets. Their loan-books became increasingly troubled, as first large property developers and then ordinary citizens began to struggle with loan payments. The Irish Government guaranteed the debt of all domestic banks, believing they were solvent but suffering from a short-term liquidity problem. In fact, the banks were insolvent, and the €64bn bank rescue was the result of what was – given the size of the country – one of the biggest banking failures in world financial history.[2]

Citizens meanwhile suffered sharp declines in incomes and living standards. Hardest hit, in general, were new homeowners and construction workers, but the impact struck Irish people of every background and social class. Some of the country's richest citizens were forced into bankruptcy, and new homeowners faced negative equity. At the same time, Irish tax revenues fell dramatically. Successive Irish governments had increased state spending over the previous decade. A number of emergency budgets followed that reduced government spending, but government revenue continued to collapse from a high of €71bn in 2007 to €57bn in 2011. Meanwhile, government debt, previously one of the lowest in Europe as a percentage of GDP, exploded from €35bn in 2007 to €191bn in 2013, and the unemployment rate soared to a high of 14.7 per cent in 2012 from a low of 4.6 per cent in 2007. Although Ireland had experienced recessions previously, particularly in the 1980s, none had seen as sharp a drop in economic activity.

By the summer of 2010, the Irish Government was still considered solvent by international lenders, but the financial meltdown was beginning to threaten its position. As the news about Ireland's banks became worse, depositors panicked, withdrawing €31bn in September 2010.[3] Overall, deposits declined by roughly €125bn from a peak of €600bn in late 2008 (O'Callaghan, 2011: 9). Eventually, the ECB signalled that it would not support the Irish banking system indefinitely unless the Government addressed the crisis (Breen, 2013: 115). Mounting political pressure from the ECB and EC pushed the Government gently at first, but then forcefully, to assent to an economic adjustment programme under the supervision of the so-called 'Troika' of the IMF, EC, and ECB.

The media acted as a cheerleader for Ireland's booming property market during the Celtic Tiger era. Glossy magazines, property supplements, and lifestyle television programmes were filled with tips about buying and decorating homes and encouraged the public to become rich by investing in property. Media organisations partnered with so-called 'property experts' to spread positive news stories about property. Media hype about property was based on numbers, but it was also underpinned by blind faith in a gamble on property. The evidence-based argument supported by some economists was that Ireland's economy was still playing catch-up with the rest of Europe; rapidly increasing property prices merely reflected the pace of economic development, rising immigration, and favourable demographic changes. However, there was a strong element of blind faith that prices would eventually stabilise rather than decline significantly. The idea that the market would eventually stabilise entered the lexicon of Irish journalism as the 'soft landing'. The latter argument was the conventional wisdom until approximately mid-2007. Only a small minority of commentators did point to the possibility of a 'hard landing'. The Taoiseach Bertie Ahern was highly critical of these views, arguing: 'Sitting on the sidelines, cribbing and moaning is a lost opportunity. I don't know how people who engage in that don't commit suicide because frankly the only thing that motivates me is being able to actively change something.'

Ordinary homebuyers were faced with a problem: to buy there and then at a high price, or potentially miss out on owning property if prices rose too much before the promised soft landing. The majority of media commentators supported this gamble with the usual caveats, but some threw caution to the wind. Just as the market was beginning to collapse in the summer of 2007, the *Irish Independent* published an article entitled 'The smart, ballsy guys are buying up property right now' (O'Connor, 29 July 2007).[4]

Previous research supports the argument that the media played an important role in the spread of property mania. According to Mercille (2014), news organisations failed to present alternative viewpoints about economic policy, particularly those that made it seem like a hard landing was on the horizon. Mercille goes on to say that the media was not critical of property mania because of its strong links (and shared interests) with the political and corporate establishment, as well as pressure from advertisers. Indeed, property advertising had become an increasingly important source of revenue for many newspapers, helping to offset some of the losses from dwindling sales, as consumers shifted from print to online media in the 2000s.

The collapse of the Irish property market had serious consequences for the Irish media sector. Like newspapers elsewhere, Irish papers – already under pressure from digital disruption – lost circulation, which fell by 22 per cent between 2007 and 2011. Advertising revenues fell by 56 per cent in the same period. Some of the papers had become dependent on lucrative property supplements during the boom and, like the Irish State itself, faced a massive shortfall in revenue when the property market crashed. Even those papers that remained profitable were left with large boom-era debts. These commercial pressures should have increased their incentive to reduce costs and sell more papers, which the international literature suggested could be achieved by framing elections as a game. Indeed, unprecedented numbers of opinion polls and leader debates in 2011 made it easier than ever for the media to provide game-oriented coverage.

The official inquiry into Ireland's banking collapse heard evidence from eight senior media executives who held positions in four media organisations in Ireland during the Celtic Tiger era and the subsequent collapse. According to Rafter (2017), their evidence displayed little regret about coverage in the boom years, and some executives pointed to news programmes which they had commissioned that questioned the 'soft landing' hypothesis. Nonetheless, Rafter argues that the banking inquiry was deeply flawed and contained little objective evidence on media behaviour during the boom, except for data on property advertising revenue which largely confirmed the importance of property-related revenue to the Irish media sector.

Crises and election coverage

The context in which an election takes place matters. A crisis is a time of exceptional difficulty or danger brought about by a sudden change. When an election takes place during a crisis, then media play an important role in helping citizens to attribute responsibility, assign blame, and make decisions about how to resolve the crisis through supporting new leadership and policies.

In this section, we put forward three arguments about how the media reacts to crisis events. The first is that the media reacts by providing more crisis-relevant coverage based on consumer demand. There is money to be made from crisis-relevant news: readers/listeners/viewers are interested in why it happened, whether it will become worse, and how it might be resolved. Which information is relevant depends critically on the nature of the crisis and the context in which it takes place. In an economic crisis, for example, the roots of the failure are usually a combination of domestic policy mistakes and external forces (often financial market pressure). News and speculation about the causes of the economic crisis and its broader effects on society is more valuable than other types of news, raising the premium on economic information and possibly reducing it for other types of information. In this regard, we anticipate that, everything else being equal, the volume of policy-relevant news is greater during elections that take place in the shadow of a crisis.

Our second argument focuses on media frames in crisis elections. When there is a great sense of crisis or system failure, we expect that the election will be treated in a qualitatively different way by competing parties and the voters they aim to convince. This contrasts with elections during periods of contentment, where politicians might compete on who is best able to maintain and manage the status quo. The crisis election will be about more than just the choice between the parties; it will be about policy choices. Certain policy issues are nearly always important, e.g. economic issues, but only at times are these issues regarded as important problems (Wlezien, 2005). When issues can be conceived as problems facing society – and when those problems are significant – then we should see greater policy focus by politicians and greater policy interest from the general public. As well as demand from the public driving a greater policy focus, parties may have less money to spend on marketing and so may have to rely on policy for attention. Similarly, media outlets may have less money to spend on opinion polls.

We also have expectations about media coverage where there are these greater levels of uncertainty and disorder. The electorate will expect that the media reflects this debate in its electoral coverage to a greater extent than in a 'contentment election'. This is consistent with Zaller's (2003) idea of a 'burglar alarm standard of news quality', in which he proposes that modern mass media cannot and need not be expected to provide high-quality coverage of all relevant political events on a routine basis. Instead, Zaller argues that soft-news coverage, which emphasises drama and the game and strategy frame, is appropriate for the coverage of 'non-emergency but important events', while the 'burglar alarm' will be rung and citizens be alerted 'to matters requiring urgent attention' (2003: 122). The concept of a crisis election constitutes a special case of this burglar alarm notion. Thus, we hypothesise that, everything else being equal, media frames of elections will become more policy-focused during elections that take place in the shadow of a crisis.

Our third argument focuses on media tone in crisis elections. Since a crisis is a time of exceptional difficulty or danger, we expect to observe a more negative tone in editorial coverage. Uncertainty and anxiety rule in a crisis. Therefore, the change in media tone should underline the seriousness of the crisis. Like the shift to more policy-focused journalism, we expect that the negative tone is both a signal that fulfils the media's professional watchdog role and is driven by market considerations in profiting from the crisis. Thus, we anticipate that, everything else being equal, the tone of election coverage is more negative during elections that take place in a crisis period.

In summary, the more serious the crisis, the more it has the potential to change the nature of election coverage. But we should not lose sight of other explanations when we are analysing the impact of a crisis on media coverage. The material impact of the crisis on incomes and people's standard of living is only one channel through which a crisis can change media coverage. What seems impossible before the crisis can become the new post-crisis reality. Slow-moving variables like party system and media fragmentation can become the locus of change, ideas that were once considered extreme or radical can become the new orthodox, and institutions that are normally resistant to change can take on new features.

Media coverage and economic crisis: evidence from Ireland

We are interested in coverage in the *Irish Times* and the *Irish Independent* before, during, and after Ireland's Celtic Tiger era. Previous research has argued that the elections before the crash – in 2002 and 2007 – were unusually contented by the standard of most Irish elections (O'Malley *et al.*, 2014). By contrast, the 2011 election was mired in crisis and produced one of the most dramatic results in Irish electoral history, with the two government parties losing badly – Fianna Fáil lost fifty-one of its seventy Dáil seats, and the Green Party lost all of their seats. As mentioned previously, the election result in 2011 was the third most volatile in terms of changes in party support in post-war European history and the most volatile in which no new party emerged (Mair, 2011).

By way of contrast, the 2016 election was fought by the incumbent Fine Gael–Labour coalition on a platform of recovery.[5] This campaign provides an intermediate case between boom and bust because the Irish State was still dealing with the legacy of the crisis. Many parts of the economy had recovered to pre-crisis levels, but there was lasting damage to some parts of society and some economic sectors had not fully recovered. Furthermore, Ireland's economy had recovered in new ways, shifting from a construction-led boom to a foreign-direct-investment-led recovery concentrating on positioning Ireland within global value chains. The focus on capturing innovative foreign direct investment within global value chains led to a spectacular recovery, but the recovery was concentrated primarily in selected economic sectors in the greater Dublin area with strong global links.

Before the crisis: 2002 and 2007

We now consider the emphasis, tone, and framing of election coverage before the crisis. Table 8.1 shows the emphasis of coverage across four elections from 2002 to 2016. The figures in this table are benchmarked against the average emphasis in our study of these two titles from 1969 to 2016. Thus, the table shows that macroeconomic policy news was 5 per cent above average in the *Irish Times* and 1 per cent above average in the *Irish Independent* in 2002. In 2007, economic policy news coverage is greater than average in the *Irish Times* but less than average in the *Irish Independent*. The emphasis of coverage in 2002 and 2007 is broadly similar to the average trend for all elections between 1969 and 2016. In summary, the emphasis of media coverage in 2002 and 2007 is not substantially different from the average election in a sample that stretches over a forty-seven-year period. Figure 8.1 illustrates the tone of coverage across elections in the *Irish Times* and the *Irish Independent*. It shows that 2002 and 2007 were relatively contented by the standard of most Irish elections. The tone of the *Irish Times* coverage, in particular, is 21 per cent less negative than our sample average in 2002, and 13 per cent less than in 2007.

Table 8.1 Emphasis and tone (% over sample mean), *Irish Times* and *Irish Independent* 2002–16

Election	Emphasis macro. *Times*	Emphasis macro. *Indep.*	Emphasis micro. *Times*	Emphasis micro. *Indep.*	Tone *Times*	Tone *Indep.*
2002	0.05	0.01	0.00	0.03	−0.21	0.06
2007	0.03	−0.06	0.05	−0.02	−0.13	−0.09
2011	0.17	0.14	0.07	0.04	0.17	0.75
2016	0.07	−0.06	0.02	−0.05	−0.20	−0.27

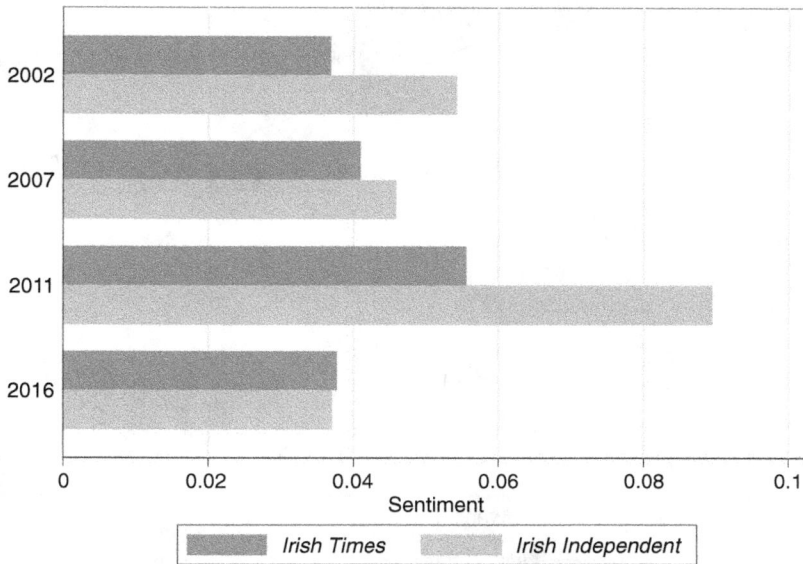

Figure 8.1 Tone and the Celtic Tiger, *Irish Times* and *Irish Independent* 2002–16

Figure 8.2 illustrates the framing of media content across elections. It shows the proportion of 'game' news paragraphs, i.e. paragraphs that frame politics as a game between opposing factions rather than a choice between substantive macroeconomic policy issues. Since both of these newspapers are considered quality sources, they always contain a higher proportion of news that is framed in terms of policy than game. Figure 8.2 shows that both titles used a similar amount of game framing in 2002. However, the *Irish Times* used more game framing than the *Irish Independent* in 2007. Both titles begin to use a lower proportion of the game frame in 2011, before using a similar proportion in 2016.

While the content of the two newspapers is broadly similar across most of our indicators in 2002 and 2007, the news stories that feature most prominently on the front pages of both newspapers are different. The *Irish Times* placed more economic news on its front page and tended to provide more balanced coverage, framing developments based on changes in real economic indicators. For example, the *Irish Times* correctly emphasised positive trends in the global economy with front-page headlines such as 'ESRI says growth will rise to 5% by end of year' (McManus and Brennan, 2002) and 'Global economy recovering quicker than expected – IMF' (O'Clery, 2002).

Coverage in the *Irish Times* also focused on the main parties' spending proposals in the 2002 election. The paper recorded the 'tit-for-tat' game of increasingly generous promises to increase public spending, as virtually all of the main parties

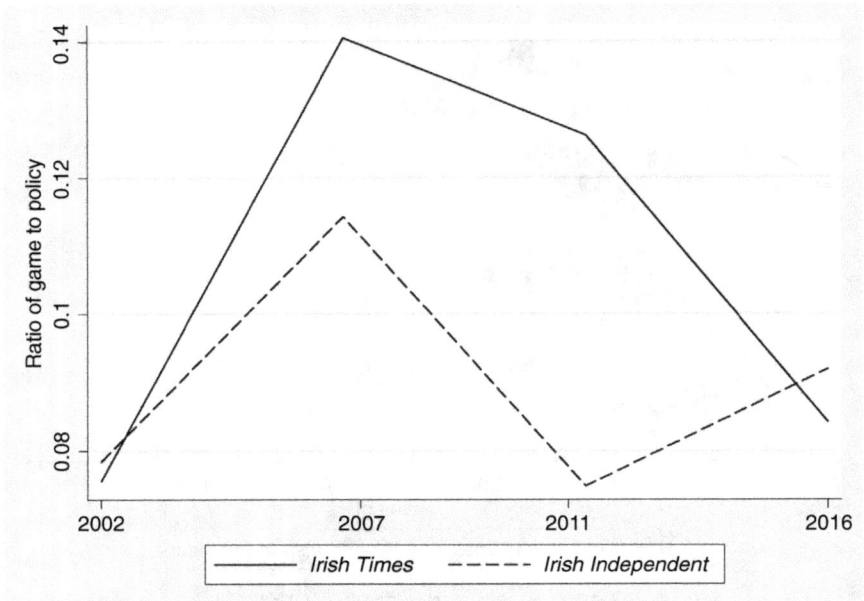

Figure 8.2 Framing and the Celtic Tiger, *Irish Times* and *Irish Independent* 2002–16

promised major public expenditure programmes in health, education, and infrastructure. The largest opposition party in 2002, Fine Gael, promised big income tax cuts and pledged to take minimum-wage earners from the tax net, while the incumbent Fianna Fáil and Progressive Democratic coalition promised to raise the old-age pension and unemployment support.

By contrast, the *Irish Independent* featured less economic news and policy discussion on its front page. When this newspaper did cover the economy, it tended to ignore positive developments. With the economy at virtually full employment and showing no signs of slowing down, readers of the *Irish Independent* were treated to scaremongering headlines, such as 'Slump in jobs to become an election issue' (Donaghy, 2002), and headlines focused on turning good news into bad news, like 'Jobless figures show big drop but devastation as 375 workers laid off' (Glennon and Black, 2002).

By the 2007 election, however, the *Irish Times* was increasingly following the *Irish Independent's* decision to relegate economic news from its front page. We found only a few major front-page stories in 2007, with one prominent story covering the dispute between the Government and opposition parties over tax and spending, and a prominent headline announcing that average house prices had fallen for the first time in five years.[6] There is virtually no economic coverage on the front page of the *Irish Independent* in the run-up to the 2007 election.

The lack of interest in the economy and economic policy issues may have been because the 2007 contest was a much closer election than that in 2002, which was seen as something of a foregone conclusion (Murphy 2003: 17–18). Instead, the main headlines focused on abortion, foreign affairs, and the scandal around Fianna Fáil leader Bertie Ahern's personal finances. The only front-page headline of substance relating to the economy in the *Irish Independent* in 2007 is a Fianna Fáil promise to backdate stamp duty cuts for new buyers.

The 2011 crisis election

The media reacted to the 2011 economic crisis by changing substantially the emphasis, tone, and framing of its coverage. Across both newspapers, we observe a shift to what can be described as more responsible, policy-focused journalism. Table 8.1 shows a large increase in news emphasising economic policy: macroeconomic policy coverage is 17 per cent greater than average in the *Irish Times* and 14 per cent greater in the *Irish Independent*. Furthermore, the news during the 2011 campaign was delivered in a more negative tone, underlining the seriousness of the crisis. Figure 8.1 illustrates the increasingly negative tone, and Figure 8.2 shows that both newspapers used less game framing, although the reduction in the *Irish Times* is not as much as in the *Irish Independent*. This evidence in our content analysis data is supported by a 2011 election survey (Lansdowne/RTÉ exit poll) which confirms the importance of the criterion of 'policies set out by the parties' to voters. Support for this criterion increased from 25 per cent to 43 per cent since the 2007 election (Marsh and Cunningham, 2011: 185). In summary, all of the main indicators illustrate the impact of the crisis and point in the direction of an increased focus on policy and the economy.[7]

In order to complement our content analysis data, we reviewed the front pages of both newspapers every day during the month of the 2011 election campaign. Both titles covered the economy in great detail in this campaign. In this regard, their commentary helped to explain to the public why the Irish State needed to take urgent action to deal with the collapse of the banking system. Complex technical and policy issues were front-page news throughout the 2011 campaign. For example, there were headlines on bank recapitalisation, taxation, government spending and borrowing, debt restructuring, job cuts, asset sales, and the activities of the ECB, European Commission, and the IMF. Several articles focused on passage through Parliament of the Finance Bill, which the outgoing Government was determined to pass before leaving office. Furthermore, there was extensive coverage of the meltdown in the housing market.

In line with these changes in editorial coverage in the *Irish Times* and *Irish Independent*, we also find a shift in attitudes and opinions. In an election survey, 35.6 per cent of voters mentioned the economic crisis as the single most important issue or problem, and a further 13.5 per cent mentioned related economic issues, such as unemployment (Lansdowne/RTÉ exit poll, 2011). This stands in sharp contrast to 2007, when 35 per cent of voters selected the proposed Taoiseach and set of government ministers as an important criterion. The latter option was not a top priority in 2011, as the figure fell to 20 per cent.

The 2016 post-crisis election

Ireland's economy and public finances had largely recovered from the crisis by the time voters went to the polls in 2016. The media's portrayal of the election has elements of continuity with the type of coverage observed in the 2011 crisis election but also some reversion to previous coverage. In 2016, the *Irish Times* maintained some of its emphasis on economic policy news. Table 8.1 shows that this type of coverage was higher than average across both policy news types. By contrast, the *Irish Independent* reversed its position on economic policy coverage. In our analysis, we detected 5 to 6 per cent less than average coverage. Furthermore, the *Irish Times* and the *Irish Independent* moved towards using the same proportion of the game frame. Both newspapers, however, revert to 2007 levels of tone, presumably because the level of uncertainty and anxiety regarding Ireland's economic future had been replaced by more optimism about the future.

Our reading of the front pages of both newspapers confirms the findings from our automatic content analysis. For example, the *Irish Times* exhibits more continuity with the crisis period than the *Irish Independent*. While the tone of the newspaper suggests a return to previous coverage, the type of news stories that featured prominently on the front page show that Ireland was still dealing with the legacy of the crisis. Many of the complex policy issues that were salient during the 2011 campaign also made headlines in 2016. In the *Irish Times*, there were headlines about the clean-up of the banking system, the depressed housing market, and the legacy of the bailout, while many news stories urged the need for caution regarding economic policy. Furthermore, Ireland's economic recovery was not a simple return to old ways. In the period between the crisis and the recovery, new economic sectors flourished and old sectors withered. The character of the economy changed, shifting focus from property and construction to high technology sectors driven by large inflows of foreign direct investment. The changing circumstances of the Irish economy attracted significant media attention during the 2016 campaign, with several prominent news stories on Ireland's corporate tax regime and attractiveness to global corporations. For example, the *Irish Times* featured headlines such as 'Google moved 28.7bn through Ireland in tax scheme' (Beesley, 2016a) and 'Facebook warns of potential tax claims dating back to 2009' (Beesley, 2016b).

In the 2016 campaign, the *Irish Independent* featured less economic coverage on its front pages, and its coverage tended to focus on the game of politics rather than the difference between substantive policy choices. For example, in the run-up to the election, it mounted a concerted attack on Sinn Féin's competence as an economic manager, with headlines such as 'How Adams will cut your pension' (Doyle *et al.*, 2016) and headlines that completely abandoned any sense of impartial analysis, including 'We'll end up like Greece if SF, motley crew take power' (McQuinn and Doyle, 2016).

Conclusion

This chapter has offered new insights into the effect of financial and economic crises on media coverage. Drawing together several trends of scholarship on politics, media and economic crises, we tested three hypotheses regarding the impact of a crisis on the emphasis, tone, and framing of media content during elections. We tested these hypotheses through an empirical examination of elections surrounding the rise and fall of Ireland's Celtic Tiger, focusing in particular on election campaigns from 2002 to 2016. Our findings – based on the content of the *Irish Times* and the *Irish Independent* during the campaigns – show that the media reacts to crises by changing the emphasis and framing of coverage to reflect greater demand for crisis-relevant information, as well as delivering content in an increasingly negative tone to reflect higher levels of uncertainty and anxiety. These findings underline the importance of exogenous factors in influencing media coverage of elections. The effects that we observe could also be explained by the interaction of these exogenous factors with Ireland's dominant media system. The underlying norms of critical impartiality may have been reinforced and amplified during the crisis, particularly as the media itself was held responsible for its initial failure to question the emergence of a massive speculative bubble in the property market in 2007.

Our approach could be extended, for example, to the 1979 British general election, which could be regarded as having taken place in an economic crisis, as could the 2012 parliamentary election in Greece. While this chapter focused on economic performance, researchers should further explore the impact of other types of crises on media content – e.g. the 2001 Israeli election that took place during the second Intifada. Sheafer *et al.* (2008) observe a spike in press coverage from just over 20 per cent in 1999 to approximately 40 per cent in the 2001 election. Another example is the Italian elections which took place under the shadow of the Tangentopoli corruption allegations in 1994 and 1996. These are examples of elections during a systemic crisis which saw a move from the First to the Second Italian Republic.

A second conclusion is a more general one on the nature of media coverage. Our study of Ireland shows that, when it matters, the media can shift focus quite dramatically and concentrate on policy – in Zaller's (2003) words, it raises the 'alarm' and moves to lessen dramatic and entertaining routine coverage to more focused coverage that alerts the otherwise 'monitorial citizen', whose urgent attention is required. In our analysis of two national newspapers over four recent elections, we observe that, in special circumstances, that trend can be reversed

– and in a dramatic fashion. Specifically, our data on the 2002, 2007, 2011, and 2016 elections in Ireland shows that media focus on the election predictably tends to follow the context of the elections. This outcome questions the argument that the media drives the public agenda more than real-world indicators and lends support to our argument regarding the role of exogenous factors in shaping campaign coverage (Funkhouser, 1973; Dearing and Rogers, 1996).

A third conclusion relates to the qualities of democracy. Sen (1999) and many others argue that democracy can prevent catastrophes because policies are observed and questioned earlier by a free press and other institutions. That the Irish media moved so firmly to cover policy in the 2011 crisis election might support Sen's argument. Accepting this point, we could have a less pessimistic outlook on the media than other commentators have had: the media can be responsive and responsible. Unfortunately, this attention came too late to prevent the economic collapse as, like elsewhere, the Irish media did not sufficiently discuss or question the policies that ultimately provoked the crisis until after the event.

Notes

1 The figure pertaining to house prices is from Dirk Schoenmaker (2015). The figure pertaining to the banking system is from David McWilliams (2013).
2 The €64bn figure is based on the initial cost of recapitalising the banks. As of 2015, the Irish Comptroller and Auditor General estimated the final cost at €43bn. The exact cost will depend on future financial market conditions. The €43bn estimate is from Cliff Taylor (2015).
3 From domestic banks, €18bn, and €13bn from non-domestic banks.
4 A less critical view of the media would argue that a range of views were presented by the media, from reckless hyping of property to articles urging caution, but that otherwise the media merely reflected the mania that gripped wider Irish society.
5 Fine Gael's campaign slogan in 2016 was 'Let's Keep The Recovery Going'.
6 The conventional wisdom was that stamp duty reform had undermined the housing market and shaken potential buyers' and sellers' confidence. It would become clear after the election that the housing market had collapsed and that house prices would decrease further in the years ahead.
7 Furthermore, our estimates are likely to be conservative because the true impact of the crisis is difficult for our automatic news classifier to detect. The reason it is difficult to detect is that the collapsing economy and the need for corrective action is a central theme in many articles, across many different topics and issues. All of the new associations between economic policy language and language used to discuss other topics are not part of our classifier.

Conclusion

In this project, we generated unprecedented amounts of data on the Irish media. Indeed, we leveraged far more data than has been used for most large comparative projects in political communication. There is a substantial amount of nuance and considerable detail throughout the volume. In this final chapter, we stand back and consider the evolution of Irish election coverage as a whole over the last fifty years. We found that critical impartiality remains a convincing description of Irish election coverage and that the much-discussed cluster of arguments that we call hypercritical infotainment does not apply to Ireland.

Ireland's media system has cleaved to critical impartiality in spite of substantial changes to its environment that are associated with the emergence of hypercritical infotainment. Television and radio were liberalised. All outlets and sectors of the media have faced increased competition, short-term economic crisis, and a long-term crisis of the industry as a whole, the latter being an effect of the greatest technological shock in over fifty years. All of this surely tempted the Irish media sufficiently to adopt an approach that was more contemporary and supposedly more profitable. Professional norms and structures, however, point in the opposite direction. Our period has seen third-level institutions, including universities, invest in journalism courses. Their graduates have gone on to form a significant proportion of Irish journalists. Almost inevitably, these courses taught critical impartiality as a journalistic norm. Indeed, the subject of academic journalism is full of warnings about the dangers of infotainment, in spite of hypercriticism. The formalisation of critical impartiality in third-level training is a classic example of an increasing returns process. Nonetheless, it is hard to see this as the principal explanation why the Irish media has maintained its tight consensus on critical impartiality.

Previous shifts in media system subtype in Ireland have been ultimately political. Deferential partisanship was a product of the new independent Ireland. The new State claimed the loyalty of the newspapers, and the eventually dominant Fianna Fáil party set up the *Irish Press* to be its mouthpiece. Critical impartiality was an unintended consequence of a political reorganisation of broadcasting prior to the establishment of a national television station. The new medium was probably a mere catalyst. Impartiality was enshrined in legislation, and the independence of the broadcaster allowed it to defend its own critical interpretation of what impartiality meant in practice. The liberalisation of the 1990s introduced competition to broadcasting but required new entrants to adhere to the existing norms. Similarly, the broadcast sector was under the same legislative obligations when struggling with the sudden debt crisis and the gradual internet crisis. Were newspapers to defect to hypercritical infotainment, RTÉ would still be more constrained to stick with critical impartiality. Even so, Ireland does not appear to fit the theory in which a dominant public broadcaster continues to set responsible norms for the rest of the media sector. Contrary to this theory, RTÉ's output is not more policy-focused than its private-sector competitors. Given the importance of political intervention to previous shifts and the system's seeming imperviousness to economic pressures, it is unsurprising that social media has not yet transformed Ireland's traditional media. Moreover, the small size of constituencies and the continued importance of candidates mean that Ireland has yet to have an election where social media would be truly influential. Nonetheless, it is remarkable to discover, as we did, that social media has had virtually no impact on coverage of Irish elections. Actually, rather than a change in the economics of the media, which it is as a bare minimum, social media appears more as an exogenous factor that has had no discernible effect on election coverage.

Truly exogenous factors have a limited effect on the nature of Irish election coverage, even at the level of variation that has little or no bearing on the type of media system. Some change can be absorbed into the normative structures and professional routines of critical impartiality. Irish newspapers were able to drastically reduce systematic bias in coverage of female candidates without any significant change in the overall nature of election coverage. In a political system dominated by parties, critical impartiality is compatible with both gender bias and gender neutrality. When Irish society and politics turned against condescending portrayals of women politicians, Irish newspapers could easily adapt accordingly. It is mysterious that the jump in the proportion of women candidates in the quota election of 2016 proved too much for the media to catch up with, while a considerable shift in the framing of elections during the crisis of 2011 was possible right across the sector. Other exogenous effects are probably too obvious or too subtle to provide an indication of the nature of the Irish media system. The obvious: if political parties feed the media less content about their leader, then mentions of that leader will surely decline. The subtle: political journalists, presumably unknowingly, reflect the mood of the general public in the tone of their election coverage.

We think that the nature of our data and the nature of the Irish case mean that our findings have implications for other countries. Ireland is an extreme case in the Western World in relation to exogenous factors, economic performance, the nature of the political system, and social change. If they had limited impact in Ireland, we can expect them to have had even more limited or virtually no impact elsewhere. It may be that, due to the path dependency of media systems, such exogenous factors matter more across, rather than within, national media systems. Nonetheless, comparative research has not discovered strong consistent patterns (de Vreese *et al.*, 2016). The liberalisation of the sector, combined with its small scale and economic crisis meant that, if there was an economic basis to hypercritical infotainment, Ireland would have been a likely case. Indeed, Ireland's unusual level of economic and cultural penetration by Britain and the United States opens it up to a business strategy with American roots. Again, the implication is that the link between the shifting economic basis of the mass media and hypercritical infotainment is tenuous elsewhere, too. This finding echoes much comparative research.

It appears that Ireland's national media systems are resilient to styles of journalism that have been commercially successful in the US (Benson and Hallin, 2007; Umbricht and Esser, 2014). Related to these negative findings is our positive finding of the remarkable resilience of critically impartial election coverage in Ireland. The imperviousness of this set of norms and routines to many changes, including profound changes in the media itself, suggests that the increasing returns process is chiefly located in the profession of journalism. Deviations from the norm by individuals or organisations are likely to be inefficient and, at least initially, unrewarding. Our theoretical emphasis on media systems as an argument about path dependency underpinned by increasing returns is somewhat distinctive. The existing literature tends to emphasise how content is linked to a complex set of factors at different levels (Hallin and Mancini, 2004; de Vreese *et al.*, 2016). The collective professional autonomy, which seems to go some way towards explaining the stability of Ireland's election coverage, may be useful in studying other countries with long histories of an independent media.

A shock that will disrupt Ireland's media system may originate in technology, culture, or the economy, but may have to be transmitted through the political system, as happened in the 1920s and 1960s. Ireland's journalists have no choice but to use social media as part of the research for, and promotion of, their core work in traditional formats. However, if Ireland's proudly critical, impartial journalists are so self-referential, they may continue to refuse to engage with social media as a subject of election coverage. If this indicates something about the media system more generally, they may allow the traditional media to slowly fade into irrelevance. In other words, critical impartiality may be the last branch of Ireland's liberal media system.

The resilience of journalistic norms is good news. It means that national democratic and media cultures can resist the intense pressures of commercialisation and Americanisation. Resilience does not imply power. Our work suggests that the Irish media has not set the agenda in many respects. It does not favour one party over another. It did not seem to foist gender equality in election coverage on a conservative society. The media reacted to economic events instead of framing them proactively. There is no straightforward election reality for journalists to report. Nonetheless, critically impartial Irish journalists have largely succeeded in election reporting that is broadly fair in relation to the existing political parties.

Resilient reporting is also potentially bad news. Conservatism with a small 'c' is probably not an effective response to the existential threat from social media. The current response centres on monetising traditional content provided online. Social media is treated as a way of promoting and researching traditional content, not something that is thought to require a change in the way elections are covered. In the short term, this perhaps makes sense. The traditional media continues to dominate political debate. Indeed, journalists are at the centre of mainstream political discussion online. In the medium to long term, this strategy is more questionable. Social media is surely a major change in the nature of election campaigning and public debate, which will be multiplied by generational change (Harder *et al.*, 2016; Broersma *et al.*, 2016). The political discussion online cannot be restricted to professional journalists and therefore cannot merely be the occasion for an extension of the existing consensus to a new brand of journalists. It should be an opportunity for the renegotiation of journalistic norms. It seems unlikely that the traditional media can adapt to the technological and economic shock without some substantial change in content. However, that change has to be the next branch on the liberal tree after critical impartiality. In order to remain resilient, liberal media systems will need to be imaginative.

Appendix 1: An overview of elections in Ireland since 1969

The 1969 general election can be regarded as an election that saw a generational change in Irish politics. Fianna Fáil had held power continuously since 1957, though with two changes of leader. In late 1966, Seán Lemass resigned as Taoiseach and leader of Fianna Fáil. He had been one of the revolutionary generation, who became prominent in the War of Independence and a founding member of Fianna Fáil. He was replaced by Jack Lynch. Lynch was a popular sporting figure in Ireland and an experienced and cautious minister. He was reluctant to take on the leadership but agreed to do so under pressure from Lemass to avoid a damaging contest in which Charles Haughey, Lemass's dynamic young son-in-law, and George Colley, also young but seen as traditional Fianna Fáil, would compete for the leadership against a 'greener' nationalist, Neil Blaney. Fine Gael also saw a leadership transition from James Dillon, a son of the last leader of the Irish Parliamentary Party, to Liam Cosgrave, the son of W. T. Cosgrave, the first Prime Minister of independent Ireland. Cosgrave was a traditional, conservative Fine Gael politician, but the party was debating a move to more social democratic policies. Labour had moved decisively to the left in 1969, with a plan to nationalise building land and the assertion that the 'seventies will be socialist'. The party expected this to be a breakthrough election, with a group of senior members in the party very prominent in the media. Fianna Fáil responded with the warnings that Labour would turn Ireland into a Cuba-style state. Despite Lynch's modest personality, the Fianna Fáil campaign centred on him. It used the slogan 'Let's Back Jack'; he engaged in a nationwide tour and it was clear that he was popular.

But in 1969 the media was an important political actor. The newspapers had become much less deferential, and RTÉ had found a more independent and critical voice. That criticism was largely of a Government that had become complacent and too close to business. It had been at the forefront of a small economic boom, and there was a rise in new self-made businessmen who – as some within the party and outside the party considered – had too cosy a relationship with the party. The problem for the opposition was that it was not clear what alternative government there was. Fine Gael and Labour moved further apart in policy terms, and the memory of the somewhat chaotic interparty governments of the late 1940s and 1950s was still fresh. Fianna Fáil presented itself as a stable option. The party unexpectedly (opinion polls were not yet an electoral feature) won an overall majority, allowing Lynch to dispel ideas that he was just a caretaker in a divided party.

By 1973, the divisions within Fianna Fáil that Lynch's choice as leader had avoided were in full view. In mid-1970, the 'Arms Crisis' became public, in which two ministers, Haughey and Blaney, were sacked and later accused of involvement in the illegal importation of arms for the purpose of supply to the IRA. Fianna Fáil managed to remain mostly intact – Blaney left the party, as did another prominent member. Labour had dropped a no-coalition rule in 1970 and was working with Fine Gael at going into the subsequent election as a potential alternative government. They struggled to agree a programme and Taoiseach Jack Lynch hoped to benefit from this by calling an early election. With the election looming, Fine Gael and Labour quickly agreed a fourteen-point plan, aiming to form a 'National Coalition' should they gain sufficient seats. This offered the electorate a viable alternative government for the first time in many years. The question of Northern Ireland might have been a central issue, given the Troubles in the North, but the economy appears to have been more important, and contemporary observers point to a debate between George Colley and Garret FitzGerald as a crucial step.

The 'National Coalition' won the election in the sense that they formed a Government and Fianna Fáil lost seats. But this was to a large extent an artefact of the transfer agreement between the two parties which increased their seat share. In fact, Fianna Fáil increased its vote share slightly in 1973. The Government that was formed worked well and was comfortable within itself, but it was perhaps unlucky to have a series of crises in the spiking oil price and a collapse in beef prices which affected a large area of the still relatively agricultural country. Unemployment rose, and though the Government argued that this was due to factors outside its control, opinion polls show voters disagreed. Few trusted those polls, and the Government called an election in June 1977, somewhat earlier than it needed to. Fianna Fáil's campaign was again centred on its leader, Jack Lynch, but in 1977 that effort was supplemented by a more modern research-based campaign strategy (see Rafter, 2017). Fianna Fáil published a manifesto in which it developed policies to appeal to key demographic groups, especially the young (see Rafter, 2017). This was the first election under the amended electoral legislation that reduced the voting age to eighteen (from twenty-one). Fianna Fáil promised tax cuts and spending increases to be funded by borrowing. To the surprise of most election observers, Fianna Fáil took over 50 per cent of the votes cast and won a clear legislative majority. Despite Lynch's triumph, it was to be his last as leader.

Lynch found himself under pressure. Much of the new intake of TDs had been groomed and charmed by Charles Haughey, who successfully fomented restlessness among the backbenchers, who knew that, given the unusually large majority, many of them were unlikely to survive the subsequent general election. Following a number of by-election defeats, Lynch announced his resignation in 1979. Haughey won the contest to replace him, though most senior party members preferred George Colley. Haughey's election was never accepted, and it started years of internecine battles.

Haughey called an election in 1981, three months later than he had hoped. Haughey was forced to cancel a planned 'snap election' because of a tragic fire in a Dublin nightclub. The plan had been to call the election on the back of a relatively positive budget and a 'special relationship' that Haughey claimed to have cultivated with Margaret Thatcher. By 21 May, when the election was announced, the special relationship was compromised by the continued deaths of IRA hunger strikers, two more on the day the election was called. The election was announced, Haughey said, 'because of the grave and tragic situation in Northern Ireland', but he could not clearly offer a solution. Despite this, the economy was the more important topic according to contemporary sources.

Haughey faced a rejuvenated Fine Gael, under Garret FitzGerald, which had done much work to professionalise and modernise a party that had traditionally been run by part-time grandees. He advanced the interests and careers of younger members and women. FitzGerald pushed the party in a slightly social democratic and comparatively socially liberal direction, putting clear water between Fine Gael and Fianna Fáil.

Unlike in 1973 and 1977, Fine Gael and Labour did not have an agreement on coalition. Fine Gael offered change and reforms of the tax code. Labour focused on unemployment and inflation. Fine Gael was campaigning, like Fianna Fáil, with a nationwide leader tour. Fianna Fáil emphasised the precarious nature of the economy, and that only a stable government could deliver the necessary measures. This did beg the question why there was a need for an early election, given the Government's significant majority. The parties failed to agree any head-to-head TV debate, instead being individually interrogated by print journalists on TV. The press also used the slightly more common opinion polls to suggest that the election was on a knife edge. Opinion polls gained extra credibility in the early 1980s' elections as a result of the pundits' failure to predict the 1977 Fianna Fáil landslide.

The election delivered a poor result for Fianna Fáil, not just in comparison with 1977 but in terms of its lowest vote since 1961. Fine Gael achieved its best result since 1927, despite the increased fragmentation of the vote. The 1981 election also represented a step change in the election of women. Eleven women TDs were elected, and in the main these were different to the traditional 'widows and daughters', who had made up the largest share of women TDs in earlier elections.

Fine Gael and Labour formed a minority coalition government with FitzGerald as Taoiseach, helped by a change in the leadership of the Labour Party, but dependent on a left-wing independent for its survival. The nation's finances were in worse shape than previously, though, and the Government did not last long, as the independent withdrew support on a budgetary issue early in 1982, causing a fresh election held in February 1982 (in graphs referred to as 1982a).

It was a clear choice between the outgoing Government and Fianna Fáil. The outgoing Government was hardly united on the issue of the budget, but they shifted ground to give the appearance of unity. One of the issues in the election was the suitability of Haughey for the position of Taoiseach. Fianna Fáil had, some claimed cynically, opposed the budget as too austere, but failed to produce an alternative. There were grave misgivings within Fianna Fáil, whereas Fine Gael supporters were united in their support for FitzGerald. Fine Gael made him the centrepiece of its campaign. The parties also suffered from having an election so soon after the last, and so the parties' finances could not stretch to fund extensive leader tours. Two days before the poll, there was a head-to-head leader debate, which attracted a large viewership. That event, however, failed to convince the public in significant numbers, and for two weeks after the election it was unclear what government could be formed.

Eventually, Haughey put together a local 'pork-barrel' arrangement with an independent TD, and with the support of the small Workers' Party he managed to be elected as Taoiseach. The Government soon became embroiled in scandal and division. The Labour Party also saw a change, with the leader leaving the party and a young, untested leader with little experience, Dick Spring, taking over. With increased unemployment, the Government was forced to introduce austerity policies. In this context, the Workers' Party withdrew support, and a third election in eighteen months was called for November 1982 (in graphs referred to as 1982b). Given that Fine Gael also supported the austerity policies, the economy was somewhat neutralised as a campaign issue. Abortion was also defused, as both main parties agreed to propose a referendum to place a constitutional ban on abortion. Haughey's suitability for office was not defused. Given the fractious nature of his party and the way in which his Government fell, Haughey could not claim a Fianna Fáil Government to be the choice of those hoping for stability. Northern Ireland became an issue, with Fianna Fáil attempting to paint FitzGerald as an instrument of the British. The election was more decisive. Fianna Fáil lost support and Fine Gael gained support, making a Fine Gael–Labour coalition possible.

That Government failed to deal with the economic crisis, and debt and unemployment increased. Fianna Fáil became more unified under Haughey mainly because a number of members were expelled or resigned to form the Progressive Democrats in 1985. The PDs campaigned on a relatively liberal platform, proposing cuts in spending and taxation. Fianna Fáil campaigned against the cuts that the Fine Gael–Labour Government had introduced. That Government fell apart in 1987, and the ensuing election once again pitted Haughey against FitzGerald.

There was an expectation that Fine Gael and Labour would both lose support, and they did. The PDs did well, polling 14 per cent, but mainly damaging Fine Gael. Fianna Fáil failed, however, to achieve an overall majority.

The Fianna Fáil minority Government formed on the tacit agreement of the new Fine Gael leader, Alan Dukes, in what was called the 'Tallaght Strategy', i.e. that his party would not oppose legislative actions to bring the country's budgetary situation under control. Despite having this free hand, Haughey wanted an overall majority, and when Fianna Fáil was polling at close to 50 per cent in early 1989, he used the occasion of a defeat on an opposition motion to have money set aside to compensate people who had been infected by blood transfusions, to call an election (Murphy, 2016: 34–5).

There was suspicion at Haughey's desire for an overall majority, particularly since the Tallaght Strategy gave him a stable majority. Immediately, Fianna Fáil's poll position fell and in the election was dominated by the issue of health, particularly the cuts that had been imposed. This might be surprising given that those cuts were by and large supported by Fine Gael and the PDs, who agreed a pact to govern together should they have the numbers. Fianna Fáil lost seats, though so did the PDs and Fine Gael, and Labour's gains were small. The Workers' Party grew to seven seats, putting pressure on Labour from the left flank.

The Government formed from this was a coalition of Fianna Fáil and the PDs. The arithmetic logic of this was perfect, as the two parties' combined legislative support gave the Government a bare majority, but the two parties' leaders, Charles Haughey and Des O'Malley, were long-time bitter political rivals. The coalition was formed, eventually, though it caused deep unease within Fianna Fáil, which had long campaigned on a position that coalitions were inherently unstable.

That coalition functioned reasonably well until a change of leadership in Fianna Fáil brought Albert Reynolds to the position of Taoiseach. In a dispute over evidence at the Beef Tribunal – a tribunal investigating Irish policy to underwrite the risk of exporting beef to certain countries – it became clear that trust between Reynolds and O'Malley had broken down, if it ever existed. The Government collapsed in late 1992 and an election was held in November. There was much focus on Reynolds and his role in the collapse of the Government, and Fianna Fáil had its worst result in modern times, though it still polled close to 40 per cent.

Labour under Dick Spring had been particularly critical of Reynolds in the preceding Dáil and the election itself. Labour had its best result since 1922, polling almost 20 per cent of the vote. Labour used its strong position and Reynolds' weak one to extract a deal from Fianna Fáil that gave Labour considerable control of policy. But entering government with Fianna Fáil was controversial, and some of the issues of trust that had plagued the Fianna Fáil–PD Government affected the Fianna Fáil–Labour one, too. Despite breakthroughs in the Northern Ireland peace process and a healthy economy, trust once again broke down, and

Labour left the Government in 1994. Though we normally would have seen an election ensue, the President let it be known that she would prefer to see if a government could be formed without an election. Some by-election changes made a coalition of Fine Gael, Labour, and Democratic Left (a new party that emerged from the Workers' Party) an option, which it had not been in early 1993.

That Government, under Fine Gael leader John Bruton as Taoiseach, worked better than most expected, although Fianna Fáil in opposition complained that the Government was too sensitive to the needs of unionism. It was a time of economic growth, and the Government had a decidedly left-wing bent, opting to increase public spending.

In opposition, Fianna Fáil and the PDs entered the 1997 election campaign as a government-in-waiting, offering to cut taxes significantly. The parties won the election, marginally, and formed a coalition with the help of a few independent TDs. The Government's tax-cutting agenda proved popular and effective. Despite lower rates, tax income increased, enabling the Government to increase spending. A peace agreement signed in Northern Ireland was also a significant achievement, and effectively neutralised it as an issue.

The opposition parties struggled in the face of this success. Democratic Left merged into the Labour Party, under Ruairi Quinn. Fine Gael gained little traction with campaigns highlighting the slow delivery of public services, and John Bruton was removed to be replaced by Michael Noonan in advance of the election scheduled for 2002.

Noonan was a good communicator and an effective debater, but replacing Bruton did little to improve Fine Gael's performance. The result was worse than its worst expectations: Fianna Fáil and the PDs were re-elected, and the larger party came close to an overall majority. Noonan resigned, as did Labour leader Ruairi Quinn. Fine Gael chose Enda Kenny, a relatively minor party figure who had survived the great wipeout of Fine Gael TDs. Labour picked Pat Rabbitte, a witty and acerbic debater who had been a member of Democratic Left.

The Government went on a spending spree. It increased public-sector pay, reduced taxes, and increased spending on public services. This fuelled an already booming economy and, in particular, a dangerously overheated housing market. There were significant affordability issues, as inflation rose. Immigration also rose, as Ireland became a country with a significant foreign-born population for the first time.

Neither Labour nor Fine Gael offered a significant critique of the Government's performance. The two parties agreed a pact that they would go into government together after the election scheduled for 2007. Their main selling point seemed to be that they were not Fianna Fáil. Meanwhile, Sinn Féin emerged as a growing electoral force in the State, and though to the left of Labour, it was not clear that it had a distinct policy appeal. Its attractions were populist, asserting that the wealthy were profiting most in the boom. But as the less well-off had never been so well off, it was not an argument that attracted many voters. Probably, only the Green Party offered a coherent critique of the Government's policies.

Perhaps because the Irish had become used to a booming economy, other issues emerged to replace it. The 2007 election was dominated by Bertie Ahern's finances. It was revealed that Ahern had received significant financial support when he was Minister for Finance in the early 1990s and failed to declare tax on these. He dealt with the issue poorly, and Michael McDowell, the new leader of the PDs and Tánaiste, announced that he might leave the Government. It did not make much sense, as an election had to be called anyway, and probably endeared the PDs to few voters. Ahern was lacklustre in the campaign, but Brian Cowen, the Minister for Finance, worked to put the economy firmly back on the agenda. The PDs were annihilated, but Fianna Fáil survived despite significant gains made by Fine Gael.

Fianna Fáil needed a new governing partner and found one in the Green Party, which had increased its representation. However, the allegations on Bertie Ahern's finances remained, and in 2008 he resigned, being replaced by Brian Cowen without a contest. Cowen suffered a defeat in an EU Treaty referendum almost immediately. Then the credit crunch sent Ireland into a downward spiral of austerity budgets and recession. The Government barely kept going, sustained only by the prospect of an election. By late 2010, with rising unemployment and emigration once again a feature of life, the State's finances were so bad that it was felt necessary to enter a lending programme with the Troika of the IMF, EU, and ECB. This led to the Green Party pulling out of government and an election in early 2011.

The Taoiseach, Brian Cowen, having survived an attempt on his leadership, botched a reshuffle, and his leadership was once again called into question. He resigned as leader, remaining as Taoiseach, and Fianna Fáil selected a long-serving minister, Micheál Martin, as leader. Enda Kenny, the leader of Fine Gael, had recently survived an attempt to remove him as leader. He was judged to have failed to make headway on the Government's significant woes. The Labour leader Eamon Gilmore, on the other hand, was seen as an effective leader of the opposition. Labour campaigned vigorously with the message 'Gilmore for Taoiseach', but the positive early poll showings failed to generate any momentum. Fine Gael's campaign was quite policy-based and collegiate. The leader was not the main communicator of the party policy, which was left to the party spokespersons. Fine Gael polled well, capitalising on the historic collapse in support for Fianna Fáil. But it failed to achieve an overall majority, though this was not expected. Fianna Fáil fell to just twenty seats, and the Green Party was wiped out. Sinn Féin made something of a breakthrough, though it was disappointed not to capitalise on the unprecedented crisis. The new United Left Alliance also gained seats.

Labour also performed well, getting its best vote share since 1922. In doing so, it had campaigned against Fine Gael, claiming that only with Labour in government certain cuts would be avoided. The two parties formed a Government – one with the largest majority in the history of the State, but also one with an unalloyed agenda of cuts. Many of these cuts were in areas Labour had promised to protect, and the party's support was affected by these. This drop in support materialised in the 2014 local elections, after which the leader Eamon Gilmore resigned and was replaced by Joan Burton. There was no obvious change in policy direction as a result of this, and the implementation of water charges was deeply unpopular, opposed in many protest marches. The opposition extended into Parliament, where Sinn Féin and Fianna Fáil, sensing the opposition, hardened their stance on the issue.

The 2016 election campaign was one that the outgoing Fine Gael–Labour Government campaigned to remain in power. It was one of their messages that only they could provide a coherent, stable government. The other main message was that the economy was recovering, which by objective indicators it was, and that a change in government would risk that recovery. Neither message captured the public imagination, which seemed more concerned about the pace and breadth of the recovery and the provision of public services. The opposition parties made water charges a key focus and pledged to increase funding for services. Their lines were variations on the message that they would offer a fairer economic recovery. Fianna Fáil leader Micheál Martin was seen to be popular among the public, and he performed well in leader debates. This too became an important focus of the party's campaign.

It was an election that no one won. Fianna Fáil recovered somewhat, coming close to Fine Gael's support, but it came close mainly because Fine Gael performed poorly. Not as poorly as labour, however, which was reduced to just seven seats. Sinn Féin continued to grow, as did the number of seats for small parties and independents. It was the most fragmented Dáil since the 1920s, which made forming a government difficult. It took seventy days for one to be formed, and this was a Fine-Gael-led minority government with support from independent TDs, three of whom became cabinet ministers. It also relied on the support of Fianna Fáil abstaining on key votes.

Appendix 2: Data and methodology

This project uses cutting-edge machine learning processes to prepare a large time-series dataset for analysis. The data consists of media coverage for fourteen elections from 1969 to 2016. Two print sources provide the data for thirteen elections, while a wider cross-section of print and other materials is available for 2016. For the period 1969–2011, the data focuses on the *Irish Times* and *Irish Independent*. This data was gathered as PDF scans of the original newspapers as they are stored in the Irish Newspaper Archives. All available data for the *Irish Times* (1969–92) and *Irish Independent* (1969–2011) was downloaded for the dates in each election year from the day the Taoiseach dissolved the Dáil to the day before the voting, the last day of the official campaign. The PDFs were scanned by optical character recognition software, ABBYY Fineware, to extract text from the images. All other print media covering election campaign dates was downloaded from LexisNexis. Table A.1 lists the number of paragraphs by source. Given that the analysis throughout this book examines a cross-section of data for 2016, the counts are separated into pre-2016 and 2016 columns. In total, the project utilises 1,044,822 paragraphs of text.

To analyse the data, we induce automatic content classifiers using supervised learning. The classifiers are trained to identify three distinct concepts: news about public policy and politics, political frames, and sentiment. The policy and political competition classifier identifies content focused on government policy developments, such as a new law, the budget, foreign policy, etc., and the 'game' of political competition, including commentary on elections, polls, parties, leaders, coalitions, and government formation. The political frames classifier identifies whether the election coverage is framed as being about 'Stability', 'Austerity', leadership 'Effectiveness', or 'Equality'. The data is also coded for sentiment. This classifier identifies whether sentiment is present or absent, and if present, whether the tone is positive or negative. This is presented as a three-category classification where a paragraph coded as neutral contains no sentiment, while a paragraph coded as negative or positive indicates that sentiment is present and the respective direction of the tone. We analyse this data at the paragraph level as this unit of analysis increases the reliability of our manual

Table A.1 Number of text paragraphs by source

Outlet	1969–2011	2016	Total	Medium
Irish Times	471,849	35,257	507,106	Print
Irish Independent	382,748	44,369	427,117	Print
Irish Examiner	0	31,650	31,650	Print
Irish Daily Mirror	0	47,905	47,905	Print
Irish Daily Mail	0	21,529	21,529	Print
Morning Ireland	0	1,468	1,468	Radio
Drivetime	0	1,316	1,316	Radio
Newstalk Breakfast	0	2,309	2,309	Radio
The Last Word	0	3,198	3,198	Radio
Six One	0	1,044	1,044	TV
News at 5:30	0	180	180	TV

coding and is more conducive to automated computer coding (Le and Mikolov, 2014).

Inducing automatic classifiers is a two-stage process. The first stage establishes that humans can reliably code training data from which the computer will learn the concepts. To do this, a team of coders independently code a small sample of text. An inter-coder agreement score is generated to assess the consistency with which the coders classified the same text into the relevant categories of the coding scheme. For this task, we use Krippendorff's alpha (KA) as the benchmark. This is a higher standard than 'percentage agreement'. A KA score of 0.8 or higher is the gold standard ideal, while scores over 0.67 are usable for analysis but perhaps best not to over-interpret minor variation in any analysis based on such codes. When a reliable alpha score is achieved, one or more coders then code training data independently.

Three classifiers, for topic, frames, and sentiment, are used to code thirteen categories. The topic classifier identifies the extent to which a paragraph is about political policies and competition. Here we are interested in whether the paragraph is likely to contain text pertaining to macroeconomic policy, microeconomic policy, any other policy, or political competition (news about: politics not related to policy; votes; leadership styles; strategies; etc.). If a paragraph does not contain information about these topics, we consider it likely to be non-political, or 'Other'. Several versions of the topic coding scheme were tested and a KA of 0.75 (see Table A.2) was achieved for the coding scheme employed throughout the analyses of this book.

The second classifier employed throughout the project assesses the ways in which the political coverage in the media is framed. The text may be about a topic like macroeconomic policy as determined by the topic classifier, but, simultaneously, the policy may be framed as providing stability, causing austerity,

Table A.2 Policy classifier: Inter-coder agreement

Coding scheme	Score
Political competition, Macroeconomic, Microeconomic, Other policy, Other	0.75
Political competition, Macroeconomic, Microeconomic, Other	0.73
Political competition, Economic policy, Other policy, Other	0.80
Political competition, Economic policy, Other	0.79

Note: The coefficients are KA among three coders. The data are 300 randomly selected *Financial Times* paragraphs.

Table A.3 Irish election project: Inter-coder agreement

Coding scheme	Score
Stability, Austerity, Effectiveness, Game, Equality, Other	0.73
Stability, Austerity, Game, Effectiveness, Other	0.72
Stability, Austerity, Game, Other	0.82
Stability, Austerity, Effectiveness, Game, Other	0.72
Stability, Austerity, Game, Equality, Other	0.83

Note: The coefficients are KA of the inter-coder agreement from two coders. The data are 137 paragraphs selected at random from the *Irish Times*.

or contributing to equality/inequality. We also assess whether the text relates to the effectiveness of political figures. Furthermore, we constructed a 'Game' frame, which is similar to the political competition topic in the policy classifier described above but trained on data covering Irish news and politics (Table A.3). The data was coded using the first coding which had an acceptable KA of 0.73.

Our third class of analysis is sentiment: the degree to which the tone of the text contains sentiment, and the tonal direction of the sentiment (Table A.4). One hundred paragraphs randomly selected from the *Financial Times* were used for this agreement test. The codes aim to at least differentiate between text which has no sentiment or mixed sentiment, negative sentiment or positive sentiment. While we could have used a scheme that included intensity on the negative side, we used the three-category scheme to minimise error at the automatic coding stage. The most appropriate KA test is one which treats the coding scheme as ordinal, going from most negative through negative, collapsing mixed and neutral, and then on to positive. However, we also present the KA where we treat the data as nominal. In this sense, the coding scheme and inter-coder agreement are completely unreliable. However, treating the scheme and the codes as ordinal or even interval raises the reliability to the gold standard of 0.8.

Our classifiers independently test the relevance of each paragraph to our categories of interest. The automatic process uses hand-coded data to train a

Table A.4 Sentiment: Inter-coder agreement

Coding scheme

	Nominal	Ordinal	Interval
Very negative, Negative, Mixed/neutral, Positive	0.54	0.8	0.8
Negative, Mixed/neutral, Positive	0.58	0.8	0.79

Note: The results are based on KA tests for three coders on 100 paragraphs randomly selected from the *Financial Times*.

Table A.5 Policy classifier performance

Category i	Category-i-biased classifier	
	Category i	Other
Macroeconomic policy	0.78	0.85
Other economic policy	0.71	0.71
Political competition	0.74	0.89
Other policy	0.68	0.62

Note: The classifier training data are 300 randomly selected paragraphs from the *Financial Times*, *El País*, and *Die Welt*. *EP* and *DW* paragraphs are Google-translated. Training set (N = 3,588), test set (N = 897).

Support Vector Machine (SVM) algorithm to identify whether the text relates to each of our categories. We use 80 per cent of the available data to train the computer and reserve 20 per cent of the data for testing the classifiers' accuracies. The input data for each SVM is balanced in terms of the categories. We use 80 per cent of the available data for each category in training combined with random samples of all other paragraphs of equal size. For a paragraph x, if each category-i classifier (C_i) returns a probability of less than a threshold that balances false positives and negatives, usually between 0.4 and 0.6, instead of a blunt 0.5, we assign the paragraph to 'Other' as it is of no policy or political-competition relevance. If the probability exceeds the threshold for classification for more than one C_i, we can only say that it is likely to be about either of these topics.

Our automatic classification system for policy works extremely well (Table A.5 below), with over 70 per cent of category-i paragraphs in the test sets being correctly coded and, in some cases, over 80 per cent of other paragraphs correctly coded as 'Other'. The 'Microeconomic' policy classifier is relatively weak but still produces acceptable machine learning accuracy rates.

We repeat the process for the election frame codes in Table A.6 above and for sentiment in Table A.7 below. While the classification of topics and frames classified each category iteratively against all other categories combined, the

Table A.6 Irish election classifier performance

	Category i	Other
Stability (ML)	0.73	0.82
Stability (WC)	0.77	0.88
Austerity	0.55	0.70
Effectiveness	0.67	0.69
Game	0.71	0.82
Equality	0.76	0.80

Note: The results for Stability (ML) are extracted from the normal machine learning procedure. The Stability (WC) results are simply the correlation between the presence of the truncated word 'stabil' and the paragraphs coded as 'Stability'. Results are based on the analysis of 137 paragraphs randomly selected from the *Irish Times*.

Table A.7 Sentiment analysis performance (excl. 'Mixed')

	Hand codes		
SVM codes	Negative	Neutral	Positive
Negative	0.77	0.17	0.24
Neutral	0.03	0.60	0.06
Positive	0.20	0.22	0.70

Note: Five-fold cross-validated sentiment classifier. Training sets (N = 799), test sets (N = 200).

sentiment classifier is multi-class, i.e. it trains simultaneously to identify three categories. In Table A.6, there are two versions of the stability classifier. The first is the machine learning (ML) standard method that utilises SVM classification. This has a recall rate of 0.73 for the category. The second is simply a word count (WC) that classifies based on the appearance or absence of the word 'Stability' in its truncated form 'stabil'.

Table A.7 reports the accuracy scores for a multi-class classifier that labels each paragraph's sentiment. The classifier identifies whether the paragraph contains any sentiment or is 'Neutral', and if sentiment is present, whether the tone is 'Positive' or 'Negative'. Of paragraphs coded as 'Negative' or 'Very negative' at the initial stage, 77 per cent are correctly identified by the computer; 70 per cent of positive paragraphs are correctly identified. While the accuracy for the neutral category is lower than desirable, at 60 per cent, this is partly a function of the lower proportion of neutral paragraphs in the training data (about 15 per cent). This system is more than sufficient for measuring tone over large numbers of paragraphs. While the computer cannot predict a mixed paragraph, an aggregate of paragraphs with relatively large and equal numbers of positive and negative paragraphs would be mixed.

Named-entity recognition

The final major aspect of our methodological approach is identifying the appropriate people and institutions to which paragraphs refer. We can then analyse variation in topical emphasis, frames, and sentiment between leaders, parties, candidates, or any other class of named entities in the data. To perform this function, we compiled a dictionary of party names, institutions, and relevant persons. For each election, we automatically cross-reference the names listed in the dictionary with their appearance in the text for that year. While the term 'Dáil Éireann' is relevant for all election years, the term 'Jack Lynch' is only relevant for the first three elections in the time series 1969, 1973, and 1977, as he did not run as a candidate in any election after 1977, although he was a TD until 1981. Our system tags each paragraph with the names of candidates listed in the subset of the dictionary pertaining to each year, their party or independent affiliation, whether they contested the election as an incumbent or a challenger, and their gender. Our dictionary includes 2,621 individual election candidates; they may appear multiple times in the reference list, once for each election they stood for as a candidate.

References

Aalberg, T., J. Strömbäck and C. H. de Vreese (2012) 'The framing of politics as strategy and game: A review of concepts, operationalizations and key findings', *Journalism*, 13:2, 162–78.

Ahearne, A., F. Kydland and M. A. Wynne (2006) 'Ireland's Great Depression', *Economic and Social Review*, 37:2, 215–43.

Anonymous (1969) 'Denmark's success spurs her campaign', *Irish Times* (11 June 1969).

Anonymous (2010) 'Was it for this?', *Irish Times* (18 November 2010).

Anonymous (2016) '"I'm flat out from now on but not in killer heels", vows FG's Mary', *Irish Daily Mail* (15 February 2016), p. 9.

Balmas, M., G. Rahat, T. Sheafer and S. R. Shenhav (2014) 'Two routes to personalised politics: Centralised and decentralised personalisation', *Party Politics*, 20:1, 37–51.

Barnett, S. and I. Gaber (2001) *Westminster Tales: The Twenty-First Century Crisis in Political Journalism* (London: Continuum).

Barrett, S. D. (2000) 'Competitiveness and Contestability in the Irish Media Sector', *Trinity Economic Paper Series*, 2000/3 (Dublin: Department of Economics, Trinity College).

Beesley, A. (2016a) 'Google moved €28.7bn through Ireland in tax scheme', *Irish Times* (20 February 2016), p. 1.

Beesley, A. (2016b) 'Facebook warns of potential tax claims dating back to 2009: Social media giant declares in filings it will defend "any and all such claims"', *Irish Times* (26 January 2016), p. 1.

Benson, R. and D. C. Hallin (2007) 'How states, markets and globalization shape the news: The French and US national press, 1965–97', *European Journal of Communication*, 22:1, 27–48.

Binderkrantz, A. and C. Green-Pedersen (2009) 'Policy or processes in focus?', *International Journal of Press/Politics*, 14:2, 166–85.

Blair, T. (2007) 'The Full Speech: "The media is a feral beast, tearing people to pieces"', *Independent* (13 June 2007), www.independent.co.uk/news/uk/politics/the-full-speech-the-media-is-a-feral-beast-tearing-people-to-pieces-452905.html [Accessed 13 September 2017].

Blair, T. (2010) *A Journey* (London: Random House).

Blumler, J. G. and M. Gurevitch (1995) *The Crisis in Political Communication* (New York and London: Routledge).

Brandenburg, H. (2005) 'Political bias in the Irish media: A quantitative study of campaign coverage in the 2002 general election', *Irish Political Studies*, 20:3, 297–322.

Brants, K. and P. Neijens (1998) 'The infotainment of politics', *Political Communication*, 15:2, 149–64.

Breen, M. (2013) *The Politics of IMF Lending* (Basingstoke: Palgrave Macmillan).

Breen, M. and J. Dorgan (2013) 'The death of Irish trade protectionism: A political economy analysis', *Irish Studies in International Affairs*, 24:1, 275–89.

Breen, M., I. McMenamin, M. Courtney and G. McNulty (2015) 'Daily Judgement: Political News and Financial Markets', American Political Science Association Annual Conference, San Francisco, USA, 2–7 September.

Breen, M. J. and A. E. Healy (2016) *Changing Values, Attitudes and Behaviours in Ireland: An Analysis of European Social Survey Data in Ireland, 2002–2012* (Newcastle: Cambridge Scholars Publishing).

Broersma, M., D. Jackson, E. Thorsen and T. Graham (2016) 'The Virtual Lobby: How Politicians and Journalists Interact on Twitter During Election Campaigns', paper presented to the International Journal of Press/Politics Annual Conference, Oxford, 28–30 September.

Buckley, F. and M. O'Connor (2016) 'Implementation of Gender Quotas in Ireland', paper presented to the Annual Conference of the Political Studies Association of Ireland, Belfast, October 7–9.

Cappella, J. N. and K. H. Jamieson (1997) *Spiral of Cynicism: The Press and the Public Good* (New York and Oxford: Oxford University Press).

Clarke, H. D., D. Sanders, M. C. Stewart and P. Whiteley (2004) *Political Choice in Britain* (New York: Oxford University Press).

Coakley, J. and M. Gallagher (eds) (2010) *Politics in the Republic of Ireland* (London: Routledge, 5th edn), p. 266.

Collins, L. (1981) Liam Collins, 'Sir Oliver sweeps by in his Pope Mobile', *Irish Independent* (30 May 1981).

Collins, S. (2009) 'Rotating taoiseach not in Labour plan, *Irish Times* (15 June 2009).Mercille

Costa-Lobo, M. and J. Curtice (eds) (2015) *Personality Politics? The Role of Leader Evaluations in Democratic Elections* (Oxford: Oxford University Press).

Curran, J. (2011) *Media and Democracy* (London: Routledge).

Cushion, S. (2014) 'Assessing, measuring and applying "public value" tests beyond new media: Interpreting impartiality and plurality in debates about journalism standards', in L. Barkho (ed.), *From Theory to Practice: How to Assess and Apply Impartiality in News and Current Affairs* (Chicago: Chicago University Press), pp. 363–80.

Cushion, S. (2015) *News and Politics: The Rise of Live and Interpretive Journalism* (London: Routledge).

Cushion, S., A. Kilby, R. Thomas, M. Morani and R. Sambrook (2018) 'Newspapers, impartiality, and television news', *Journalism Studies*, 19:2, 162–81.

Dahlgren, P. and C. Sparks (eds) (1991) *Communication and Citizenship: Journalism and the Public Sphere in the New Media Age* (London: Routledge).

Dáil Debates, 224:1085 (12 October 1966).

Daly, M. E. (2016) *Sixties Ireland: Reshaping the Economy, State and Society, 1957–1973* (Cambridge: Cambridge University Press).

Davis, A. (2009) 'Journalist–source relations, mediated reflexivity and the politics of politics', *Journalism Studies*, 10:2, 204–19.

de Saint-Georges, I. (2017) 'Generalizing from case studies: A commentary', *Integrative Psychological and Behavioral Science*, 52:1, 94–103.

Dearing, J. W. and E. M. Rogers (1996) *Agenda Setting* (Thousand Oaks: Sage).

Dee, R. (2016) 'Having a baby is magical – but a decent maternity service should not be just a fairytale', *Irish Daily Mail* (18 February 2016), p. 12.

De Bréadún, D. (2002) 'Kinder, gentler Noonan takes getting used to', *Irish Times* (29 April 2002).

de Vreese, C., F. Esser and D. N. Hopmann (eds) (2016) *Comparing Political Journalism* (London and New York: Routledge).

Dimitrova, D. V. and P. Kostadinova (2013) 'Identifying antecedents of the strategic game frame: A longitudinal analysis', *Journalism & Mass Communication Quarterly*, 90 (1):75–88.

Donaghy, K. (2002) 'Slump in jobs to become an election issue', *Irish Independent* (6 May 2002), p. 1.

Donovan, D. and A. E. Murphy (2013) *The Fall of the Celtic Tiger: Ireland and the Euro Debt Crisis* (Oxford: Oxford University Press).

Downey, J. (2009) *In My Own Time* (Dublin: Gill & MacMillan).

Downie Jr, L. and R. G. Kaiser (2002) *The News about the News: American Journalism in Peril* (New York: Alfred A. Knopf).

Doyle, K., C. McQuinn and N. O'Connor (2016) 'How Adams will cut your pension', *Irish Independent* (22 February 2016), p. 1.

Eichengreen, B. (2008) *The European Economy Since 1945: Coordinated Capitalism and Beyond* (Princeton: Princeton University Press).

Eurostat. (2015) *People in the EU: Who are we and where do we live?* Luxembourg: Publications office of the European Union.

Fahey, T., H. Russell and C. T. Whelan (2007) 'Quality of life after the boom', in T. Fahey, H. Russell and C. T. Whelan (eds), *Best of Times? The Social Impact of the Celtic Tiger* (Dublin: Institute of Public Administration).

Fallows, J. (1997) *Breaking the News: How the Media Undermine American Democracy* (New York: Vintage).

Farrell, D. M. and P. Webb (2000) 'Political parties as campaign organizations', in R. J. Dalton and M. P. Wattenberg, *Parties Without Partisans: Political Change in Advanced Industrial Democracies* (Oxford: Oxford Scholarship), 102–28.

Farrell, D. M. and J. Suiter (2016) 'The election in context', in M. Gallagher and M. Marsh (eds), *How Ireland Voted 2016: The Election that Nobody Won* (Cham, CH: Palgrave Macmillan).

Ferris, J. S., S. L. Winer and B. Grofman (2014) 'Measuring Electoral Competitiveness: The Parliamentary System of Canada, 1867–2011', unpublished paper, Carleton University, http://http-server.carleton.ca/~winers/papers/FWG-Measurement-Competitiveness-13–10–14v2.pdf [Accessed January 2017].

Foley, M. (2000) *The British Presidency* (Manchester: Manchester University Press).

Fowler, L. L. and J. Lawless (2009) 'Looking for sex in all the wrong places: Press coverage and the electoral fortunes of gubernatorial candidates', *Perspectives on Politics*, 7:3, 519–36.

Franklin, B. (2004) *Packaging Politics: Political Communications in Britain's Media Democracy* (London: Arnold).

Funkhouser, R. G. (1973) 'The issues of the sixties: An exploratory study in the dynamics of public opinion', *Public Opinion Quarterly*, 37:1, 62–75.

Gallagher, M. (2017) *Election Indices Dataset*, Trinity College Dublin, www.tcd.ie/Political_Science/staff/michael_gallagher/ElSystems/index.php [Accessed 10 January 2017].

Galtung, J. and M. Ruge (1965) 'The structure of foreign news: The presentation of the Congo, Cuba and Cyprus crises in four Norwegian newspapers', *Journal of Peace Research*, 2:1, 64-91.

Gans, H. (1979) *Deciding What's News: A Study of* CBS Evening News, NBC Nightly News, Newsweek *and* Time (New York: Vintage).

Garvin, T. (2004) *Preventing the Future: Why Was Ireland so Poor for so Long?* (Dublin: Gill & Macmillan).

Garzia, D. (2014) *Personalization of Politics and Electoral Change* (Basingstoke: Palgrave Macmillan).

Gill, R. (2007) *Gender and the Media* (Cambridge: Polity).

Glennon, C. (1982) 'Garret's U-turn: V.A.T. removed from children's clothes', *Irish Independent* (30 January 1982), p. 1.

Glennon, C. and F. Black (2002) 'Jobless figures show big drop but devastation as 375 workers laid off', *Irish Independent* (4 May 2002), p. 1.

Goodbody, W. (2016) '#GE16 – The first real social media election here', RTÉ News (29 February 2016), www.rte.ie/business/2016/02/29/ge16-the-first-social-media-election/ [Accessed 10 March 2017].

Government of Ireland (1960) *Programme for Economic Expansion: Laid by the Government Before Each House of the Oireachtas, November 1958* (Dublin: Stationery Office).

Green, J. (2007) 'When voters and parties agree: Valence issues and party competition', *Political Studies*, 55:3, 629–55.

Grogan, D. (1973) 'Cats among pigeons: Where classes change at every corner', *Irish Times* (22 February 1973), p. 8.

Hallin, D. C. and P. Mancini (2004) *Comparing Media Systems: Three Models of Media and Politics* (New York: Cambridge University Press).

Hamilton, J. T. (2004) *All the News That's Fit to Sell: How the Market Transforms Information into News* (Princeton, NJ: Princeton University Press).

Harcup, T. and D. O'Neill (2001) 'What is news? Galtung and Ruge revisited', *Journalism Studies*, 2:2, 261–80.

Harder, R., P. Van Aelst, J. Sevenans and S. Paulussen (2016) 'Inter-Media Agenda-Setting in the Social Media Age: How Twitter Influences the Media Agenda in Election Times', paper presented to the International Journal of Press/Politics Annual Conference, Oxford, 28–30 September.

Harris, E. (1992) 'One for the strategists, not spin doctors', *Irish Independent* (7 November 1992), p. 15.

Hayes, D. and J. L. Lawless (2016) *Women on the Run: Gender, Media, and Political Campaigns in a Polarized Era* (Cambridge: Cambridge University Press).

Holt, E. (1989) 'Carte blanche for a cliché contest', *Irish Independent* (29 May 1989).

Holtz-Bacha, C., A. I. Langer and S. Merkle (2014) 'The personalisation of politics in comparative perspective: Campaign coverage in Germany and the United Kingdom', *European Journal of Communication*, 29:2, 153–70.

Honohan, P. and B. M. Walsh (2002) 'Catching up with the leaders: The Irish hare', *Brookings Papers on Economic Activity*, 1, 1–57.

Hopmann, D. N., P. Van Aelst, S. Salgado and G. Legnante (2017) 'Political Balance', in C. de Vreese, F. Esser and D. N. Hopmann (eds), *Comparing Political Journalism* (London: Routledge), pp. 92–111.

Horgan, J. (2001) *Irish Media: A Critical History* (London: Routledge).

Humphries, T. (2007) 'Mary Lou tells it straight on black and white issues', *Irish Times* (12 May 2007), p. 7.

Ingle, R. (2007) 'Change brewing and Clune may be electorate's cup of tea', *Irish Times* (18 May 2007), p. 9.

International Monetary Fund (1983) 'Minutes of Executive Board Meeting', 83/110, 25 July 1983, Washington, D.C., Chairman: J. de Larosière.

International Monetary Fund, *World Economic Outlook (WEO) Database*, www.imf.org/external/pubs/ft/weo/2018/01/weodata/index.aspx [Accessed 30 August 2018].

Johnson, C. (2015) 'Playing the gender card: The uses and abuses of gender in Australian politics', *Politics and Gender*, 11:2, 291–319.

Kahneman, D. and A. Tversky (1979) 'Prospect theory: An analysis of decision under risk', *Econometrica*, 47:2, 263–91.

Kappe, R. and M. Schoonvelde (2013) 'A Behavioral Model of Asymmetric Retrospective Voting', European Consortium for Political Research Annual Conference, Bordeaux, 4–7 September.

Kayser, M. A. and R. Lindstädt (2015) 'A cross-national measure of electoral competitiveness', *Political Analysis*, 23:2, 242–53.

Keenan, B. (1997) 'Borrowings halved as tax cash pours in', *Irish Independent* (30 May 1997), p. 1.

Keenan, L. and G. McElroy (2016) 'Who supports gender quotas in Ireland?', *Irish Political Studies*, 32:3, 382–403.

Kindleberger, C. and R. O'Keefe (2001) *Manias, Panics, and Crashes* (Basingstoke: Palgrave Macmillan).

Kovach, B. and T. Rosenstiel (2007) *The Elements of Journalism: What Newspeople Should Know and the Public Should Expect* (New York: Three Rivers Press, rev. ed.).

Kriesi, H. (2012) 'Personalisation of national election campaigns', *Party Politics*, 18:6, 825–44.

Laakso, M. and R. Taagepera (1979) 'Effective number of parties: A measure with application to West Europe', *Comparative Political Studies*, 12:1, 3–27.

Lains, P. (2006) 'Growth in the "Cohesion Countries": The Irish Tortoise and the Portuguese Hare, 1979–2002', Departamento de Economia, Gestão e Engenharia Industrial, Universidade de Aveiro, Working Papers de Economia No. 37, Aveiro, Portugal.

Langer, A. (2007) 'A historical exploration of the personalisation of politics and print media: The British prime ministers (1945–1999)', *Parliamentary Affairs*, 60:3, 371–87.

Lawrence, R. G. (2000) 'Game-framing the issues: Tracking the strategy frame in public policy news, *Political Communication*, 17, 93–114.

Le, Q. and T. Mikolov (2014) 'Distributed Representations of Sentences and Documents', *Proceedings of the 31st International Conference on Machine Learning*, Beijing, China, 21–26 June.

Leahy, P. (2016) 'Campaign strategies: How the campaign was won and lost', in M. Gallagher and M. Marsh (eds), *How Ireland Voted 2016: The Election that Nobody Won* (Chem, CH: Palgrave Macmillan), pp. 75–97.

Lenihan, H. (2016) 'Ballot capers: Battle of the bands as "No Direction" takes on Status Quo', *Irish Times* (19 February 2016).

Leparmentier, A. and V. Schneider (2012) 'Sarkozy et la presse, une longue fâcherie', *Le Monde* (7 February 2012), www.lemonde.fr/election-presidentielle-2012/article/2012/02/07/sarkozy-et-la-presse-une-longue-facherie_1639860_1471069.html [Accessed 18 September 2017].

Leung, D. K. K. and F. L. F. Lee (2015) 'How journalists value positive news', *Journalism Studies*, 16:2, 289–304.

Lewis-Beck, M. S. and M. Stegmaier (2007) 'Economic models of voting', in R. J. Dalton and H. Klingemann (eds), *The Oxford Handbook of Political Behavior* (Oxford: Oxford University Press).

Lloyd, J. (2004) *What the Media Are Doing to Our Politics* (London: Constable).

Lord, M. (1992b) 'Sprint for the finishing line', *Irish Independent* (24 January 1992).

Lord, M. (1992a) 'A right bunch on the banana trail', *Irish Independent* (21 November 1992), p. 49.

Louwerse, T. (2016) 'General election poll of polls: Has FG's momentum stalled?', *Irish Times* (15 February 2016), www.irishtimes.com/news/politics/general-election-poll-of-polls-has-fg-s-momentum-stalled-1.2535934 [Accessed 19 September 2018].

Lyons, F. S. L. (1971) *Ireland Since the Famine* (London: Weidenfeld and Nicolson).

MacCormaic, M. (1992) 'A long wait for the man of the hour', *Irish Independent* (11 November 1992), p. 13.

MacGoris, M. (1973) 'Fighting Alice tries for a seat', *Irish Independent* (15 February 1973), p. 8.

Mair, P. (2011) 'The election in context', in M. Gallagher and M. Marsh (eds), *How Ireland Voted 2011: The Full Story of Ireland's Earthquake Election* (Basingstoke: Palgrave Macmillan).

Marsh, M. (2017) 'After 2011: Continuing the revolution', in M. Marsh, D. M. Farrell and G. McElroy (eds), *A Conservative Revolution? Electoral Change in Twenty-First Century Ireland* (Oxford: Oxford University Press).

Marsh, M. and K. Cunningham (2011) 'A positive choice, or anyone but Fianna Fáil?', in M. Gallagher and M. Marsh (eds), *How Ireland Voted 2011: The Full Story of Ireland's Earthquake Election* (Basingstoke: Palgrave Macmillan).

McCarthy, K. (1973) 'Patient Peigin furious at those high rents', *Irish Independent* (23 February 1973), p. 11.

McCaughren, S. (2017) 'RTE to axe TV news channel as services hit by financial woes', *Irish Independent* (10 December 2017).

McConnell, D. (2016) 'Fine Gael: A party with two political corpses left in charge', *Irish Examiner* (8 July 2016).

McElroy, G. (2016) 'Gender and the Vote', paper presented to the Annual Conference of the Political Studies Association of Ireland, Belfast, October 7–9.

McEnroe, J. (2016) 'Election campaigns go off in a whole new direction…', *Irish Examiner* (19 February 2016).

McGing, C. (2011) 'How women fared in the 2011 general election', National Women's Council of Ireland, www.nwci.ie/index.php/learn/blog-article/how_women_fared_in_ the_2011_general_election (28 February 2011) [Accessed 19 April 2018].

McManus, J. and C. Brennan (2002) 'ESRI says growth will rise to 5% by end of year', *Irish Times* (23 April 2002), p. 1.

McMenamin, I., R. Flynn, E. O'Malley and K. Rafter (2013) 'Commercialism and election framing: A content analysis of twelve newspapers in the 2011 Irish general election', *International Journal Press/Politics*, 18:2, 167–87.

McQuail, D. (2003) *Media Accountability and Freedom of Publication* (Oxford: Oxford University Press).

McQuinn, C. and K. Doyle (2016) 'We'll end up like Greece if SF, motley crew take power', *Irish Independent* (17 February 2016), p. 1.

McWilliams, D. (2013) 'A heavy price for banking failure' (9 September 2013), www.davidmcwilliams.ie/a-heavy-price-for-banking-failure/ [Accessed 23 October 2018].

Melia, P. (2016) 'Women are second choice in General Election 2016', *Irish Independent* (28 February 2016), www.independent.ie/irish-news/election-2016/women-are-second-choice-in-general-election-2016-34493382.html [Accessed 19 April 2018].

Mercille, J. (2014) *The Political Economy and Media Coverage of the European Economic Crisis: The Case of Ireland* (New York: Routledge).

Millward Brown Lansdowne and Raidió Teilifís Éireann (2011) *Exit Poll 2011 – Data set* (Dublin: Millward Brown Lansdowne and RTÉ).

Molony, S. (2016) 'NOW you know she's in', *Irish Daily Mail* (23 February 2016).

Mughan, A. (2000) *Media and the Presidentialization of Parliamentary Elections* (Basingstoke: Palgrave Macmillan).

Murphy, G. (2003) 'The background to the election', in M. Gallagher, M. Marsh and P. Mitchell (eds), *How Ireland Voted 2002* (Basingstoke: Palgrave Macmillan).

Murphy, G. (2016) *Electoral Competition in Ireland Since 1987* (Manchester: Manchester University Press).

Murray, R. (2010) *Parties, Gender Quotas and Candidate Selection in France* (London: Palgrave Macmillan).

Nealon, T. (1974) *Ireland: A Parliamentary Directory 1973–74* (Dublin: IPA), p. 119.

Neumann, W. R. (2010) 'Theories of media evolution', in W. R. Neumann (ed.), *Media, Technology, and Society: Theories of Media Evolution* (Ann Arbor: University of Michigan Press), pp. 1–21.

O'Brien, M. (2017) *The Fourth Estate* (Manchester: Manchester University Press).

O'Brien, T. (1992) 'Harney calls for closer control over the OPW', *Irish Independent* (21 November 1992), p. 12.

O'Callaghan, G. (2011) 'Did the ECB Cause a Run on Irish Banks? Evidence from Disaggregated Data', Irish Economy Note No.13, 2011, www.irisheconomy.ie/Notes/ IrishEconomyNote13.pdf [Accessed 16 December 2016].

O'Clery, C. (2002) 'Global economy recovering quicker than expected – IMF', *Irish Times* (19 April 2002), p. 1.

O'Connor, B. (2007) 'The smart, ballsy guys are buying up property right now', *Irish Independent* (29 July 2007), www.independent.ie/opinion/analysis/the-smart-ballsy-guys-are-buying-up-property-right-now-26307728.html [Accessed 16 March 2017].

O'Malley, E., H. Brandenburg, R. Flynn, I. McMenamin and K. Rafter (2014) 'The impact of the economic crisis on media framing: Evidence from three elections in Ireland', *European Political Science Review*, 6:3, 407–26.

O'Malley, E. and R. K. Carty (2017) 'A Conservative revolution? The disequilibrium of Irish politics', in M. Marsh, D. M. Farrell and G. McElroy (eds), *A Conservative Revolution? Electoral Change in Twenty-First Century Ireland* (Oxford: Oxford University Press).

O'Malley, E. and S. McGraw (eds.) (2017) *One Party Dominance: Fianna Fáil and Irish Politics, 1926-2016* (London: Routledge).

O'Neill, S. (1981) 'Taking people at their face value', *Irish Independent* (9 June 1981).

O'Regan, E. 'Jaunty sleeping spring exits from scrum with Labour jersey intact', *Irish Independent* (31 January 1987).

O'Reilly, R. (2016a) 'Laugh? I nearly spoiled my ballot paper!', *Irish Daily Mail* (20 February 2016), pp. 14–15.

O'Reilly, R. (2016b) 'A force to be reckoned with? Not even close', *Irish Daily Mail* (15 February 2016), p. 17.

Parry-Giles, S. J. (2000) 'Mediating Hillary Rodham Clinton: Television news practices and image-making in the postmodern age', *Critical Studies in Media Communication*, 17:2, 205–26.

Patterson, T. (1994) *Out of Order* (New York: Vintage).

Patterson, T. E. (2002) 'The vanishing voter: Why are the voting booths so empty?', *National Civic Review*, 91:4, 367–77.

Pedersen, M. N. (1979) 'The dynamics of European party systems: Changing patterns of electoral volatility', *European Journal of Political Research*, 7:1, 1–26.

Pierson, P. (2000) 'Increasing returns, path dependence and the study of politics', *American Political Science Review*, 94:2, 251–67.

Polska Agencja Prasowa (2011) 'PiS poskarżył się na Lisa i nic mu to nie dało' (12 October 2011), www.fakt.pl/wydarzenia/polityka/pis-poskarzyl-sie-na-lisa-i-nic-mu-to-nie-dalo/qn5w21r [Accessed 18 September 2017].

Quinlan, S. (2016) 'Identity formation and political generations: Age, cohort, and period effects in Irish elections', in D. Farrell and J. A. Elkink (eds), *The Act of Voting: Identities, Institutions, and Locale* (Abingdon: Routledge), pp. 255–75.

Rafter, K. (2015) 'Regulating the airwaves: How political balance is achieved in practice in election news coverage', *Irish Political Studies*, 30:4, 575–94.

Rafter, K. (2017) '"Insufficient critique"' – The Oireachtas Banking Inquiry and the media', *Administration*, 65:2, 89–107.

Rafter, K., R. Flynn, E. O'Malley and I. McMenamin (2014) 'Does commercial orientation matter for policy-game framing? A content analysis of radio and television news on public and private stations', *European Journal of Communications*, 29:4, 433–48.

Rafter, K. and S. Dunne (2016) *The Irish Journalist Today* (Dublin: Dublin City University).

Rapple, C. (1982) 'Make budget harsh warns Bank', *Irish Independent* (19 January 1982).

Regan, A. (2010) 'McDowell criticises media on politicians', *Irish Times* (22 May 2010).

Reidy, T., J. Suiter and M. Breen (2017) 'Boom and bust: Economic voting in Ireland', *Politics*, first published online at https://doi.org/10.1177/0263395716680827 [Accessed 23 October 2018].

Ross, K. (2010) 'Dance macabre: Politicians, journalists, and the complicated rumba of relationships', *International Journal of Press/Politics*, 15:3, 272–94.

Ross, K., D. Ging and C. Barlow (2017) 'UK and Ireland: Employment, representation and the 30 per cent cul-de-sac', in K. Ross and C. Padovani (eds), *Gender Equality and the Media: A Challenge for Europe* (London: Routledge), pp. 221–32.

Ross, K. and C. Padovani (eds) (2017) *Gender Equality and the Media: A Challenge for Europe* (London: Routledge).

RTÉ (2016) *Morning Ireland* (20 February 2016).

RTÉ – Raidió Teilifís Éireann (2007) 'Ahern apologises for suicide remark' (4 July 2007), www.rte.ie/news/2007/0704/90808-economy/ [Accessed 13 September 2017].

Safire, W. (1976) 'Shucking the tamale', *New York Times* (3 May 1976), p. 31.

Savage, R. (2010) *A Loss of Innocence: Television and Irish society, 1960–72* (Manchester: Manchester University Press).

Schoenmaker, D. (2015) 'Stabilising and Healing the Irish Banking System: Policy Lessons', Duisenberg School of Finance, paper prepared for the CBI-CEPR-IMF Conference 2015: Ireland – Lessons from its Recovery from the Bank-Sovereign Loop, Dublin, 19 January 2015.

Schudson, M. (2008) *Why Democracies Need an Unlovable Press* (Cambridge: Polity).

Sen, A. (1999) 'Democracy as a universal value', *Journal of Democracy*, 10:3, 3–17.

Sheafer, T., G. Weimann and Y. Tsfati (2008) 'Campaigns in the Holy Land: The content and effects of election news coverage in Israel', in J. Strömbäck and L. L. Kaid (eds), *The Handbook of Election News Coverage around the World* (New York: Routledge).

Shipman, T. (2017) *All Out War: The Full Story of How Brexit Sank Britain's Political Class* (London: William Collins).

Shoemaker, P. J. and A. A. Cohen (2012) *News Around the World: Content, Practitioners, and the Public* (New York: Routledge).

Sinnott, R. (1995) *Irish Voters Decide: Voting Behaviour in Elections and Referendums Since 1918* (Manchester: Manchester University Press).

Snow, J. (2017) 'Populism's lessons for journalism', in J. Mair, T. Clark, N. Fowler and R. Snoddy (eds) *Brexit, Trump and the Media* (Bury St Edmunds: Abramis).

Soroka, S. N. (2012) 'The gatekeeping function: Distributions of information in media and the real world', *Journal of Politics*, 74:2, 514–28.

Soroka, S. N., D. A. Stecula and C. Wlezien (2015) 'It's (change in) the (future) economy, stupid: Economic indicators, the media, and public opinion', *American Journal of Political Science*, 59:2, 457–74.

Sreberny, A. and L. van Zoonen (2000) 'Gender, politics, and communication: An introduction', in A. Sreberny and L. van Zoonen (eds), *Gender, Politics, and Communication* (Cresskill, NJ: Hampton), pp. 1–21.

Stokes, D. E. (1963) 'Spatial models of party competition', *American Political Science Review*, 57:2, 368–77.

Strömbäck, J. and T. Aalberg (2008) 'Election news coverage in democratic corporatist countries: A comparative study of Sweden and Norway', *Scandinavian Political Studies*, 31:1, 91–106.

Strömbäck, J. and P. Van Aelst (2010) 'Exploring some antecedents of the media's framing of election news: A comparison of Swedish and Belgian election news', *International Journal of Press/Politics*, 14:1, 41–59.

Taylor, C. (2015) 'Bailout final cost depends on what we can get for AIB', *Irish Times* (7 November 2015), www.irishtimes.com/opinion/cliff-taylor-bailout-final-cost-depends-on-what-we-can-get-for-aib-1.2420313 [Accessed 24 September 2018].

The Economist (2004) 'The luck of the Irish' (14 October 2004), www.economist.com/node/3261071 [Accessed 16 December 2016].

The Economist (2015) 'Celtic Phoenix – Ireland shows there is economic life after death' (19 November 2015), www.economist.com/news/finance-and-economics/21678830-ireland-shows-there-economic-life-after-death-celtic-phoenix [Accessed 16 December 2016].

Time (1963) 'Ireland: New spirit in the Ould Sod', 82:2 (12 July 1963), cover page.

Umbricht, A. and F. Esser (2014) 'Changing political news? Long-term trends in American, British, French, Italian, German, and Swiss press reporting', in R. Kuhn and R. K. Neilsen (eds), *Political Journalism in Transition: Western Europe in a Comparative Perspective* (London: IB Tauris), pp. 195–218.

Webb, P. and T. Poguntke (2013) 'The presidentialisation of politics thesis defended', *Parliamentary Affairs*, 66:3, 646–54.

Wlezien, C. (2005) 'On the salience of political issues: The problem with "most important problem"', *Electoral Studies*, 24:4, 555–79.

World Bank (2016) *World Development Indicators – Online (WDI) database*, https://data.worldbank.org/products/wdi [Accessed 30 August 2018].

Zaller, J. (2003) 'A new standard of news quality: Burglar alarms for the monitorial citizen', *Political Communications*, 20:2, 109–30.

Zeh, R. and D. N. Hopmann (2013) 'Indicating mediatization? Two decades of election campaign television coverage', *European Journal of Communications*, 28:3, 225–40.

Index

EU authorised representative for GPSR:
Easy Access System Europe, Mustamäe tee 50,
10621 Tallinn, Estonia
gpsr.requests@easproject.com

www.ingramcontent.com/pod-product-compliance
Lightning Source LLC
Chambersburg PA
CBHW070338270326
41926CB00017B/3910